# THE AMERICAN EXPERIENCE: DRAMA

ADVISORY EDITORIAL BOARD

Dora V. Smith
Richard Corbin
John D. Ebbs


THE AMERICAN EXPERIENCE: FICTION

THE AMERICAN EXPERIENCE: NONFICTION

THE AMERICAN EXPERIENCE: POETRY

THE AMERICAN EXPERIENCE: DRAMA

# THE AMERICAN EXPERIENCE: DRAMA

Marjorie Wescott Barrows
*Formerly, General Editor*
*Macmillan Literary Heritage*

H. Lincoln Foster
*Housatonic Valley Regional High School*
*Falls River, Connecticut*

Frank E. Ross
*Professor of English*
*Eastern Michigan University*
*Ypsilanti, Michigan*

Eva Marie Van Houten
*Formerly, Head of English Department*
*Mumford High School*
*Detroit, Michigan*

Clarence W. Wachner
*Formerly, Divisional Director*
*Language Education Department*
*Detroit Public Schools*

A revision of *Contemporary American Drama*, previously published by Macmillan Publishing Co., Inc.

MACMILLAN PUBLISHING CO., INC.
NEW YORK
COLLIER MACMILLAN PUBLISHERS
LONDON

Copyright © 1974 Macmillan Publishing Co., Inc.

All rights reserved. No part of this book may be reproduced or transmitted in any form or by any means, electronic or mechanical, including photocopying, recording, or by any information storage and retrieval system, without permission in writing from the Publisher. Earlier editions copyright © 1968, 1964 Macmillan Publishing Co., Inc.

ACKNOWLEDGMENTS

For permission to reprint copyright material in this book, grateful acknowledgment is made to the following:

Harper & Row: For "The Matchmaker" from *Three Plays* by Thornton Wilder. Copyright © 1955, 1957 by Thornton Wilder. Copyright 1939 by Thornton Wilder, an earlier version under the title of *The Merchant of Yonkers*. Reprinted by permission of Harper & Row, Publishers.

CAUTION: *The Matchmaker* is the sole property of the author and is fully protected by copyright. It may not be acted by professionals or amateurs without formal permission and the payment of a royalty. All rights, including professional, amateur, stock, radio and television, broadcasting, motion picture, recitation, lecturing, public reading, and the rights of translation into foreign languages are reserved. All professional inquiries should be addressed to the author's agent: Harold Freedman, Brandt & Brandt Dramatic Department, Inc., 101 Park Avenue, New York, New York 10017. All requests for amateur rights should be addressed to Samuel French, 25 West 45th Street, New York, New York 10019.

Random House: For *The Glass Menagerie* by Tennessee Williams. Copyright 1945 by Tennessee Williams and Edwina D. Williams. For *The Little Foxes* by Lillian Hellman. Copyright 1939 by Lillian Hellman. For *The Subject Was Roses* from *About Those Roses and The Subject Was Roses* by Frank D. Gilroy. Copyright © 1965 by Frank D. Gilroy. All selections reprinted by permission of Random House, Inc.

NOTE: Amateurs and professionals are warned that *none* of the plays reprinted in this book may be acted, read in public, or presented as a radio or television broadcast without special permission of the author or his agent.

Cover design by Leo and Diane Dillon

Macmillan Publishing Co., Inc.
866 Third Avenue, New York, New York 10022
Collier-Macmillan Canada, Ltd.

Printed in the United States of America

# Contents

*Introduction*
vii

THE LITTLE FOXES
Lillian Hellman
3

THE MATCHMAKER
Thornton Wilder
86

THE SUBJECT WAS ROSES
Frank D. Gilroy
178

THE GLASS MENAGERIE
Tennessee Williams
268

*About the Playwrights*
354

# INTRODUCTION

The first two decades of the twentieth century witnessed a reawakening of creativity and experimentation that gave new vitality and direction to American literature. The result was not only a "new poetry" and a "new fiction," but also a "new drama." The first two were "new" in that they broke with earlier traditions in subject matter, form, and style, but as types of literature, poetry and fiction were well established as early as 1855. Such was not the case with drama. Throughout the nineteenth century, and especially in the eighties and nineties, a number of plays were written by American playwrights. With rare exceptions, these plays were dramatic entertainment, not dramatic literature. Not until the creation of a "new drama" in the 1920's and 1930's did drama take its place beside poetry and fiction as an important part of American literature.

Even before expansion and industrialization had changed the face of this nation, the commercial theater was helping to shape the cultural life of Atlantic Coast cities like New York, Boston, Philadelphia, and Charleston. As the nation grew and flourished, so did the commercial theater. Soon playhouses were doing a thriving business in large cities of the South and West. Even smaller cities established theaters, and showboats brought to frontier towns along the Mississippi River the plays of Shakespeare as well as sentimental comedies, melodramas, and minstrel shows. Following the Civil War, Americans could boast of theaters which rivaled in architecture and elaborate decoration the opera houses of Europe. Great dramatic masterpieces of the past were given inspired, often spectacular, performances by distinguished actors.

Unfortunately, the plays on which the commercial theater thrived were revivals of old romantic or heroic favorites, or new plays patterned after them. Playwrights found it all but impossible to break through the limitations of a very narrow theatrical tradition; thus few plays dealt with themes closely related to contemporary life. The drama of entertainment did, however, serve an important purpose, for it "accustomed the American people to dramatic productions, developed a body of competent actors, and brought into being a theater with physical resources sufficient for the presentation of any play."[1] By 1900, largely through the efforts of a half dozen outstanding dramatists, America was ready for a new kind of drama, one that "gave deeper meaning to the theater, portrayed modern character and life with fidelity, and pointed the way toward imaginative maturity."[2]

The impetus for this drama was provided in part by the European dramatic revival and in part by the "little theater" movement in the United States, especially in the decade from 1910 to 1920. The revival fostered experimentation and daringly extended the subject matter of drama; it also introduced new types of drama such as the problem play, the naturalistic play, the expressionistic play, and the folk drama. The little theaters not only produced these new types of drama but also offered American playwrights the chance to explore with freedom the possibilities of the twentieth-century theater

[1] Walter Fuller Taylor, *The Story of American Letters* (Chicago: Henry Regnery Company, 1956), pp. 376-377.

[2] Sculley Bradley, "The Emergence of the Modern Drama," *Literary History of the United States*, ed. Robert E. Spiller *et al.* (rev. ed.; New York: The Macmillan Company, 1960), p. 1015.

and to present their work before enthusiastic, highly discriminating audiences.

A milestone in the development of a "new American theater" was the New York City performance in 1916 by the Provincetown Players of *Bound East for Cardiff*, one of a series of short sea plays by Eugene O'Neill, the first American dramatist of major literary stature.[3] These plays won critical acclaim, but for O'Neill they were merely the first steps. Never satisfied and always experimenting, O'Neill made use of startling forms and styles to give dramatic expression to his chief concern: "the eternal predicament of man struggling for some understanding and some justification of himself in a universe always mysterious and often seemingly inimical."[4] Few, if any, of his plays are without fault, but in their tragic power, they surpass most plays of his time. With O'Neill, the American theater came of age.

By 1923, even the formerly timid commercial theater was presenting not only major works by modern European dramatists but also American plays which once would have been thought too "advanced," among them O'Neill's *The Hairy Ape* and *The Adding Machine* by Elmer Rice, one of the "new dramatists."

Two plays of the 1924-1925 season merit special attention: *What Price Glory?* by Maxwell Anderson and Lawrence Stallings and *They Knew What They Wanted* by Sidney Howard. Both were theoretically as shocking as the plays of Ibsen and Shaw had been to earlier audiences, but so sophisticated had the general public become in the years following World War I that these plays — and others like them — were enthusiastically received.

In the two decades following 1925, experimentation was encouraged by the increasing willingness of Broadway audiences to accept allegory, fantasy, symbolism, and poetry in drama. Equally acceptable were "settings and methods of staging which would have seemed merely laughable to mem-

---

[3] The editor regrets that permission to include a full-length O'Neill play in this volume could not be secured.

[4] Joseph Wood Krutch, "Eugene O'Neill," *Literary History of the United States*, p. 1244.

bers of an earlier generation who had complacently accepted the box set and the convention of the fourth wall as the ultimate in theatrical art."[5] Taking part in this experimentation were some of America's most distinguished playwrights, including Maxwell Anderson. Like O'Neill, Anderson persistently attempted tragedy, specifically the formal tragedy in verse exemplified by *Elizabeth the Queen* and by *Winterset*. Also like O'Neill, he explored other forms of dramatic expression, ranging from romantic tragedy and historical drama to fantastic comedy—even musical comedy.

By the late 1920's America had achieved a drama of literary as well as theatrical distinction. The playwrights who created it had felt free to experiment with already proven forms and methods and to develop new ones of their own. They had also dared to explore such untraditional subjects as (1) the complexities of human experience, (2) the moral and social values of American life, and (3) the economic and political problems created by technological changes and a great world war. In general, the playwrights of the 1920's were portrayers of life rather than critics. The few who tended to regard criticism as a function of the theater usually directed their criticism at the shortcomings of American culture. Their purpose was not to provoke action but to invite "compassionate or ironic contemplation."

Criticism was, however, to become the dominant tone of American drama, and even established playwrights like Maxwell Anderson and Elmer Rice were drawn into the arena of social protest. During the depression years of the 1930's, the propaganda play and social-message play were especially popular. Two playwrights who created both successful and literary drama of social criticism were Clifford Odets, with his plays about struggling, lower-middle-class people, and Lillian Hellman, with her tightly constructed dramas such as *The Little Foxes*, a play about a predatory Southern family at the turn of the century.

---

[5]Joseph Wood Krutch, "An American Drama," *Literary History of the United States*, p. 1331.

The 1930's and 1940's saw the development of many kinds of drama. O'Neill continued to experiment with tragedy, Anderson with poetic drama. Philip Barry and S. N. Behrman wrote comedies that were witty and polished and, at their best, made sharp social comments. A surprising number of plays were unrealistic or symbolic, like Thornton Wilder's *Our Town* and *The Skin of our Teeth,* or Tennessee Williams' *The Glass Menagerie.* Satire and folk drama were also represented, and many of the most successful plays were adapted from novels and biographies. Strong, realistic drama was also popular, however, as witnessed by the work of Arthur Miller. His play, *All My Sons,* focused on man's social responsibilities.

In the 1950's, the question was no longer whether or not America could achieve the dramatic literature envisioned by the "new dramatists" of the 1920's. The question was what kind of plays the present generation of playwrights would write. Tennessee Williams continued to write powerful plays that explored, in a poetic style, some of the darker aspects of human psychology. Arthur Miller wrote two important plays: *Death of a Salesman,* about the fate of the "little man" in modern society, and *The Crucible,* about the witch trials in Puritan New England. And there were other serious playwrights, including William Inge and William Gibson.

Then, in the 1960's and 1970's such rebels as Edward Albee experimented with fresh concepts and techniques, including the abstract style of the Theater of the Absurd. He also brought a new and boldly critical view of American life to the stage, in *Who's Afraid of Virginia Woolf?*

The theater has also become a vehicle for exploring major social problems in American life, such as the decay of traditional values, the inability of different generations to "communicate," and race relations. Particularly notable in this connection is the work of black playwrights, such as Lorraine Hansberry, LeRoi Jones, and Ed Bullins.

Finally, the establishment of resident theaters in major cities throughout the country proves that the American theater is a living theater. These acting companies, made up of professional actors, present classical as well as modern plays staged by Broadway directors. And America, more than ever before, is enjoying Shakespeare, Chekhov, Molière, and Shaw, as well as Albee, Tennessee Williams, and the new experimental playwrights from abroad, such as Harold Pinter, Samuel Beckett, Arnold Wesker, Eugène Ionesco, and Friedrich Dürrenmatt.

# THE AMERICAN EXPERIENCE: DRAMA

# Lillian Hellman

Always complex, the relationship between literature and life often reminds one of the question: which came first, the chicken or the egg? It is usually difficult for the student to tell which was cause and which was effect in the case of particular literary myths about certain ways of life. The literature about the Old-Southern-Way-of-Life is a case in point. Most stories describing life in the South before the Civil War were written two or even three decades after the conflict ended, and by authors who were very young or not yet born at the time of the war. Their purpose was to rationalize the military defeat of the South, to defend its old way of life against pietistic accusations by Northerners, and to glamorize a region stripped bare of its resources and wealth. Once the South had been so glowingly described, however, Southerners often tried to act as they were told Southerners once did. And Northern audiences—who bought such stories from Northern publishers—eagerly accepted tales of a romantic, magnolia-scented era with its handsome families on ancestral plantations. These assumptions that such an era once existed were soon accepted uncritically on both sides of the Mason-

Dixon Line. For years Southern audiences were urged to be true to "our Southern way of life." It was only through the painstaking research of many courageous historians and sociologists of the twentieth century that the actual uniqueness and uniform beauty of the Old South were questioned.

Because of the nation-wide popularity during 1870-1900 of tales about the Old South, thousands of such stories were written, published, and read. Gradually a highly varied set of statements congealed to form a complex myth about what life was like in the "good old days." And writers not only of the late nineteenth century but also of the twentieth drew on this myth in their work. Lillian Hellman's *The Little Foxes* illustrates the use of such a legend by a contemporary dramatist.

A large part of the Old South myth described the plantation owner's family. His daughter, for example, was always beautiful, gracious, and charming, an accomplished pianist who appreciated the "finer things" of life, such as music and the arts. Above all she was innocent: an unbruised flower to be admired by the grosser men whom she inspired. Those who acknowledged her worth proved themselves "gentlemen." Her brother was noble, accomplished in riding and dancing, and well-read in philosophy. His one major failing—and an appealing, aristocratic failing it was—was his ineptness in business matters. Known for his honesty, integrity, and generosity, he simply did not have in his expansive soul the ability to drive a hard bargain or to worry about pennies. Such occupations were the concerns of the merchants and storekeepers, with whom he did not fraternize socially. Consequently, when fate forced him to deal with dishonest men—or even with shrewd traders—he was apt to lose his money. But the loss only proved that he was accustomed to more genteel associates.

The stories written in the latter third of the nineteenth century to support the Old South myth make unequivocally clear that family strength, loyalty, and solidity are major values in all strata of Southern society. Among the aristocrats, however, it was asserted that the family servants became so cherished a part of the household that they too were adored as if they were almost members of the family. This mutually respectful and even loving relationship between Negro slave and white master became a matter of central importance in the Old South legend. In fact, the myth often asserted, the mark of a true gentleman was the affection he held for—and in which he was held by—his servants. The index of less noble natures was the less kindly way in which they treated Negroes. One who abused helpless Negroes was considered loathsome, untrue to the best Southern traditions. Harsh treatment of the slaves was thought so unSouthern that it was blamed, in stories, on Northern plantation overseers.

Another (numerically small) class in the South—the upstart "poor whites"—supposedly hated Negroes because the Negroes considered them "trash"; the myth makes clear, however, that such people also hated the aristocrats. To the depths of their mean souls, they envied the greater privileges of the plantation owners, and schemed whenever possible to usurp such positions. According to the legend, their cheating sometimes enabled them to bring financial ruin to the plantation owner. But the tradition asserted that they were never able, however much of his property they stole, to duplicate his manners and graceful way of life.

The importance of any myth lies not in its factual accuracy but in its expression of a meaningful dream or wish which exists apart from the mundane world of statistics. In the case of the Old South myth, the dream expressed was the human possibility of living a graceful and beautiful life free from the pressure of economic values with their emphasis on the pursuit of money. Such a dream was important especially to Northern audiences, one of whose major traditions was the sharp business ability of the fabled "Yankee trader." Consequently, all sections of the nation joined in their reverence for a South which never was.

A second fact about myth is its ability to survive. If it really expresses a human truth or hope, then the myth will not die, however often it is assailed by factual evidence contradicting it. Thus, after several thousand years, the Greek myths are still vitally alive even though nobody any longer believes in the Greek gods and goddesses.

The Old South myth, too, shows remarkable vitality. As sentimental idealism went out of fashion at the turn of the century, writers took a different view of the assertions made in that myth. They often stressed the pathetic struggles of weak men and women to maintain their "finer" values in the face of a corrupting society, or the destructive inner compulsions which foredoomed these struggles. But the basic assertions of the Old South myth—that once in the South there lived a great many wealthy and cultured aristocrats who acted according to a noble vision of human life and whose positions of authority and respect were gradually usurped by smaller and less admirable men—these assertions have never been significantly attacked in literature. Presumably, artists know that the "truth" exists apart from fact and cannot be subdued by fact.

Lillian Hellman's play *The Little Foxes* is an excellent example of the twentieth century use of a nineteenth century myth. In the play, she *assumes* the validity of assertions made within the Old South legend. Miss Hellman asks what implications those assertions have for the twentieth century, and to what extent the mythical Old South casts a reflection on the less colorful Southern present which she, as a Southerner, finds lacking in grace. The play provides a very valuable study. It illustrates the way in which the writer's work is inevitably shaped by popular traditions, and the way those traditions are reused to fit the changing tastes and needs of other eras. The play also illuminates a large and important part of American literature and of American cultural history.

# The Little Foxes

*"Take us the foxes, the little foxes, that spoil the vines; for our vines have tender grapes."*

### CHARACTERS

ADDIE
CAL
BIRDIE HUBBARD
OSCAR HUBBARD
LEO HUBBARD
REGINA GIDDENS
WILLIAM MARSHALL
BENJAMIN HUBBARD
ALEXANDRA GIDDENS
HORACE GIDDENS

SCENE: *The scene of the play is the living room of the Giddens house, in a small town in the South.*
TIME: *The spring of 1900.*

There has been no attempt to write Southern dialect. It is to be understood that the accents are Southern.
The word nigger appears in The Little Foxes because it was used in the South, and still is, by the kind of people who appear in the play.

# Act I

SCENE: *The living room of the Giddens home, in a small town in the deep South, the spring of 1900. Upstage is a staircase leading to the second story. Upstage, right, are double doors to the dining room. When these doors are open we see a section of the dining room and the furniture. Upstage, left, is an entrance hall with a coat rack and umbrella stand. There are large lace-curtained windows on the left wall. The room is lit by a center gas chandelier and painted china oil lamps on the tables. Against the wall is a large piano. Downstage, right, are a high couch, a large table, several chairs. Against the left back wall are a table and several chairs. Near the window there are a smaller couch and tables. The room is good-looking, the furniture expensive; but it reflects no particular taste. Everything is of the best and that is all.*

AT RISE: ADDIE, *a tall, nice-looking Negro woman of about fifty-five, is closing the windows. From behind the closed dining-room doors there is the sound of voices. After a second,* CAL, *a middle-aged Negro, comes in from the entrance hall carrying a tray with glasses and a bottle of port.* ADDIE *crosses, takes the tray from him, puts it on the table, begins to arrange it.*

ADDIE (*pointing to the bottle*). You gone stark out of your head?
CAL. No, smart lady, I ain't. Miss Regina told me to get out that bottle. (*Points to bottle.*) That very bottle for the mighty honored guest. When Miss Regina changes orders like that you can bet your dime she got her reason.
ADDIE (*points to dining room*). Go on. You'll be needed.
CAL. Miss Zan she had two helpings frozen fruit cream and she tell that honored guest, she tell him that you make the

best frozen fruit cream in all the South.
ADDIE *(smiles, pleased).* Did she? Well, see that Belle saves a little for her. She like it right before she go to bed. Save a few little cakes, too, she like—

*(The dining room doors are opened and quickly closed again by* BIRDIE HUBBARD. BIRDIE *is a woman of about forty, with a pretty, well-bred, faded face. Her movements are usually nervous and timid, but now, as she comes running into the room, she is gay and excited.* CAL *turns to* BIRDIE.*)*

BIRDIE. Oh, Cal. *(Closes door.)* I want you to get one of the kitchen boys to run home for me. He's to look in my desk drawer and— *(To* ADDIE.*)* My, Addie. What a good supper! Just as good as good can be.
ADDIE. You look pretty this evening, Miss Birdie, and young.
BIRDIE *(laughing).* Me, young? *(Turns back to* CAL.*)* Maybe you better find Simon and tell him to do it himself. He's to look in my desk, the left drawer, and bring my music album right away. Mr. Marshall is very anxious to see it because of his father and the opera in Chicago. *(To* ADDIE.*)* Mr. Marshall is such a polite man with his manners and very educated and cultured and I've told him all about how my mama and papa used to go to Europe for the music— *(Laughs. To* ADDIE.*)* Imagine going all the way to Europe just to listen to music. Wouldn't that be nice, Addie? Just to sit there and listen and— *(Turns and steps to* CAL.*)* Left drawer, Cal. Tell him that twice because he forgets. And tell him not to let any of the things drop out of the album and to bring it right in here when he comes back.

*(The dining room doors are opened and quickly closed by* OSCAR HUBBARD. *He is a man in his late forties.)*

CAL. Yes'm. But Simon he won't get it right. But I'll tell him.
BIRDIE. Left drawer, Cal, and tell him to bring the blue book and—

OSCAR *(sharply).* Birdie.
BIRDIE *(turning nervously).* Oh, Oscar. I was just sending Simon for my music album.
OSCAR *(to* CAL*).* Never mind about the album. Miss Birdie has changed her mind.
BIRDIE. But, really, Oscar. Really I promised Mr. Marshall. I—

(CAL *looks at them, exits.*)

OSCAR. Why do you leave the dinner table and go running about like a child?
BIRDIE *(trying to be gay).* But, Oscar, Mr. Marshall said most specially he *wanted* to see my album. I told him about the time Mama met Wagner, and Mrs. Wagner gave her the signed program and the big picture. Mr. Marshall wants to see that. Very, very much. We had such a nice talk and—
OSCAR *(taking a step to her).* You have been chattering to him like a magpie. You haven't let him be for a second. I can't think he came South to be bored with you.
BIRDIE *(quickly, hurt).* He wasn't bored. I don't believe he was bored. He's a very educated, cultured gentleman. *(Her voice rises.)* I just don't believe it. You always talk like that when I'm having a nice time.
OSCAR *(turning to her, sharply).* You have had too much wine. Get yourself in hand now.
BIRDIE *(drawing back, about to cry, shrilly).* What am I doing? I am not doing anything. What am I doing?
OSCAR *(taking a step to her, tensely).* I said get yourself in hand. Stop acting like a fool.
BIRDIE *(turns to him, quietly).* I don't believe he was bored. I just don't believe it. Some people like music and like to talk about it. That's all I was doing.

(LEO HUBBARD *comes hurrying through the dining room door. He is a young man of twenty, with a weak kind of good looks.*)

LEO. Mama! Papa! They are coming in now.

OSCAR *(softly).*   Sit down, Birdie. Sit down now. (BIRDIE *sits down, bows her head as if to hide her face.)*

*(The dining room doors are opened by* CAL. *We see people beginning to rise from the table.* REGINA GIDDENS *comes in with* WILLIAM MARSHALL. REGINA *is a handsome woman of forty.* MARSHALL *is forty-five, pleasant-looking, self-possessed. Behind them comes* ALEXANDRA GIDDENS, *a very pretty, rather delicate-looking girl of seventeen. She is followed by* BENJAMIN HUBBARD, *fifty-five, with a large jovial face and the light graceful movements that one often finds in large men.)*

REGINA.   Mr. Marshall, I think you're trying to console me. Chicago may be the noisiest, dirtiest city in the world but I should still prefer it to the sound of our horses and the smell of our azaleas. I should like crowds of people, and theaters, and lovely women — *Very* lovely women, Mr. Marshall?

MARSHALL *(crossing to sofa).*   In Chicago? Oh, I suppose so. But I can tell you this: I've never dined there with *three* such lovely ladies.

*(*ADDIE *begins to pass the port.)*

BEN.   Our Southern women are well favored.

LEO *(laughs).*   But one must go to Mobile for the ladies, sir. Very elegant worldly ladies, too.

BEN *(looks at him very deliberately).*   Worldly, eh? *Worldly,* did you say?

OSCAR *(hastily, to* LEO).   Your uncle Ben means that worldliness is not a mark of beauty in any woman.

LEO *(quickly).*   Of course, Uncle Ben. I didn't mean —

MARSHALL.   Your port is excellent, Mrs. Giddens.

REGINA.   Thank you, Mr. Marshall. We had been saving that bottle, hoping we could open it just for you.

ALEXANDRA *(as* ADDIE *comes to her with the tray).*   Oh. May I *really,* Addie?

ADDIE.   Better ask Mama.

ALEXANDRA. May I, Mama?
REGINA (*nods, smiles*). In Mr. Marshall's honor.
ALEXANDRA (*smiles*). Mr. Marshall, this will be the first taste of port I've ever had.

(ADDIE *serves* LEO.)

MARSHALL. No one ever had their first taste of a better port. (*He lifts his glass in a toast; she lifts hers; they both drink.*) Well, I suppose it is all true, Mrs. Giddens.
REGINA. What is true?
MARSHALL. That you Southerners occupy a unique position in America. You live better than the rest of us, you eat better, you drink better. I wonder you find time, or want to find time, to do business.
BEN. A great many Southerners don't.
MARSHALL. Do all of you live here together?
REGINA. Here with me? (*Laughs.*) Oh, no. My brother Ben lives next door. My brother Oscar and his family live in the next square.
BEN. But we are a very close family. We've always wanted it that way.
MARSHALL. That is very pleasant. Keeping your family together to share each other's lives. My family moves around too much. My children seem never to come home. Away at school in the winter; in the summer, Europe with their mother—
REGINA (*eagerly*). Oh, yes. Even down here we read about Mrs. Marshall in the society pages.
MARSHALL. I dare say. She moves about a great deal. And all of you are part of the same business? Hubbard Sons?
BEN (*motions to* OSCAR). Oscar and me. (*Motions to* REGINA.) My sister's good husband is a banker.
MARSHALL (*looks at* REGINA, *surprised*). Oh.
REGINA. I am so sorry that my husband isn't here to meet you. He's been very ill. He is at Johns Hopkins. But he will be home soon. We think he is getting better now.
LEO. I work for Uncle Horace. (REGINA *looks at him.*) I mean I work for Uncle Horace at his bank. I keep an eye on things while he's away.

REGINA *(smiles).* Really, Leo?

BEN *(looks at* LEO, *then to* MARSHALL*).* Modesty in the young is as excellent as it is rare. *(Looks at* LEO *again.)*

OSCAR *(to* LEO*).* Your uncle means that a young man should speak more modestly.

LEO *(hastily, taking a step to* BEN*).* Oh, I didn't mean, sir—

MARSHALL. Oh, Mrs. Hubbard. Where's that Wagner autograph you promised to let me see? My train will be leaving soon and—

BIRDIE. The autograph? Oh. Well. Really, Mr. Marshall, I didn't mean to chatter so about it. Really I—*(Nervously, looking at* OSCAR.*)* You must excuse me. I didn't get it because, well, because I had—I—I had a little headache and—

OSCAR. My wife is a miserable victim of headaches.

REGINA *(quickly).* Mr. Marshall said at supper that he would like you to play for him, Alexandra.

ALEXANDRA *(who has been looking at* BIRDIE*).* It's not I who play well, sir. It's my aunt. She plays just wonderfully. She's my teacher. *(Rises. Eagerly.)* May we play a duet? May we, Mama?

BIRDIE *(taking* ALEXANDRA'S *hand).* Thank you, dear. But I have my headache now. I—

OSCAR *(sharply).* Don't be stubborn, Birdie. Mr. Marshall wants you to play.

MARSHALL. Indeed I do. If your headache isn't—

BIRDIE *(hesitates, then gets up, pleased).* But I'd like to, sir. Very much. *(She and* ALEXANDRA *go to the piano.)*

MARSHALL. It's very remarkable how you Southern aristocrats have kept together. Kept together and kept what belonged to you.

BEN. You misunderstand, sir. Southern aristocrats have *not* kept together and have *not* kept what belonged to them.

MARSHALL *(laughs, indicates room).* You don't call this keeping what belongs to you?

BEN. But we are not aristocrats. *(Points to* BIRDIE *at the piano.)* Our brother's wife is the only one of us who belongs to the Southern aristocracy.

(BIRDIE *looks toward* BEN.*)*

MARSHALL (*smiles*). My information is that you people have been here, and solidly here, for a long time.
OSCAR. And so we have. Since our great-grandfather.
BEN (*smiles*). Who was *not* an aristocrat, like Birdie's.
MARSHALL (*a little sharply*). You make great distinctions.
BEN. Oh, they have been made for us. And maybe they are important distinctions. (*Leans forward, intimately.*) Now you take Birdie's family. When my great-grandfather came here they were the highest-tone plantation owners in this state.
LEO (*steps to* MARSHALL. *Proudly*). My mother's grandfather was *governor* of the state before the war.
OSCAR. They owned the plantation, Lionnet. You may have heard of it, sir?
MARSHALL (*laughs*). No, I've never heard of anything but brick houses on a lake, and cotton mills.
BEN. Lionnet in its day was the best cotton land in the South. It still brings us in a fair crop. (*Sits back.*) Ah, they were great days for those people—even when I can remember. They had the best of everything. (BIRDIE *turns to them.*) Cloth from Paris, trips to Europe, horses you can't raise any more, niggers to lift their fingers—
BIRDIE (*suddenly*). We were good to our people. Everybody knew that. We were better to them than—

(MARSHALL *looks up at* BIRDIE.)

REGINA. Why, Birdie. You aren't playing.
BEN. But when the war comes these fine gentlemen ride off and leave the cotton, *and* the women, to rot.
BIRDIE. My father was killed in the war. He was a fine soldier, Mr. Marshall. A fine man.
REGINA. Oh, certainly, Birdie. A famous soldier.
BEN (*to* BIRDIE). But that isn't the tale I am telling Mr. Marshall. (*To* MARSHALL.) Well, sir, the war ends. (BIRDIE *goes back to piano.*) Lionnet is almost ruined, and the sons finish ruining it. And there were thousands like them. Why? (*Leans forward.*) Because the Southern aristocrat can adapt himself to nothing. Too high-tone to try.
MARSHALL. Sometimes it is difficult to learn new ways.

(BIRDIE *and* ALEXANDRA *begin to play.* MARSHALL *leans forward, listening.*)

BEN.   Perhaps, perhaps. (*He sees that* MARSHALL *is listening to the music. Irritated, he turns to* BIRDIE *and* ALEXANDRA *at the piano, then back to* MARSHALL.) You're right, Mr. Marshall. It is difficult to learn new ways. But maybe that's why it's profitable. *Our* grandfather and *our* father learned the new ways and learned how to make them pay. (*Smiles nastily.*) *They* were in trade. Hubbard Sons, Merchandise. Others, Birdie's family, for example, looked down on them. (*Settles back in chair.*) To make a long story short, Lionnet now belongs to *us*. (BIRDIE *stops playing.*) Twenty years ago we took over their land, their cotton, and their daughter.

(BIRDIE *rises and stands stiffly by the piano.* MARSHALL, *who has been watching her, rises.*)

MARSHALL.   May I bring you a glass of port, Mrs. Hubbard?

BIRDIE (*softly*).   No, thank you, sir. You are most polite.

REGINA (*sharply, to* BEN).   You are boring Mr. Marshall with these ancient family tales.

BEN.   I hope not. I hope not. I am trying to make an important point— (*Bows to* MARSHALL.) for our future business partner.

OSCAR (*to* MARSHALL).   My brother always says that it's folks like us who have struggled and fought to bring to our land some of the prosperity of your land.

BEN.   Some people call that patriotism.

REGINA (*laughs gaily*).   I hope you don't find my brothers too obvious, Mr. Marshall. I'm afraid they mean that this is the time for the ladies to leave the gentlemen to talk business.

MARSHALL (*hastily*).   Not at all. We settled everything this afternoon. (MARSHALL *looks at his watch.*) I have only a few minutes before I must leave for the train. (*Smiles at her.*) And I insist they be spent with you.

REGINA.   And with another glass of port.

MARSHALL.   Thank you.

BEN (*to* REGINA). My sister is right. (*To* MARSHALL.) I am a plain man and I am trying to say a plain thing. A man ain't only in business for what he can get out of it. It's got to give him something here. (*Puts hand to his breast.*) That's every bit as true for the nigger picking cotton for a silver quarter, as it is for you and me. (REGINA *gives* MARSHALL *a glass of port.*) If it don't give him something here, then he don't pick the cotton right. Money isn't all. Not by three shots.

MARSHALL. Really? Well, I always thought it was a great deal.

REGINA. And so did I, Mr. Marshall.

MARSHALL (*leans forward. Pleasantly, but with meaning*) Now you don't have to convince me that you are the right people for the deal. I wouldn't be here if you hadn't convinced me six months ago. You want the mill here, and I want it here. It isn't my business to find out why you want it.

BEN. To bring the machine to the cotton, and not the cotton to the machine.

MARSHALL (*amused*). You have a turn for neat phrases, Hubbard. Well, however grand your reasons are, mine are simple: I want to make money and I believe I'll make it on you. (*As* BEN *starts to speak, he smiles.*) Mind you, I have no objections to more high-minded reasons. They are mighty valuable in business. It's fine to have partners who so closely follow the teachings of Christ. (*Gets up.*) And now I must leave for my train.

REGINA. I'm sorry you won't stay over with us, Mr. Marshall, but you'll come again. Any time you like.

BEN (*motions to* LEO, *indicating the bottle*). Fill them up, boy, fill them up. (LEO *moves around filling the glasses as* BEN *speaks.*) Down here, sir, we have a strange custom. We drink the *last* drink for a toast. That's to prove that the Southerner is always still on his feet for the last drink. (*Picks up his glass.*) It was Henry Frick, your Mr. Henry Frick, who said, "Railroads are the Rembrandts of investments." Well, *I* say, "Southern cotton mills *will be* the Rembrandts of investment." So I give you the firm of Hubbard Sons and Marshall, Cotton Mills, and to it a long

and prosperous life. (*They all pick up their glasses.* MAR-
SHALL *looks at them, amused. Then he, too, lifts his
glass, smiles.*)

OSCAR. The children will drive you to the depot. Leo! Alexandra! You will drive Mr. Marshall down.

LEO (*eagerly, looks at* BEN *who nods*). Yes, sir. (*To* MAR-SHALL.) Not often Uncle Ben lets *me* drive the horses. And a beautiful pair they are. (*Starts for hall.*) Come on, Zan.

ALEXANDRA. May I drive tonight, Uncle Ben, please? I'd like to and—

BEN (*shakes his head, laughs*). In your evening clothes? Oh, no, my dear.

ALEXANDRA. But Leo always— (*Stops, exits quickly.*)

REGINA. I don't like to say good-bye to you, Mr. Marshall.

MARSHALL. Then we won't say good-bye. You have promised that you would come and let me show you Chicago. Do I have to make you promise again?

REGINA (*looks at him as he presses her hand*). I promise again.

MARSHALL (*touches her hand again, then moves to* BIRDIE). Good-bye, Mrs. Hubbard.

BIRDIE (*shyly, with sweetness and dignity*). Good-bye, sir.

MARSHALL (*as he passes* REGINA). Remember.

REGINA. I will.

OSCAR. We'll see you to the carriage. (MARSHALL *exits, followed by* BEN *and* OSCAR. *For a second* REGINA *and* BIRDIE *stand looking after them. Then* REGINA *throws up her arms, laughs happily.*)

REGINA. And there, Birdie, goes the man who has opened the door to our future.

BIRDIE (*surprised at the unaccustomed friendliness*). What?

REGINA (*turning to her*). Our future. Yours and mine, Ben's and Oscar's, the children— (*Looks at* BIRDIE'S *puzzled face, laughs.*) Our future! (*Gaily.*) You were charming at supper, Birdie. Mr. Marshall certainly thought so.

BIRDIE (*pleased*). Why, Regina! Do you think he did?

REGINA. Can't you tell when you're being admired?

BIRDIE. Oscar said I bored Mr. Marshall. (*Then quietly.*) But he admired *you*. He told me so.

REGINA. What did he say?
BIRDIE. He said to me, "I hope your sister-in-law will come to Chicago. Chicago will be at her feet." He said the ladies would bow to your manners and the gentlemen to your looks.
REGINA. Did he? He seems a lonely man. Imagine being lonely with all that money. I don't think he likes his wife.
BIRDIE. Not like his wife? What a thing to say.
REGINA. She's away a great deal. He said that several times. And once he made fun of her being so social and high-tone. But that fits in all right. (*Sits back, arms on back of sofa, stretches.*) Her being social, I mean. She can introduce me. It won't take long with an introduction from her.
BIRDIE (*bewildered*). Introduce you? In Chicago? You mean you really might go? Oh, Regina, you can't leave here. What about Horace?
REGINA. Don't look so scared about everything, Birdie. I'm going to live in Chicago. I've always wanted to. And now there'll be plenty of money to go with.
BIRDIE. But Horace won't be able to move around. You know what the doctor wrote.
REGINA. There'll be millions, Birdie, millions. You know what I've always said when people told me we were rich? I said I think you should either be a nigger or a millionaire. In between, like us, what for? (*Laughs. Looks at* BIRDIE.) But I'm not going away tomorrow, Birdie. There's plenty of time to worry about Horace when he comes home. If he ever decides to come home.
BIRDIE. Will we be going to Chicago? I mean, Oscar and Leo and me?
REGINA. You? I shouldn't think so. (*Laughs.*) Well, we must remember tonight. It's a very important night and we mustn't forget it. We shall plan all the things we'd like to have and then we'll really have them. Make a wish, Birdie, any wish. It's bound to come true now.

(BEN *and* OSCAR *enter.*)

BIRDIE (*laughs*). Well. Well, I don't know. Maybe. (REGINA

*turns to look at* BEN.) Well, I guess I'd know right off what I wanted.

(OSCAR *stands by the upper window, waves to the departing carriage.*)

REGINA (*looks up at* BEN, *smiles. He smiles back at her*). Well, you did it.

BEN.  Looks like it might be we did.

REGINA (*springs up, laughs*).  Looks like it! Don't pretend. You're like a cat who's been licking the cream. (*Crosses to wine bottle.*) Now we must all have a drink to celebrate.

OSCAR.  The children, Alexandra and Leo, make a very handsome couple, Regina. Marshall remarked himself what fine young folks they were. How well they looked together!

REGINA (*sharply*).  Yes. You said that before, Oscar.

BEN.  Yes, sir. It's beginning to look as if the deal's all set. I may not be a subtle man — but — (*Turns to them. After a second.*) Now somebody ask me how I know the deal is set.

OSCAR.  What do you mean, Ben?

BEN.  You remember I told him that down here we drink the *last* drink for a toast?

OSCAR (*thoughtfully*).  Yes. I never heard that before.

BEN.  Nobody's ever heard it before. God forgives those who invent what they need. I already had his signature. But we've all done business with men whose word over a glass is better than a bond. Anyway it don't hurt to have both.

OSCAR (*turns to* REGINA).  You understand what Ben means?

REGINA (*smiles*).  Yes, Oscar. I understand. I understood immediately.

BEN (*looks at her admiringly*).  Did you, Regina? Well, when he lifted his glass to drink, I closed my eyes and saw the bricks going into place.

REGINA.  And *I* saw a lot more than that.

BEN.  Slowly, slowly. As yet we have only our hopes.

REGINA.  Birdie and I have just been planning what we want. I know what I want. What will you want, Ben?

BEN. Caution. Don't count the chickens. (*Leans back, laughs.*) Well, God would allow us a little daydreaming. Good for the soul when you've worked hard enough to deserve it. (*Pauses.*) I think I'll have a stable. For a long time I've had my good eyes on Carter's in Savannah. A rich man's pleasure, the sport of kings, why not the sport of Hubbards? Why not?

REGINA (*smiles*). Why not? What will you have, Oscar?

OSCAR. I don't know. (*Thoughtfully.*) The pleasure of seeing the bricks grow will be enough for me.

BEN. Oh, of course. Our greatest pleasure will be to see the bricks grow. But we are all entitled to a little side indulgence.

OSCAR. Yes, I suppose so. Well, then, I think we might take a few trips here and there, eh, Birdie?

BIRDIE (*surprised at being consulted*). Yes, Oscar. I'd like that.

OSCAR. We might even make a regular trip to Jekyll Island. I've heard the Cornelly place is for sale. We might think about buying it. Make a nice change. Do you good, Birdie, a change of climate. Fine shooting on Jekyll, the best.

BIRDIE. I'd like—

OSCAR (*indulgently*). What would you like?

BIRDIE. Two things. Two things I'd like most.

REGINA. Two! I should like a thousand. You are modest, Birdie.

BIRDIE (*warmly, delighted with the unexpected interest*). I should like to have Lionnet back. I know you own it now, but I'd like to see it fixed up again, the way Mama and Papa had it. Every year it used to get a nice coat of paint—Papa was very particular about the paint—and the lawn was so smooth all the way down to the river, with the trims of zinnias and red-feather plush. And the figs and blue little plums and the scuppernongs— (*Smiles. Turns to* REGINA.) The organ is still there and it wouldn't cost much to fix. We could have parties for Zan, the way Mama used to have for me.

BEN. That's a pretty picture, Birdie. Might be a most pleasant way to live. (*Dismissing* BIRDIE.) What do you want, Regina?

BIRDIE (*very happily, not noticing that they are no longer listening to her*). I could have a cutting garden. Just where Mama's used to be. Oh, I do think we could be happier there. Papa used to say that *nobody* had ever lost their temper at Lionnet, and *nobody* ever would. Papa would never let anybody be nasty-spoken or mean. No, sir. He just didn't like it.

BEN. What do you want, Regina?

REGINA. I'm going to Chicago. And when I'm settled there and know the right people and the right things to buy — because I certainly don't now — I shall go to Paris and buy them. (*Laughs.*) I'm going to leave you and Oscar to count the bricks.

BIRDIE. Oscar. Please let me have Lionnet back.

OSCAR (*to* REGINA). You are serious about moving to Chicago?

BEN. She is going to see the great world and leave us in the little one. Well, we'll come and visit you and meet all the great and be proud you are our sister.

REGINA (*gaily*). Certainly. And you won't even have to learn to be subtle, Ben. Stay as you are. You will be rich and the rich don't have to be subtle.

OSCAR. But what about Alexandra? She's seventeen. Old enough to be thinking about marrying.

BIRDIE. And, Oscar, I have one more wish. Just one more wish.

OSCAR (*turns*). What is it, Birdie? What are you saying?

BIRDIE. I want you to stop shooting. I mean, so much. I don't like to see animals and birds killed just for the killing. You only throw them away —

BEN (*to* REGINA). It'll take a great deal of money to live as you're planning, Regina.

REGINA. Certainly. But there'll be plenty of money. You have estimated the profits very high.

BEN. I have —

BIRDIE (OSCAR *is looking at her furiously*). And you never let anybody else shoot, and the niggers need it so much to keep from starving. It's wicked to shoot food just because you like to shoot, when poor people need it so —

BEN (*laughs*). I have estimated the profits very high — for myself.

REGINA. What did you say?

BIRDIE. I've always wanted to speak about it, Oscar.

OSCAR (*slowly, carefully*). What are you chattering about?

BIRDIE (*nervously*). I was talking about Lionnet and — and about your shooting —

OSCAR. You are exciting yourself.

REGINA (*to* BEN). I didn't hear you. There was so much talking.

OSCAR (*to* BIRDIE). You have been acting very childish, very excited, all evening.

BIRDIE. Regina asked me what I'd like.

REGINA. What did you say, Ben?

BIRDIE. Now that we'll be so rich everybody was saying what they would like, so *I* said what *I* would like, too.

BEN. I said — (*He is interrupted by* OSCAR.)

OSCAR (*to* BIRDIE). Very well. We've all heard you. That's enough now.

BEN. I am waiting. (*They stop.*) I am waiting for you to finish. You and Birdie. Four conversations are three too many. (BIRDIE *slowly sits down.* BEN *smiles, to* REGINA.) I said that I had, and I do, estimate the profits very high — for myself, and Oscar, of course.

REGINA (*slowly*). And what does that mean? (BEN *shrugs, looks toward* OSCAR.)

OSCAR (*looks at* BEN, *clears throat*). Well, Regina, it's like this. For forty-nine per cent Marshall will put up four hundred thousand dollars. For fifty-one per cent — (*Smiles archly.*) a controlling interest, mind you, we will put up two hundred and twenty-five thousand dollars besides offering him certain benefits that our (*Looks at* BEN.) local position allows us to manage. Ben means that two hundred and twenty-five thousand dollars is a lot of money.

REGINA. I know the terms and I know it's a lot of money.

BEN (*nodding*). It is.

OSCAR. Ben means that we are ready with our two-thirds

of the money. Your third, Horace's I mean, doesn't seem to be ready. (*Raises his hand as* REGINA *starts to speak*.) Ben has written to Horace, I have written, and you have written. He answers. But he never mentions this business. Yet we have explained it to him in great detail, and told him the urgency. Still he never mentions it. Ben has been very patient, Regina. Naturally, you are our sister and we want you to benefit from anything we do.

REGINA. And in addition to your concern for me, you do not want control to go out of the family. (*To* BEN.) That right, Ben?

BEN. That's cynical. (*Smiles*.) Cynicism is an unpleasant way of saying the truth.

OSCAR. No need to be cynical. We'd have no trouble raising the third share, the share that you want to take.

REGINA. I am sure you could get the third share, the share you were saving for me. But that would give you a strange partner. And strange partners sometimes want a great deal. (*Smiles unpleasantly*.) But perhaps it would be wise for you to find him.

OSCAR. Now, now. Nobody says we *want* to do that. We would like to have you in and you would like to come in.

REGINA. Yes. I certainly would.

BEN (*laughs, puts up his hand*). But we haven't heard from Horace.

REGINA. I've given my word that Horace will put up the money. That should be enough.

BEN. Oh, it was enough. I took your word. But I've got to have more than your word now. The contracts will be signed this week, and Marshall will want to see our money soon after. Regina, Horace has been in Baltimore for five months. I know that you've written him to come home, and that he hasn't come.

OSCAR. It's beginning to look as if he doesn't want to come home.

REGINA. Of course he wants to come home. You can't move around with heart trouble at any moment you choose.

You know what doctors are like once they get their hands on a case like this —

OSCAR. They can't very well keep him from answering letters, can they? (REGINA *turns to* BEN.) They couldn't keep him from arranging for the money if he wanted to —

REGINA. Has it occurred to you that Horace is also a good businessman?

BEN. Certainly. He is a shrewd trader. Always has been. The bank is proof of that.

REGINA. Then, possibly, he may be keeping silent because he doesn't think he is getting enough for his money. (*Looks at* OSCAR.) Seventy-five thousand he has to put up. That's a lot of money, too.

OSCAR. Nonsense. He knows a good thing when he hears it. He knows that we can make *twice* the profit on cotton goods manufactured here than can be made in the North.

BEN. That isn't what Regina means. (*Smiles.*) May I interpret you, Regina? (*To* OSCAR.) Regina is saying that Horace wants *more* than a third of our share.

OSCAR. But he's only putting up a third of the money. You put up a third and you get a third. What else could he expect?

REGINA. Well, *I* don't know. I don't know about these things. It would seem that if you put up a third you should only get a third. But then again, there's no law about it, is there? I should think that if you knew your money was very badly needed, well, you just might say, I want more, I want a bigger share. You boys have done that. I've heard you say so.

BEN (*after a pause, laughs*). So you believe he has deliberately held out? For a larger share? (*Leaning forward.*) Well, I don't believe it. But I do believe that's what *you* want. Am I right, Regina?

REGINA. Oh, I shouldn't like to be too definite. But I could say that I wouldn't like to persuade Horace unless he did get a larger share. I must look after his interests. It seems only natural —

OSCAR. And where would the larger share come from?

REGINA. I don't know. That's not my business. (*Giggles.*)

But perhaps it could come off your share, Oscar. (REGINA *and* BEN *laugh*.)

OSCAR (*rises and wheels furiously on both of them as they laugh*). What kind of talk is this?

BEN. I haven't said a thing.

OSCAR (*to* REGINA). You are talking very big tonight.

REGINA (*stops laughing*). Am I? Well, you should know me well enough to know that I wouldn't be asking for things I didn't think I could get.

OSCAR. Listen. I don't believe you can even get Horace to come home, much less get money from him or talk quite so big about what you want.

REGINA. Oh, I can get him home.

OSCAR. Then why haven't you?

REGINA. I thought I should fight his battles for him, before he came home. Horace is a very sick man. And even if *you* don't care how sick he is, I do.

BEN. Stop this foolish squabbling. How can you get him home?

REGINA. I will send Alexandra to Baltimore. She will ask him to come home. She will say that she wants him to come home, and that *I* want him to come home.

BIRDIE (*suddenly*). Well, of course she wants him here, but he's sick and maybe he's happy where he is.

REGINA (*ignores* BIRDIE, *to* BEN). You agree that he will come home if she asks him to, if she says that I miss him and want him —

BEN (*looks at her, smiles*). I admire you, Regina. And I agree. That's settled now and — (*Starts to rise.*)

REGINA (*quickly*). But before she brings him home, I want to know what he's going to get.

BEN. What do you want?

REGINA. Twice what you offered.

BEN. Well, you won't get it.

OSCAR (*to* REGINA). I think you've gone crazy.

REGINA. I don't want to fight, Ben —

BEN. I don't either. You won't get it. There isn't any chance of that. (*Roguishly.*) You're holding us up, and that's not pretty, Regina, not pretty. (*Holds up his hand as he sees she is about to speak.*) But we need you, and I don't want to fight. Here's what I'll do: I'll give Horace forty per cent, instead of the thirty-three and a third he really should get. I'll do that, provided he is home and his money is up within two weeks. How's that?

REGINA. All right.

OSCAR. I've asked before: where is this extra share coming from?

BEN (*pleasantly*). From you. From your share.

OSCAR (*furiously*). From me, is it? That's just fine and dandy. That's my reward. For thirty-five years I've worked my hands to the bone for you. For thirty-five years I've done all the things you didn't want to do. And this is what I—

BEN (*turns slowly to look at* OSCAR. OSCAR *breaks off*). My, my. I am being attacked tonight on all sides. First by my sister, then by my brother. And I ain't a man who likes being attacked. I can't believe that God wants the strong to parade their strength, but I don't mind doing it if it's got to be done. (*Leans back in his chair.*) You ought to take these things better, Oscar. I've made you money in the past. I'm going to make you more money now. You'll be a very rich man. What's the difference to any of us if a little more goes here, a little less goes there—it's all in the family. And it will stay in the family. I'll never marry. (ADDIE *enters, begins to gather the glasses from the table.* OSCAR *turns to* BEN.) So my money will go to Alexandra and Leo. They may even marry some day and— (ADDIE *looks at* BEN.)

BIRDIE (*rising*). Marry—Zan and Leo—

OSCAR (*carefully*). That would make a great difference in my feelings. If they married.

BEN. Yes, that's what I mean. Of course it would make a difference.

OSCAR (*carefully*). Is that what *you* mean, Regina?

REGINA. Oh, it's too far away. We'll talk about it in a few years.

OSCAR. I want to talk about it now.

BEN (*nods*). Naturally.

REGINA. There's a lot of things to consider. They are first cousins, and—

OSCAR. That isn't unusual. Our grandmother and grandfather were first cousins.
REGINA (*giggles*). And look at us. (BEN *giggles*.)
OSCAR (*angrily*). You're both being very gay with my money.
BEN (*sighs*). These quarrels. I dislike them so. (*Leans forward to* REGINA.) A marriage might be a very wise arrangement, for several reasons. And then, Oscar has given up something for you. You should try to manage something for him.
REGINA. I haven't said I was opposed to it. But Leo is a wild boy. There were those times when he took a little money from the bank and—
OSCAR. That's all past history—
REGINA. Oh, I know. And I know all young men are wild. I'm only mentioning it to show you that there are considerations—
BEN (*irritated because she does not understand that he is trying to keep* OSCAR *quiet*). All right, so there are. But please assure Oscar that you will think about it very seriously.
REGINA (*smiles, nods*). Very well. I assure Oscar that I will think about it seriously.
OSCAR (*sharply*). That is not an answer.
REGINA (*rises*). My, you're in a bad humor and you shall put me in one. I have said all that I am willing to say now. After all, Horace has to give his consent, too.
OSCAR. Horace will do what you tell him to.
REGINA. Yes, I think he will.
OSCAR. And I have your word that you will try to—
REGINA (*patiently*). Yes, Oscar. You have my word that I will think about it. Now do leave me alone. (*There is the sound of the front door being closed.*)
BIRDIE. I—Alexandra is only seventeen. She—
REGINA (*calling*). Alexandra? Are you back?
ALEXANDRA. Yes, Mama.
LEO (*comes into the room*). Mr. Marshall got off safe and sound. Weren't those fine clothes he had? You can always spot clothes made in a good place. Looks like maybe they were done in England. Lots of men in the North send all the way to England for their stuff.

BEN (*to* LEO). Were you careful driving the horses?
LEO. Oh, yes, sir. I was. (ALEXANDRA *has come in on* BEN'S *question, hears the answer, looks angrily at* LEO.)
ALEXANDRA. It's a lovely night. You should have come, Aunt Birdie.
REGINA. Were you gracious to Mr. Marshall?
ALEXANDRA. I think so, Mama. I liked him.
REGINA. Good. And now I have great news for you. You are going to Baltimore in the morning to bring your father home.
ALEXANDRA (*gasps, then delighted*). Me? Papa said I should come? That must mean— (*Turns to* ADDIE.) Addie, he must be well. Think of it, he'll be back home again. We'll bring him home.
REGINA. You are going alone, Alexandra.
ADDIE (ALEXANDRA *has turned in surprise*). Going alone? Going by herself? A child that age! Mr. Horace ain't going to like Zan traipsing up there by herself.
REGINA (*sharply*). Go upstairs and lay out Alexandra's things.
ADDIE. He'd expect me to be along—
REGINA. I'll be up in a few minutes to tell you what to pack. (ADDIE *slowly begins to climb the steps. To* ALEXANDRA.) I should think you'd like going alone. At your age it certainly would have delighted me. You're a strange girl, Alexandra. Addie has babied you so much.
ALEXANDRA. I only thought it would be more fun if Addie and I went together.
BIRDIE (*timidly*). Maybe I could go with her, Regina. I'd really like to.
REGINA. She is going alone. She is getting old enough to take some responsibilities.
OSCAR. She'd better learn now. She's almost old enough to get married. (*Jovially, to* LEO, *slapping him on shoulder.*) Eh, son?
LEO. Huh?
OSCAR (*annoyed with* LEO *for not understanding*). Old enough to get married, you're thinking, eh?
LEO. Oh, yes, sir. (*Feebly.*) Lots of girls get married at Zan's age. Look at Mary Prester and Johanna and—

REGINA. Well, she's not getting married tomorrow. But she is going to Baltimore tomorrow, so let's talk about that. (*To* ALEXANDRA.) You'll be glad to have Papa home again.

ALEXANDRA. I wanted to go before, Mama. You remember that. But you said *you* couldn't go, and that *I* couldn't go alone.

REGINA. I've changed my mind. (*Too casually.*) You're to tell Papa how much you missed him, and that he must come home now—for your sake. Tell him that you *need* him home.

ALEXANDRA. Need him home? I don't understand.

REGINA. There is nothing for you to understand. You are simply to say what I have told you.

BIRDIE (*rises*). He may be too sick. She couldn't do that—

ALEXANDRA. Yes. He may be too sick to travel. I couldn't make him think he had to come home for me, if he is too sick to—

REGINA (*looks at her, sharply, challengingly*). You *couldn't* do what I tell you to do, Alexandra?

ALEXANDRA (*quietly*). No. I couldn't. If I thought it would hurt him.

REGINA (*after a second's silence, smiles pleasantly*). But you are doing this for Papa's own good. (*Takes* ALEXANDRA'S *hand.*) You must let me be the judge of his condition. It's the best possible cure for him to come home and be taken care of here. He mustn't stay there any longer and listen to those alarmist doctors. You are doing this entirely for his sake. Tell your papa that I want him to come home, that I miss him very much.

ALEXANDRA (*slowly*). Yes, Mama.

REGINA (*to the others. Rises*). I must go and start getting Alexandra ready now. Why don't you all go home?

BEN (*rises*). I'll attend to the railroad ticket. One of the boys will bring it over. Good night, everybody. Have a nice trip, Alexandra. The food on the train is very good. The celery is so crisp. Have a good time and act like a little lady. (*Exits.*)

REGINA. Good night, Ben. Good night, Oscar— (*Playfully.*) Don't be so glum, Oscar. It makes you look as if you had chronic indigestion.

BIRDIE. Good night, Regina.
REGINA. Good night, Birdie. (*Exits upstairs.*)
OSCAR (*starts for hall*). Come along.
LEO (*to* ALEXANDRA). Imagine your not wanting to go! What a little fool you are. Wish it were me. What I could do in a place like Baltimore!
ALEXANDRA (*angrily, looking away from him*). Mind your business. I can guess the kind of things *you* could do.
LEO (*laughs*). Oh, no, you couldn't. (*He exits.*)
REGINA (*calling from the top of the stairs*). Come on, Alexandra.
BIRDIE (*quickly, softly*). Zan.
ALEXANDRA. I don't understand about my going, Aunt Birdie. (*Shrugs.*) But anyway, Papa will be home again. (*Pats* BIRDIE'S *arm.*) Don't worry about me. I can take care of myself. Really I can.
BIRDIE (*shakes her head, softly*). That's not what I'm worried about. Zan—
ALEXANDRA (*comes close to her*). What's the matter?
BIRDIE. It's about Leo—
ALEXANDRA (*whispering*). He beat the horses. That's why we were late getting back. We had to wait until they cooled off. He always beats the horses as if—
BIRDIE (*whispering frantically, holding* ALEXANDRA'S *hands*). He's my son. My own son. But you are more to me— more to me than my own child. I love you more than anybody else—
ALEXANDRA. Don't worry about the horses. I'm sorry I told you.
BIRDIE (*her voice rising*). I am not worrying about the horses. I am worrying about *you*. You are *not* going to marry Leo. I am not going to let them do that to you—
ALEXANDRA. Marry? To Leo? (*Laughs.*) I wouldn't marry, Aunt Birdie. I've never even thought about it—
BIRDIE. But they have thought about it. (*Wildly.*) Zan, I couldn't stand to think about such a thing. You and—

(OSCAR *has come into the doorway on* ALEXANDRA'S *speech. He is standing quietly, listening.*)

ALEXANDRA (*laughs*). But I'm not going to marry. And I'm certainly not going to marry Leo.

BIRDIE. Don't you understand? They'll make you. They'll make you—

ALEXANDRA (*takes* BIRDIE'S *hands, quietly, firmly*). That's foolish, Aunt Birdie. I'm grown now. Nobody can make me do anything.

BIRDIE. I just couldn't stand—

OSCAR (*sharply*). Birdie. (BIRDIE *looks up, draws quickly away from* ALEXANDRA. *She stands rigid, frightened. Quietly.*) Birdie, get your hat and coat.

ADDIE (*calls from upstairs*). Come on, baby. Your mama's waiting for you, and she ain't nobody to keep waiting.

ALEXANDRA. All right. (*Then softly, embracing* BIRDIE.) Good night, Aunt Birdie. (*As she passes* OSCAR.) Good night, Uncle Oscar. (BIRDIE *begins to move slowly toward the door as* ALEXANDRA *climbs the stairs.* ALEXANDRA *is almost out of view when* BIRDIE *reaches* OSCAR *in the doorway. As* BIRDIE *quickly attempts to pass him, he slaps her hard, across the face.* BIRDIE *cries out, puts her hand to her face. On the cry,* ALEXANDRA *turns, begins to run down the stairs.*) Aunt Birdie! What happened? What happened? I—

BIRDIE (*softly, without turning*). Nothing, darling. Nothing happened. (*Quickly, as if anxious to keep* ALEXANDRA *from coming close.*) Now go to bed. (OSCAR *exits.*) Nothing happened. I only—I only twisted my ankle. (*She goes out.* ALEXANDRA *stands on the stairs looking after her as if she were puzzled and frightened.*)

*Curtain*

# Act II

SCENE: *Same as Act I. A week later, morning.*

AT RISE. *The light comes from the open shutter of the right window; the other shutters are tightly closed.* ADDIE *is standing at the window, looking out. Near the dining room doors are brooms, mops, rags, etc. After a second,* OSCAR *comes into the entrance hall, looks in the room, shivers, decides not to take his hat and coat off, comes into the room. At the sound of the door,* ADDIE *turns.*

ADDIE (*without interest*). Oh, it's you, Mr. Oscar.

OSCAR. What is this? It's not night. What's the matter here? (*Shivers.*) Fine thing at this time of the morning. Blinds all closed. (ADDIE *begins to open shutters.*) Where's Miss Regina? It's cold in here.

ADDIE. Miss Regina ain't down yet.

OSCAR. She had any word?

ADDIE (*wearily*). No, sir.

OSCAR. Wouldn't you think a girl that age could get on a train at one place and have sense enough to get off at another?

ADDIE. Something must have happened. If Zan say she was coming last night, she's coming last night. Unless something happened. Sure fire disgrace to let a baby like that go all that way alone to bring home a sick man without—

OSCAR. You do a lot of judging around here, Addie, eh? Judging of your white folks, I mean.

ADDIE (*looks at him, sighs*). I'm tired. I been up all night watching for them.

REGINA (*speaking from the upstairs hall*). Who's downstairs, Addie? (*She appears in a dressing gown, peers down from the landing.* ADDIE *picks up broom, dustpan and brush and exits.*) Oh, it's you, Oscar. What are you doing here so early? I haven't been down yet. I'm not finished dressing.

OSCAR (*speaking up to her*). You had any word from them?

REGINA. No.

OSCAR. Then something certainly has happened. People don't just say they are arriving on Thursday night, and they haven't come by Friday morning.

REGINA. Oh, nothing has happened. Alexandra just hasn't got sense enough to send a message.

OSCAR. If nothing's happened, then why aren't they here?

REGINA. You asked me that ten times last night. My, you do fret so, Oscar. Anything might have happened. They may have missed connections in Atlanta, the train may have been delayed—oh, a hundred things could have kept them.

OSCAR. Where's Ben?

REGINA (*as she disappears upstairs*). Where should he be? At home, probably. Really, Oscar, I don't tuck him in his bed and I don't take him out of it. Have some coffee and don't worry so much.

OSCAR. Have some coffee? There isn't any coffee. (*Looks at his watch, shakes his head. After a second* CAL *enters with a large silver tray, coffee urn, small cups, newspaper.*) Oh, there you are. Is everything in this fancy house always late?

CAL (*looks at him surprised*). You ain't out shooting this morning, Mr. Oscar?

OSCAR. First day I missed since I had my head cold. First day I missed in eight years.

CAL. Yes, sir. I bet you. Simon he say you had a mighty good day yesterday morning. That's what Simon say.

(*Brings* OSCAR *coffee and newspaper.*)

OSCAR. Pretty good, pretty good.

CAL (*laughs, slyly*). Bet you got enough bobwhite and squirrel to give every nigger in town a Jesus-party. Most of 'em ain't had no meat since the cotton picking was over. Bet they'd give anything for a little piece of that meat—

OSCAR (*turns his head to look at* CAL). Cal, if I catch a nigger in this town going shooting, you know what's going to happen. (LEO *enters.*)

CAL (*hastily*). Yes, sir, Mr. Oscar. I didn't say nothing about nothing. It was Simon who told me and— Morning, Mr. Leo. You gentlemen having your breakfast with us here?

LEO. The boys in the bank don't know a thing. They haven't had any message. (CAL *waits for an answer, gets none, shrugs, moves to door, exits.*)

OSCAR (*peers at* LEO). What you doing here, son?

LEO. You told me to find out if the boys at the bank had any message from Uncle Horace or Zan—

OSCAR. I told you if they had a message to bring it here. I told you that if they didn't have a message to stay at the bank and do your work.

LEO. Oh, I guess I misunderstood.

OSCAR. You didn't misunderstand. You just were looking for any excuse to take an hour off. (LEO *pours a cup of coffee.*) You got to stop that kind of thing. You got to start settling down. You going to be a married man one of these days.

LEO. Yes, sir.

OSCAR. You also got to stop with that woman in Mobile. (*As* LEO *is about to speak.*) You're young and I haven't got no objections to outside women. That is, I haven't got no objections so long as they don't interfere with serious things. Outside women are all right in their place, but *now* isn't their place. You got to realize that.

LEO (*nods*). Yes, sir, I'll tell her. She'll act all right about it.

OSCAR. Also, you got to start working harder at the bank. You got to convince your Uncle Horace you going to make a fit husband for Alexandra.

LEO. What do you think has happened to them? Supposed to be here last night— (*Laughs.*) Bet you Uncle Ben's mighty worried. Seventy-five thousand dollars worried.

OSCAR (*smiles happily*). Ought to be worried. Damn well ought to be. First he don't answer the letters, then he don't come home— (*Giggles.*)

LEO. What will happen if Uncle Horace don't come home or don't—

OSCAR. Or don't put up the money? Oh, we'll get it from outside. Easy enough.

LEO (*surprised*). But *you* don't want outsiders.

OSCAR. What do I care who gets my share? I been shaved already. Serve Ben right if he had to give away some of his.

LEO. Damn shame what they did to you.

OSCAR (*looking up the stairs*). Don't talk so loud. Don't you worry. When I die, you'll have as much as the rest. You might have yours *and* Alexandra's. I'm not so easily licked.

LEO.  I wasn't thinking of myself, Papa —
OSCAR.  Well, you should be, you should be. It's every man's duty to think of himself.
LEO.  You think Uncle Horace don't want to go in on this?
OSCAR (*giggles*).  That's my hunch. He hasn't showed any signs of loving it yet.
LEO (*laughs*).  But he hasn't listened to Aunt Regina yet, either. Oh, he'll go along. It's too good a thing. Why wouldn't he want to? He's got plenty and plenty to invest with. He don't even have to sell anything. Eighty-eight thousand worth of Union Pacific bonds sitting right in his safe deposit box. All he's got to do is open the box.
OSCAR (*after a pause. Looks at his watch*).  Mighty late breakfast in this fancy house. Yes, he's had those bonds for fifteen years. Bought them when they were low and just locked them up.
LEO.  Yeah. Just has to open the box and take them out. That's all. Easy as easy can be. (*Laughs.*) The things in that box! There's all those bonds, looking mighty fine. (OSCAR *slowly puts down his newspaper and turns to* LEO.) Then right next to them is a baby shoe of Zan's and a cheap old cameo on a string, and, *and* — nobody'd believe this — a piece of an old violin. Not even a whole violin. Just a piece of an old thing, a piece of a violin.
OSCAR (*very softly, as if he were trying to control his voice*).  A piece of a violin! What do you think of that!
LEO.  Yes, sirree. A lot of other crazy things, too. A poem, I guess it is, signed with his mother's name, and two old schoolbooks with notes and — (LEO *catches* OSCAR'S *look. His voice trails off. He turns his head away.*)
OSCAR (*very softly*).  How do you know what's in the box, son?
LEO (*stops, draws back, frightened, realizing what he has said*).  Oh, well. Well, er. Well, one of the boys, sir. It was one of the boys at the bank. He took old Manders' keys. It was Joe Horns. He just up and took Manders' keys and, and — well, took the box out. (*Quickly.*) Then they all asked me if I wanted to see, too. So I looked a little, I guess, but then I made them close up the box quick and I told them never —

OSCAR (*looks at him*). Joe Horns, you say? He opened it?
LEO. Yes, sir, yes, he did. My word of honor. (*Very nervously looking away.*) I suppose that don't excuse *me* for looking— (*Looking at* OSCAR.) but I did make him close it up and put the keys back in Manders' drawer—
OSCAR (*leans forward, very softly*). Tell me the truth, Leo. I am not going to be angry with you. Did you open the box yourself?
LEO. No, sir, I didn't. I told you I didn't. No, I—
OSCAR (*irritated, patient*). I am *not* going to be angry with you. (*Watching* LEO *carefully.*) Sometimes a young fellow deserves credit for looking round him to see what's going on. Sometimes that's a good sign in a fellow your age. (OSCAR *rises.*) Many great men have made their fortune with their eyes. Did you open the box?
LEO (*very puzzled*). No. I—
OSCAR (*moves to* LEO). Did you open the box? It may have been—well; it may have been a good thing if you had.
LEO (*after a long pause*). I opened it.
OSCAR (*quickly*). Is that the truth? (LEO *nods.*) Does anybody else know that you opened it? Come, Leo, don't be afraid of speaking the truth to me.
LEO. No. Nobody knew. Nobody was in the bank when I did it. But—
OSCAR. Did your Uncle Horace ever know you opened it?
LEO (*shakes his head*). He only looks in it once every six months when he cuts the coupons, and sometimes Manders even does that for him. Uncle Horace don't even have the keys. Manders keeps them for him. Imagine not looking at all that. You can bet if I had the bonds, I'd watch 'em like—
OSCAR. If you had them. (LEO *watches him.*) If you had them. Then you could have a share in the mill, you and me. A fine, big share, too. (*Pauses, shrugs.*) Well, a man can't be shot for wanting to see his son get on in the world, can he, boy?
LEO (*looks up, begins to understand*). No, he can't. Natural enough. (*Laughs.*) But I haven't got the bonds and Uncle

Horace has. And now he can just sit back and wait to be a millionaire.

OSCAR (*innocently*). You think your Uncle Horace likes you well enough to lend you the bonds if he decides not to use them himself?

LEO. Papa, it must be that you haven't had your breakfast! (*Laughs loudly.*) Lend me the bonds! My God—

OSCAR (*disappointed*). No, I suppose not. Just a fancy of mine. A loan for three months, maybe four, easy enough for us to pay it back then. Anyway, this is only April— (*Slowly counting the months on his fingers.*) and if he doesn't look at them until fall, he wouldn't even miss them out of the box.

LEO. That's it. He wouldn't even miss them. Ah, well—

OSCAR. No, sir. Wouldn't even miss them. How could he miss them if he never looks at them? (*Sighs as* LEO *stares at him.*) Well, here we are sitting around waiting for him to come home and invest his money in something he hasn't lifted his hand to get. But I can't help thinking he's acting strange. You laugh when I say he could lend you the bonds if he's not going to use them himself. But would it hurt him?

LEO (*slowly looking at* OSCAR). No. No, it wouldn't.

OSCAR. People ought to help other people. But that's not always the way it happens. (BEN *enters, hangs his coat and hat in hall. Very carefully.*) And so sometimes you got to think of yourself. (*As* LEO *stares at him*, BEN *appears in the doorway.*) Morning, Ben.

BEN. (*coming in, carrying his newspaper*). Fine sunny morning. Any news from the runaways?

REGINA (*on the staircase*). There's no news or you would have heard it. Quite a convention so early in the morning, aren't you all? (*Goes to coffee urn.*)

OSCAR. You rising mighty late these days. Is that the way they do things in Chicago society?

BEN (*looking at his paper*). Old Carter died up in Senateville. Eighty-one is a good time for us all, eh? What do you think has really happened to Horace, Regina?

REGINA. Nothing.

BEN (*too casually*). You don't think maybe he never started from Baltimore and never intends to start?
REGINA (*irritated*). Of course they've started. Didn't I have a letter from Alexandra? What is so strange about people arriving late? He has that cousin in Savannah he's so fond of. He may have stopped to see him. They'll be along today some time, very flattered that you and Oscar are so worried about them.
BEN. I'm a natural worrier. Especially when I am getting ready to close a business deal and one of my partners remains silent *and* invisible.
REGINA (*laughs*). Oh, is that it? I thought you were worried about Horace's health.
OSCAR. Oh, that too. Who could help but worry? I'm worried. This is the first day I haven't shot since my head cold.
REGINA (*starts toward dining room*). Then you haven't had your breakfast. Come along. (OSCAR *and* LEO *follow her.*)
BEN. Regina. (*She turns at dining room door.*) That cousin of Horace's has been dead for years and, in any case, the train does not go through Savannah.
REGINA (*laughs, continues into dining room, seats herself*). Did he die? You're always remembering about people dying. (BEN *rises.*) Now I intend to eat my breakfast in peace, and read my newspaper.
BEN (*goes toward dining room as he talks*). This is second breakfast for me. My first was bad. Celia ain't the cook she used to be. Too old to have taste any more. If she hadn't belonged to Mama, I'd send her off to the country.

(OSCAR *and* LEO *start to eat.* BEN *seats himself.*)

LEO. Uncle Horace will have some tales to tell, I bet. Baltimore is a lively town.
REGINA (*to* CAL). The grits isn't hot enough. Take it back.
CAL. Oh, yes'm. (*Calling into the kitchen as he exits.*) Grits didn't hold the heat. Grits didn't hold the heat.
LEO. When I was at school three of the boys and myself took a train once and went over to Baltimore. It was so big we thought we were in Europe. I was just a kid then—

REGINA.  I find it very pleasant (ADDIE *enters.*) to have breakfast alone. I hate chattering before I've had something hot. (CAL *closes the dining room doors.*) Do be still, Leo.

(ADDIE *comes into the room, begins gathering up the cups, carries them to the large tray. Outside there are the sounds of voices. Quickly* ADDIE *runs into the hall. A few seconds later she appears again in the doorway, her arm around the shoulders of* HORACE GIDDENS, *supporting him.* HORACE *is a tall man of about forty-five. He has been good looking, but now his face is tired and ill. He walks stiffly, as if it were an enormous effort, and carefully, as if he were unsure of his balance.* ADDIE *takes off his overcoat and hangs it on the hall tree. She then helps him to a chair.*)

HORACE.  How are you, Addie? How have you been?
ADDIE.  I'm all right, Mr. Horace. I've just been worried about you.

(ALEXANDRA *enters. She is flushed and excited, her hat awry, her face dirty. Her arms are full of packages, but she comes quickly to* ADDIE.)

ALEXANDRA.  Don't tell me how worried you were. We couldn't help it and there was no way to send a message.
ADDIE (*begins to take packages from* ALEXANDRA).  Yes, sir, I was mighty worried.
ALEXANDRA.  We had to stop in Mobile over night. Papa— (*Looks at him.*) Papa didn't feel well. The trip was too much for him, and I made him stop and rest— (*As* ADDIE *takes the last package.*) No, don't take that. That's father's medicine. I'll hold it. It mustn't break. Now, about the stuff outside. Papa must have his wheel chair. I'll get that and the valises—
ADDIE (*very happy, holding* ALEXANDRA'S *arms*).  Since when you got to carry your own valises? Since when I ain't old enough to hold a bottle of medicine? (HORACE *coughs.*) You feel all right, Mr. Horace?

HORACE (*nods*). Glad to be sitting down.
ALEXANDRA (*opening package of medicine*). He doesn't feel all right. (ADDIE *looks at her, then at* HORACE.) He just says that. The trip was very hard on him, and now he must go right to bed.
ADDIE (*looking at him carefully*). Them fancy doctors, they give you help?
HORACE. They did their best.
ALEXANDRA (*has become conscious of the voices in the dining room*). I bet Mama was worried. I better tell her we're here now. (*She starts for door.*)
HORACE. Zan. (*She stops.*) Not for a minute, dear.
ALEXANDRA. Oh, Papa, you feel bad again. I knew you did. Do you want your medicine?
HORACE. No, I don't feel that way. I'm just tired, darling. Let me rest a little.
ALEXANDRA. Yes, but Mama will be mad if I don't tell her we're here.
ADDIE. They're all in there eating breakfast.
ALEXANDRA. Oh, are they all here? Why do they *always* have to be here? I was hoping Papa wouldn't have to see anybody, that it would be nice for him and quiet.
ADDIE. Then let your papa rest for a minute.
HORACE. Addie, I bet your coffee's as good as ever. They don't have such good coffee up north. (*Looks at the urn.*) Is it as good, Addie? (ADDIE *starts for coffee urn.*)
ALEXANDRA. No. Dr. Reeves said not much coffee. Just now and then. I'm the nurse now, Addie.
ADDIE. You'd be a better one if you didn't look so dirty. Now go and take a bath. Change your linens, get out a fresh dress and give your hair a good brushing—go on—
ALEXANDRA. Will you be all right, Papa?
ADDIE. Go on.
ALEXANDRA (*on stairs, talks as she goes up*). The pills Papa must take once every four hours. And the bottle only when—only if he feels very bad. Now don't move until I come back and don't talk much and remember about his medicine, Addie—
ADDIE. Ring for Belle and have her help you and then I'll make you a fresh breakfast.

ALEXANDRA (*as she disappears*). How's Aunt Birdie? Is she here?

ADDIE. It ain't right for you to have coffee? It will hurt you?

HORACE (*slowly*). Nothing can make much difference now. Get me a cup, Addie. (*She looks at him, crosses to urn, pours a cup.*) Funny. They can't make coffee up north. (ADDIE *brings him a cup.*) They don't like red pepper, either. (*He takes the cup and gulps it greedily.*) God, that's good. You remember how I used to drink it? Ten, twelve cups a day. So strong it had to stain the cup. (*Then slowly.*) Addie, before I see anybody else, I want to know why Zan came to fetch me home. She's tried to tell me, but she doesn't seem to know herself.

ADDIE (*turns away*). I don't know. All I know is big things are going on. Everybody going to be high-tone rich. Big rich. You too. All because smoke's going to start out of a building that ain't even up yet.

HORACE. I've heard about it.

ADDIE. And, er— (*Hesitates—steps to him.*) And—well, Zan, she going to marry Mr. Leo in a little while.

HORACE (*looks at her, then very slowly*). What are you talking about?

ADDIE. That's right. That's the talk, God help us.

HORACE (*angrily*). What's the talk?

ADDIE. I'm telling you. There's going to be a wedding— (*Angrily turns away.*) Over my dead body there is.

HORACE (*after a second, quietly*). Go and tell them I'm home.

ADDIE (*hesitates*). Now you ain't to get excited. You're to be in your bed—

HORACE. Go on, Addie. Go and say I'm back. (ADDIE *opens dining room doors. He rises with difficulty, stands stiff, as if he were in pain, facing the dining room.*)

ADDIE. Miss Regina. They're home. They got here—

REGINA. Horace! (REGINA *quickly rises, runs into the room. Warmly.*) Horace! You've finally arrived. (*As she kisses him, the others come forward, all talking together.*)

BEN (*in doorway, carrying a napkin*). Well, sir, you had us all mighty worried. (*He steps forward. They shake hands.* ADDIE *exits.*)

OSCAR. You're a sight for sore eyes.
HORACE. Hello, Ben.

(LEO *enters, eating a biscuit.*)

OSCAR. And how you feel? Tip-top, I bet, because that's the way you're looking.
HORACE (*coldly, irritated with* OSCAR'S *lie*). Hello, Oscar. Hello, Leo, how are you?
LEO (*shaking hands*). I'm fine, sir. But a lot better now that you're back.
REGINA. Now sit down. What did happen to you and where's Alexandra? I am so excited about seeing you that I almost forgot about her.
HORACE. I didn't feel good, a little weak, I guess, and we stopped over night to rest. Zan's upstairs washing off the train dirt.
REGINA. Oh, I am so sorry the trip was hard on you. I didn't think that —
HORACE. Well, it's just as if I had never been away. All of you here —
BEN. Waiting to welcome you home.

(BIRDIE *bursts in. She is wearing a flannel kimono and her face is flushed and excited.*)

BIRDIE (*runs to him, kisses him*). Horace!
HORACE (*warmly pressing her arm*). I was just wondering where you were, Birdie.
BIRDIE (*excited*). Oh, I would have been here. I didn't know you were back until Simon said he saw the buggy. (*She draws back to look at him. Her face sobers.*) Oh, you don't look well, Horace. No, you don't.
REGINA (*laughs*). Birdie, what a thing to say —
HORACE (*looking at* OSCAR). Oscar thinks I look very well.
OSCAR (*annoyed.* **Turns on** LEO). Don't stand there holding that biscuit in your hand.
LEO. Oh, well. I'll just finish my breakfast, Uncle Horace, and then I'll give you all the news about the bank — (*He exits into the dining room.*)
OSCAR. And what is that costume you have on?

BIRDIE (*looking at* HORACE). Now that you're home, you'll feel better. Plenty of good rest and we'll take such fine care of you. (*Stops.*) But where is Zan? I missed her so much.

OSCAR. I asked you what is that strange costume you're parading around in?

BIRDIE (*nervously, backing toward stairs*). Me? Oh! It's my wrapper. I was so excited about Horace I just rushed out of the house—

OSCAR. Did you come across the square dressed that way? My dear Birdie, I—

HORACE (*to* REGINA, *wearily*). Yes, it's just like old times.

REGINA (*quickly to* OSCAR). Now, no fights. This is a holiday.

BIRDIE (*runs quickly up the stairs*). Zan! Zannie!

OSCAR. Birdie! (*She stops.*)

BIRDIE. Oh. Tell Zan I'll be back in a little while. (*Whispers.*) Sorry, Oscar. (*Exits.*)

REGINA (*to* OSCAR *and* BEN). Why don't you go finish your breakfast and let Horace rest for a minute?

BEN (*crossing to dining room with* OSCAR). Never leave a meal unfinished. There are too many poor people who need the food. Mighty glad to see you home, Horace. Fine to have you back. Fine to have you back.

OSCAR (*to* LEO *as* BEN *closes dining room doors*). Your mother has gone crazy. Running around the streets like a woman—

(*The moment* REGINA *and* HORACE *are alone, they become awkward and self-conscious.*)

REGINA (*laughs awkwardly*). Well. Here we are. It's been a long time. (HORACE *smiles.*) Five months. You know, Horace, I wanted to come and be with you in the hospital, but I didn't know where my duty was. Here, or with you. But you know how much I *wanted* to come.

HORACE. That's kind of you, Regina. There was no need to come.

REGINA. Oh, but there was. Five months lying there all by yourself, no kinfolks, no friends. Don't try to tell me you didn't have a bad time of it.

HORACE. I didn't have a bad time. (*As she shakes her head, he becomes insistent.*) No, I didn't, Regina. Oh, at first when I — when I heard the news about myself — but after I got used to that, I liked it there.

REGINA. You *liked* it? (*Coldly.*) Isn't that strange. You liked it so well you didn't want to come home?

HORACE. That's not the way to put it. (*Then, kindly, as he sees her turn her head away.*) But there I was and I got kind of used to it, kind of to like lying there and thinking. (*Smiles.*) I never had much time to think before. And time's become valuable to me.

REGINA. It sounds almost like a holiday.

HORACE (*laughs*). It was, sort of. The first holiday I've had since I was a little kid.

REGINA. And here I was thinking you were in pain and —

HORACE (*quietly*). I was in pain.

REGINA. And instead you were having a holiday! A holiday of thinking. Couldn't you have done that here?

HORACE. I wanted to do it before I came here. I was thinking about us.

REGINA. About us? About you and me? Thinking about you and me after all these years. (*Unpleasantly.*) You shall tell me everything you thought — some day.

HORACE (*there is silence for a minute*). Regina. (*She turns to him.*) Why did you send Zan to Baltimore?

REGINA. Why? Because I wanted you home. You can't make anything suspicious out of that, can you?

HORACE. I didn't mean to make anything suspicious about it. (*Hesitantly, taking her hand.*) Zan said you wanted me to come home. I was so pleased at that and touched, it made me feel good.

REGINA (*taking away her hand, turns*). Touched that I should want you home?

HORACE (*sighs*). I'm saying all the wrong things as usual. Let's try to get along better. There isn't so much more time. Regina, what's all this crazy talk I've been hearing about Zan and Leo? Zan and Leo marrying?

REGINA (*turning to him, sharply*). Who gossips so much around here?

HORACE (*shocked*). Regina!

REGINA (*annoyed, anxious to quiet him*). It's some foolishness that Oscar thought up. I'll explain later. I have no intention of allowing any such arrangement. It was simply a way of keeping Oscar quiet in all this business I've been writing you about—

HORACE (*carefully*). What has Zan to do with any business of Oscar's? Whatever it is, you had better put it out of Oscar's head immediately. You know what I think of Leo.

REGINA. But there's no need to talk about it now.

HORACE. There is no need to talk about it ever. Not as long as I live. (HORACE *stops, slowly turns to look at her.*) As long as I live. I've been in a hospital for five months. Yet since I've been here you have not once asked me about—about my health. (*Then gently.*) Well, I suppose they've written you. I can't live very long.

REGINA (*coldly*). I've never understood why people have to talk about this kind of thing.

HORACE (*there is a silence. Then he looks up at her, his face cold*). You misunderstand. I don't intend to gossip about my sickness. I thought it was only fair to tell you. I was not asking for your sympathy.

REGINA (*sharply, turns to him*). What do the doctors think caused your bad heart?

HORACE. What do you mean?

REGINA. They didn't think it possible, did they, that your fancy women may have—

HORACE (*smiles unpleasantly*). Caused my heart to be bad? I don't think that's the best scientific theory. You don't catch heart trouble in bed.

REGINA (*angrily*). I didn't think you did. I only thought you might catch a bad conscience—in bed, as you say.

HORACE. I didn't tell them about my bad conscience. Or about my fancy women. Nor did I tell them that my wife has not wanted me in bed with her for— (*Sharply.*) How long is it, Regina? (REGINA *turns to him.*) Ten years? Did you bring me home for this, to make me feel guilty again? That means you want something. But you'll not make me feel guilty any more. My "thinking" has made a difference.

REGINA. I see that it has. (*She looks toward dining room door. Then comes to him, her manner warm and friendly.*) It's foolish for us to fight this way. I didn't mean to be unpleasant. I was stupid.

HORACE (*wearily*). God knows I didn't either. I came home wanting so much not to fight, and then all of a sudden there we were. I got hurt and—

REGINA (*hastily*). It's all my fault. I didn't ask about—about your illness because I didn't want to remind you of it. Anyway I never believe doctors when they talk about— (*Brightly.*) when they talk like that.

HORACE (*not looking at her*). Well, we'll try our best with each other. (*He rises.*)

REGINA (*quickly*). I'll try. Honestly, I will. Horace, Horace, I know you're tired but, but—couldn't you stay down here a few minutes longer? I want Ben to tell you something.

HORACE. Tomorrow.

REGINA. I'd like to now. It's very important to me. It's very important to all of us. (*Gaily, as she moves toward dining room.*) Important to your beloved daughter. She'll be a very great heiress—

HORACE. Will she? That's nice.

REGINA (*opens doors*). Ben, are you finished breakfast?

HORACE. Is this the mill business I've had so many letters about?

REGINA (*to* BEN). Horace would like to talk to you now.

HORACE. Horace would not like to talk to you now. I am very tired, Regina—

REGINA (*comes to him*). Please. You've said we'll try our best with each other. I'll try. Really, I will. Please do this for me now. You will see what I've done while you've been away. How I watched your interests. (*Laughs gaily.*) And I've done very well too. But things can't be delayed any longer. Everything must be settled this week— (HORACE *sits down.* BEN *enters.* OSCAR *has stayed in the dining room, his head turned to watch them.* LEO *is pretending to read the newspaper.*) Now you must tell Horace all about it. Only be quick because he is very tired and must go to bed. (HORACE *is looking up at her.*

*His face hardens as she speaks.*) But I think your news will be better for him than all the medicine in the world.

BEN (*looking at* HORACE). It could wait. Horace may not feel like talking today.

REGINA. What an old faker you are! You know it can't wait. You know it must be finished this week. You've been just as anxious for Horace to get here as I've been.

BEN (*very jovial*). I suppose I have been. And why not? Horace has done Hubbard Sons many a good turn. Why shouldn't I be anxious to help him now?

REGINA (*laughs*). Help him! Help him when you need him, that's what you mean.

BEN. What a woman you married, Horace. (*Laughs awkwardly when* HORACE *does not answer.*) Well, then I'll make it quick. You know what I've been telling you for years. How I've always said that every one of us little Southern businessmen had great things— (*Extends his arm.*) —right beyond our finger tips. It's been my dream: my dream to make those fingers grow longer. I'm a lucky man, Horace, a lucky man. To dream and to live to get what you've dreamed of. That's *my* idea of a lucky man. (*Looks at his fingers as his arm drops slowly.*) For thirty years I've cried bring the cotton mills to the cotton. (HORACE *opens medicine bottle.*) Well, finally I got up nerve to go to Marshall Company in Chicago.

HORACE. I know all this. (*He takes the medicine.* REGINA *rises, steps to him.*)

BEN. Can I get you something?

HORACE. Some water, please.

REGINA (*turns quickly*). Oh, I'm sorry. Let me. (*Brings him a glass of water. He drinks as they wait in silence.*) You feel all right now?

HORACE. Yes. You wrote me. I know all that.

(OSCAR *enters from dining room.*)

REGINA (*triumphantly*). But you don't know that in the last few days Ben has agreed to give us—you, I mean—a much larger share.

HORACE. Really? That's very generous of him.
BEN (*laughs*). It wasn't so generous of me. It was smart of Regina.
REGINA (*as if she were signaling* HORACE). I explained to Ben that perhaps you hadn't answered his letters because you didn't think he was offering you enough, and that the time was getting short and you could guess how much he needed you—
HORACE (*smiles at her, nods*). And I could guess that he wants to keep control in the family.
REGINA (*to* BEN, *triumphantly*). Exactly. (*To* HORACE.) So I did a little bargaining for you and convinced my brothers they weren't the only Hubbards who had a business sense.
HORACE. Did you have to convince them of that? How little people know about each other! (*Laughs.*) But you'll know better about Regina next time, eh, Ben? (BEN, REGINA, HORACE *laugh together.* OSCAR'S *face is angry.*) Now, let's see. We're getting a bigger share. (*Looking at* OSCAR.) Who's getting less?
BEN. Oscar.
HORACE. Well, Oscar, you've grown very unselfish. What's happened to you?

(LEO *enters from dining room.*)

BEN (*quickly, before* OSCAR *can answer*). Oscar doesn't mind. Not worth fighting about now, eh, Oscar?
OSCAR (*angrily*). I'll get mine in the end. You can be sure of that. I've got my son's future to think about.
HORACE (*sharply*). Leo? Oh, I see. (*Puts his head back, laughs.* REGINA *looks at him nervously.*) I am beginning to see. Everybody will get theirs.
BEN. I knew you'd see it. Seventy-five thousand, and that seventy-five thousand will make you a million.
REGINA (*steps to table, leaning forward*). It will, Horace, it will.
HORACE. I believe you. (*After a second.*) Now I can understand Oscar's self-sacrifice, but what did you have to promise Marshall Company besides the money you're putting up?

BEN. They wouldn't take promises. They wanted guarantees.

HORACE. Of what?

BEN (*nods*). Water power. Free and plenty of it.

HORACE. You got them that, of course.

BEN. Cheap. You'd think the Governor of a great state would make his price a little higher. From pride, you know. (HORACE *smiles.* BEN *smiles.*) Cheap wages. "What do you mean by cheap wages?" I say to Marshall. "Less than Massachusetts," he says to me, "and that averages eight a week." "Eight a week! By God," I tell him, "*I'd* work for eight a week myself." Why, there ain't a mountain white or a town nigger but wouldn't give his right arm for three silver dollars every week, eh, Horace?

HORACE. Sure, And they'll take less than that when you get around to playing them off against each other. You can save a little money that way, Ben. (*Angrily.*) And make them hate each other just a little more than they do now.

REGINA. What's all this about?

BEN (*laughs*). There'll be no trouble from anybody, white or black. Marshall said that to me. "What about strikes? That's all we've had in Massachusetts for the last three years." I say to him, "What's a strike? I never heard of one. Come South, Marshall. We got good folks and we don't stand for any fancy fooling."

HORACE. You're right. (*Slowly.*) Well, it looks like you made a good deal for yourselves, and for Marshall, too. (*To* BEN.) Your father used to say he made the thousands and you boys would make the millions. I think he was right. (*Rises.*)

REGINA (*they are all looking at* HORACE. *She laughs nervously*). Millions for *us,* too.

HORACE. Us? You and me? I don't think so. We've got enough money, Regina. We'll just sit by and watch the boys grow rich. (*They watch* HORACE *tensely as he begins to move toward the staircase. He passes* LEO, *looks at him for a second.*) How's everything at the bank, Leo?

LEO. Fine, sir. Everything is fine.

HORACE. How are all the ladies in Mobile? (HORACE *turns*

*to* REGINA, *sharply*.) Whatever made you think I'd let Zan marry—

REGINA. Do you mean that you are turning this down? Is it possible that's what you mean?

BEN. No, that's not what he means. Turning down a fortune. Horace is tired. He'd rather talk about it tomorrow—

REGINA. We can't keep putting it off this way. Oscar must be in Chicago by the end of the week with the money and contracts.

OSCAR (*giggles, pleased*). Yes, sir. Got to be there end of the week. No sense going without the money.

REGINA (*tensely*). I've waited long enough for your answer. I'm not going to wait any longer.

HORACE (*very deliberately*). I'm very tired now, Regina.

BEN (*hastily*). Now, Horace probably has his reasons. Things he'd like explained. Tomorrow will do. I can—

REGINA (*turns to* BEN, *sharply*). I want to know his reasons now! (*Turns back to* HORACE.)

HORACE (*as he climbs the steps*). I don't know them all myself. Let's leave it at that.

REGINA. We shall not leave it at that! We have waited for you here like children. Waited for you to come home.

HORACE. So that you could invest my money. So that is why you wanted me home? Well, I had hoped— (*Quietly.*) If you are disappointed, Regina, I'm sorry. But I must do what I think best. We'll talk about it another day.

REGINA. We'll talk about it now. Just you and me.

HORACE (*looks down at her. His voice is tense*). Please, Regina, it's been a hard trip. I don't feel well. Please leave me alone now.

REGINA (*quietly*). I want to talk to you, Horace. I'm coming up. (*He looks at her for a minute, then moves on again out of sight. She begins to climb the stairs.*)

BEN (*softly.* REGINA *turns to him as he speaks*). Sometimes it is better to wait for the sun to rise again. (*She does not answer.*) And sometimes, as our mother used to tell you, (REGINA *starts up stairs.*) it's unwise for a good-looking woman to frown. (BEN *rises, moves toward stairs.*) Softness and a smile do more to the heart of men— (*She disappears.* BEN *stands looking up the stairs. There is a long silence. Then, suddenly,* OSCAR *giggles.*)

OSCAR. Let us hope she'll change his mind. Let us hope. (*After a second* BEN *crosses to table, picks up his newspaper.* OSCAR *looks at* BEN. *The silence makes* LEO *uncomfortable.*)

LEO. The paper says twenty-seven cases of yellow fever in New Orleans. Guess the flood-waters caused it. (*Nobody pays attention.*) Thought they were building the levees high enough. Like the niggers always say: a man born of woman can't build nothing high enough for the Mississippi. (*Gets no answer. Gives an embarrassed laugh.*)

(*Upstairs there is the sound of voices. The voices are not loud, but* BEN, OSCAR, LEO *become conscious of them.* LEO *crosses to landing, looks up, listens.*)

OSCAR (*pointing up*). Now just suppose she don't change his mind? Just suppose he keeps on refusing?

BEN (*without conviction*). He's tired. It was a mistake to talk to him today. He's a sick man, but he isn't a crazy one.

OSCAR (*giggles*). But just suppose he is crazy. What then?

BEN (*puts down his paper, peers at* OSCAR). Then we'll go outside for the money. There's plenty who would give it.

OSCAR. And plenty who will want a lot for what they give. The ones who are rich enough to give will be smart enough to want. That means we'd be working for them, don't it, Ben?

BEN. You don't have to tell me the things I told you six months ago.

OSCAR. Oh, you're right not to worry. She'll change his mind. She always has. (*There is a silence. Suddenly* REGINA'S *voice becomes louder and sharper. All of them begin to listen now. Slowly* BEN *rises, goes to listen by the staircase.* OSCAR, *watching him, smiles. As they listen* REGINA'S *voice becomes very loud.* HORACE'S *voice is no longer heard.*) Maybe. But I don't believe it. I never did believe he was going in with us.

BEN (*turning on him*). What the hell do you expect me to do?
OSCAR (*mildly*). Nothing. You done your almighty best. Nobody could blame you if the whole thing just dripped away right through our fingers. You can't do a thing. But there may be something I could do for us. (OSCAR *rises*.) Or, I might better say, Leo could do for us. (BEN *stops, turns, looks at* OSCAR. LEO *is staring at* OSCAR.) Ain't that true, son? Ain't it true you might be able to help your own kinfolks?
LEO (*nervously taking a step to him*). Papa, I—
BEN (*slowly*). How would he help us, Oscar?
OSCAR. Leo's got a friend. Leo's friend owns eighty-eight thousand dollars in Union Pacific bonds. (BEN *turns to look at* LEO.) Leo's friend don't look at the bonds much—not for five or six months at a time.
BEN (*after a pause*). Union Pacific. Uh, huh. Let me understand. Leo's friend would—would lend him these bonds and he—
OSCAR (*nods*). Would be kind enough to lend them to us.
BEN. Leo.
LEO (*excited, comes to him*). Yes, sir?
BEN. When would your friend be wanting the bonds back?
LEO (*very nervous*). I don't know. I—well, I—
OSCAR (*sharply. Steps to him*). You told me he won't look at them until Fall—
LEO. Oh, that's right. But I—not till Fall. Uncle Horace never—
BEN (*sharply*). Be still.
OSCAR (*smiles at* LEO). Your uncle doesn't wish to know your friend's name.
LEO (*starts to laugh*). That's a good one. Not know his name—
OSCAR. Shut up, Leo! (LEO *turns away slowly, moves to table.* BEN *turns to* OSCAR.) He won't look at them again until September. That gives us five months. Leo will return the bonds in three months. And we'll have no trouble raising the money once the mills are going up. Will Marshall accept bonds?

(BEN *stops to listen to sudden sharp voices from above. The voices are now very angry and very loud.*)

BEN (*smiling*). Why not? Why not? (*Laughs.*) Good. We are lucky. We'll take the loan from Leo's friend—I think he will make a safer partner than our sister. (*Nods toward stairs. Turns to* LEO). How soon can you get them?

LEO. Today. Right now. They're in the safe-deposit box and—

BEN (*sharply*). I don't want to know where they are.

OSCAR (*laughs*). We will keep it secret from you. (*Pats* BEN's *arm*).

BEN (*smiles*). Good. Draw a check for our part. You can take the night train for Chicago. Well, Oscar, (*Holds out his hand.*) good luck to us.

OSCAR. Leo will be taken care of?

LEO. I'm entitled to Uncle Horace's share. I'd enjoy being a partner—

BEN (*turns to stare at him*). You would? You can go to hell, you little— (*Starts toward* LEO.)

OSCAR (*nervously*). Now, now. He didn't mean that. I only want to be sure he'll get something out of all this.

BEN. Of course. We'll take care of him. We won't have any trouble about that. I'll see you at the store.

OSCAR (*nods*). That's settled then. Come on, son. (*Starts for door.*)

LEO (*puts out his hand*). I was only going to say what a great day this was for me and— (BEN *ignores his hand.*)

BEN. Go on.

(LEO *looks at him, turns, follows* OSCAR *out.* BEN *stands where he is, thinking. Again the voices upstairs can be heard.* REGINA's *voice is high and furious.* BEN *looks up, smiles, winces at the noise.*)

ALEXANDRA (*upstairs*). Mama—Mama—don't . . . (*The noise of running footsteps is heard and* ALEXANDRA *comes running down the steps, speaking as she comes.*) Uncle Ben!

Uncle Ben! Please go up. Please make Mama stop. Uncle Ben, he's sick, he's so sick. How can Mama talk to him like that—please, make her stop. She'll—

BEN. Alexandra, you have a tender heart.

ALEXANDRA (*crying*). Go on up, Uncle Ben, please—

(*Suddenly the voices stop. A second later there is the sound of a door being slammed.*)

BEN. Now you see. Everything is over. Don't worry. (*He starts for the door.*) Alexandra, I want you to tell your mother how sorry I am that I had to leave. And don't worry so, my dear. Married folk frequently raise their voices, unfortunately. (*He starts to put on his hat and coat as* REGINA *appears on the stairs.*)

ALEXANDRA (*furiously*). How can you treat Papa like this? He's sick. He's very sick. Don't you know that? I won't let you.

REGINA. Mind your business, Alexandra. (*To* BEN. *Her voice is cold and calm.*) How much longer can you wait for the money?

BEN (*putting on his coat*). He has refused? My, that's too bad.

REGINA. He will change his mind. I'll find a way to make him. What's the longest you can wait now?

BEN. I could wait until next week. But I can't wait until next week. (*He giggles, pleased at the joke.*) I could but I can't. Could and can't. Well, I must go now. I'm very late—

REGINA (*coming downstairs toward him*). You're not going. I want to talk to you.

BEN. I was about to give Alexandra a message for you. I wanted to tell you that Oscar is going to Chicago tonight, so we can't be here for our usual Friday supper.

REGINA (*tensely*). Oscar is going to Chi— (*Softly.*) What do you mean?

BEN. Just that. Everything is settled. He's going on to deliver to Marshall—

REGINA (*taking a step to him*). I demand to know what—You are lying. You are trying to scare me. *You haven't got the money.* How could you have it? You can't have— (BEN *laughs.*) You will wait until I—

(HORACE *comes into view on the landing.*)

BEN. You are getting out of hand. Since when do I take orders from you?
REGINA. Wait, you— (BEN *stops.*) How *can* he go to Chicago? Did a ghost arrive with the money? (BEN *starts for the hall.*) I don't believe you. Come back here. (REGINA *starts after him.*) Come back here, you— (*The door slams. She stops in the doorway, staring, her fists clenched. After a pause she turns slowly.*)
HORACE (*very quietly*). It's a great day when you and Ben cross swords. I've been waiting for it for years.
ALEXANDRA. Papa, Papa, please go back! You will—
HORACE. And so they don't need you, and so you will not have your millions, after all.
REGINA (*turns slowly*). You hate to see anybody live now, don't you? You hate to think that I'm going to be alive and have what I want.
HORACE. I should have known you'd think that was the reason.
REGINA. Because you're going to die and you know you're going to die.
ALEXANDRA (*shrilly*). Mama! Don't— Don't listen, Papa. Just don't listen. Go away—
HORACE. Not to keep you from getting what you want. Not even partly that. (*Holding to the rail.*) I'm sick of you, sick of this house, sick of my life here. I'm sick of your brothers and their dirty tricks to make a dime. There must be better ways of getting rich than cheating niggers on a pound of bacon. Why should I give you the money? (*Very angrily.*) To pound the bones of this town to make dividends for you to spend? You wreck the town, you and your brothers, *you* wreck the town and live on it. Not me.

Maybe it's easy for the dying to be honest. But it's not my fault I'm dying. (ADDIE *enters, stands at door quietly.*) I'll do no more harm now. I've done enough. I'll die my own way. And I'll do it without making the world any worse. I leave that to you.
REGINA (*looks up at him slowly, calmly*).   I hope you die. I hope you die soon. (*Smiles.*) I'll be waiting for you to die.
ALEXANDRA (*shrieking*).   Papa! Don't— Don't listen— Don't—
ADDIE.   Come here, Zan. Come out of this room.

(ALEXANDRA *runs quickly to* ADDIE, *who holds her.* HORACE *turns slowly and starts upstairs.*)

*Curtain*

# Act III

SCENE:   *Same as Act I. Two weeks later. It is late afternoon and it is raining.*

AT RISE:   HORACE *is sitting near the window in a wheel chair. On the table next to him is a safe-deposit box, and a small bottle of medicine.* BIRDIE *and* ALEXANDRA *are playing the piano. On a chair is a large sewing basket.*

BIRDIE (*counting for* ALEXANDRA).   One and two and three and four. One and two and three and four. (*Nods—turns to* HORACE.) We once played together, Horace. Remember?
HORACE (*has been looking out of the window*).   What, Birdie?
BIRDIE.   We played together. You and me.
ALEXANDRA.   *Papa* used to play?
BIRDIE.   Indeed he did. (ADDIE *appears at the door in a large kitchen apron. She is wiping her hands on a towel.*) He played the fiddle and very well, too.
ALEXANDRA (*turns to smile at* HORACE).   I never knew—

ADDIE.  Where's your mama?
ALEXANDRA.  Gone to Miss Safronia's to fit her dresses.

(ADDIE *nods, starts to exit.*)

HORACE.  Addie.
ADDIE.  Yes, Mr. Horace.
HORACE (*speaks as if he had made a sudden decision*).  Tell Cal to get on his things. I want him to go an errand.

(ADDIE *nods, exits.* HORACE *moves nervously in his chair, looks out of the window.*)

ALEXANDRA (*who has been watching him*).  It's too bad it's been raining all day, Papa. But you can go out in the yard tomorrow. Don't be restless.
HORACE.  I'm not restless, darling.
BIRDIE.  I remember so well the time we played together, your papa and me. It was the first time Oscar brought me here to supper. I had never seen all the Hubbards together before, and you know what a ninny I am and how shy. (*Turns to look at* HORACE.) You said you could play the fiddle and you'd be much obliged if I'd play with you. *I* was obliged to *you*, all right, all right. (*Laughs when he does not answer her.*) Horace, you haven't heard a word I've said.
HORACE.  Birdie, when did Oscar get back from Chicago?
BIRDIE.  Yesterday. Hasn't he been here yet?
ALEXANDRA (*stops playing*).  No. Neither has Uncle Ben since — since that day.
BIRDIE.  Oh, I didn't know it was *that* bad. Oscar never tells me anything —
HORACE (*smiles, nods*).  The Hubbards have had their great quarrel. I knew it would come some day. (*Laughs.*) It came.
ALEXANDRA.  It came. It certainly came all right.
BIRDIE (*amazed*).  But Oscar was in such a good humor when he got home, I didn't —
HORACE.  Yes, I can understand that.

(ADDIE *enters carrying a large tray with glasses, a carafe of elderberry wine and a plate of cookies, which she puts on the table.*)

ALEXANDRA. Addie! A party! What for?

ADDIE. Nothing for. I had the fresh butter, so I made the cakes, and a little elderberry does the stomach good in the rain.

BIRDIE. Isn't this nice! A party just for us. Let's play party music, Zan.

(ALEXANDRA *begins to play a gay piece.*)

ADDIE (*to* HORACE, *wheeling his chair to center*). Come over here, Mr. Horace, and don't be thinking so much. A glass of elderberry will do more good.

(ALEXANDRA *reaches for a cake,* BIRDIE *pours herself a glass of wine.*)

ALEXANDRA. Good cakes, Addie. It's nice here. Just us. Be nice if it could always be this way.

BIRDIE (*nods happily*). Quiet and restful.

ADDIE. Well, it won't be that way long. Little while now, even sitting here, you'll hear the red bricks going into place. The next day the smoke'll be pushing out the chimneys and by church time that Sunday every human born of woman will be living on chicken. That's how Mr. Ben's been telling the story.

HORACE (*looks at her*). They believe it that way?

ADDIE. Believe it? They use to believing what Mr. Ben orders. There ain't been so much talk around here since Sherman's army didn't come near.

HORACE (*softly*). They are fools.

ADDIE (*nods, sits down with the sewing basket*). You ain't born in the South unless you're a fool.

BIRDIE (*has drunk another glass of wine*). But we didn't play together after that night. Oscar said he didn't like me to play on the piano. (*Turns to* ALEXANDRA.) You know what he said that night?

ALEXANDRA. Who?
BIRDIE. Oscar. He said that music made him nervous. He said he just sat and waited for the next note. (ALEXANDRA *laughs*.) He wasn't poking fun. He meant it. Ah, well— (*She finishes her glass, shakes her head.* HORACE *looks at her, smiles.*) Your papa don't like to admit it, but he's been mighty kind to me all these years. (*Running the back of her hand along his sleeve.*) Often he'd step in when somebody said something and once— (*She stops, turns away, her face still.*) Once he stopped Oscar from— (*She stops, turns. Quickly.*) I'm sorry I said that. Why, here I am so happy and yet I think about bad things. (*Laughs nervously.*) That's not right, now, is it? (*She pours a drink.* CAL *appears in the door. He has on an old coat and is carrying a torn umbrella.*)
ALEXANDRA. Have a cake, Cal.
CAL (*comes in, takes a cake*). Yes'm. You want me, Mr. Horace?
HORACE. What time is it, Cal?
CAL. 'Bout ten minutes before it's five.
HORACE. All right. Now you walk yourself down to the bank.
CAL. It'll be closed. Nobody'll be there but Mr. Manders, Mr. Joe Horns, Mr. Leo—
HORACE. Go in the back way. They'll be at the table, going over the day's business. (*Points to the deposit box.*) See that box?
CAL (*nods*). Yes, sir.
HORACE. You tell Mr. Manders that Mr. Horace says he's much obliged to him for bringing the box, it arrived all right.
CAL (*bewildered*). He know you got the box. He bring it himself Wednesday. I opened the door to him and he say, "Hello, Cal, coming on to summer weather."
HORACE. You say just what I tell you. Understand?

(BIRDIE *pours another drink, stands at table.*)

CAL. No, sir. I ain't going to say I understand. I'm going down and tell a man he give you something he already know he give you, and you say "understand."

HORACE. Now, Cal.
CAL. Yes, sir. I just going to say you obliged for the box coming all right. I ain't going to understand it, but I'm going to say it.
HORACE. And tell him I want him to come over here after supper, and to bring Mr. Sol Fowler with him.
CAL (*nods*). He's to come after supper and bring Mr. Sol Fowler, your attorney-*at*-law, with him.
HORACE (*smiles*). That's right. Just walk right in the back room and say your piece. (*Slowly.*) In front of everybody.
CAL. Yes, sir. (*Mumbles to himself as he exits.*)
ALEXANDRA (*who has been watching* HORACE). Is anything the matter, Papa?
HORACE. Oh, no. Nothing.
ADDIE. Miss Birdie, that elderberry going to give you a headache spell.
BIRDIE (*beginning to be drunk. Gaily*). Oh, I don't think so. I don't think it will.
ALEXANDRA (*as* HORACE *puts his hand to his throat*). Do you want your medicine, Papa?
HORACE. No, no. I'm all right, darling.
BIRDIE. Mama used to give me elderberry wine when I was a little girl. For hiccoughs. (*Laughs.*) You know, I don't think people get hiccoughs any more. Isn't that funny? (BIRDIE *laughs.* HORACE *and* ALEXANDRA *laugh.*) I used to get hiccoughs just when I shouldn't have.
ADDIE (*nods*). And nobody gets growing pains no more. That is funny. Just as if there was some style in what you get. One year an ailment's stylish and the next year it ain't.
BIRDIE (*turns*). I remember. It was my first big party, at Lionnet I mean, and I was so excited, and there I was with hiccoughs and Mama laughing. (*Softly. Looking at carafe.*) Mama always laughed. (*Picks up carafe.*) A big party, a lovely dress from Mr. Worth in Paris, France, and hiccoughs. (*Pours drink.*) My brother pounding me on the back and Mama with the elderberry bottle, laughing at me. Everybody was on their way to come, and I was such a ninny, hiccoughing away. (*Drinks.*) You know, that was

the first day I ever saw Oscar Hubbard. The Ballongs were selling their horses and he was going there to buy. He passed and lifted his hat—we could see him from the window—and my brother, to tease Mama, said maybe we should have invited the Hubbards to the party. He said Mama didn't like them because they kept a store, and he said that was old-fashioned of her. (*Her face lights up.*) And then, and *then*, I saw Mama angry for the first time in my life. She said that wasn't the reason. She said she was old-fashioned, but not that way. She said she was old-fashioned enough not to like people who killed animals they couldn't use, and who made their money charging awful interest to poor, ignorant niggers and cheating them on what they bought. She was very angry, Mama was. I had never seen her face like that. And then suddenly she laughed and said, "Look, I've frightened Birdie out of the hiccoughs." (*Her head drops. Then softly.*) And so she had. They were all gone. (*Moves to sofa, sits.*)

ADDIE. Yeah, they got mighty well off cheating niggers. Well, there are people who eat the earth and eat all the people on it like in the Bible with the locusts. Then there are people who stand around and watch them eat it. (*Softly.*) Sometimes I think it ain't right to stand and watch them do it.

BIRDIE (*thoughtfully*). Like I say, if we could only go back to Lionnet. Everybody'd be better there. They'd be good and kind. I like people to be kind. (*Pours drink.*) Don't you, Horace; don't you like people to be kind?

HORACE. Yes, Birdie.

BIRDIE (*very drunk now*). Yes, that was the first day I ever saw Oscar. Who would have thought— (*Quickly.*) You all want to know something? Well, I don't like Leo. My very own son, and I don't like him. (*Laughs, gaily.*) My, I guess I even like Oscar more.

ALEXANDRA. Why did you marry Uncle Oscar?

ADDIE (*sharply*). That's no question for you to be asking.

HORACE (*sharply*). Why not? She's heard enough around here to ask anything.

ALEXANDRA. Aunt Birdie, why did you marry Uncle Oscar?
BIRDIE. I don't know. I thought I liked him. He was kind to me and I thought it was because he liked me too. But that wasn't the reason—(*Wheels on* ALEXANDRA.) Ask why *he* married *me*. I can tell you that: he's told it to me often enough.
ADDIE (*leaning forward*). Miss Birdie, don't—
BIRDIE (*speaking very rapidly, tensely*). My family was good and the cotton on Lionnet's fields was better. Ben Hubbard wanted the cotton and (*Rises.*) Oscar Hubbard married it for him. He was kind to me, then. He used to smile at me. He hasn't smiled at me since. Everybody knew that's what he married me for. (ADDIE *rises.*) Everybody but me. Stupid, stupid me.
ALEXANDRA (*to* HORACE, *holding his hand, softly*). I see. (*Hesitates.*) Papa, I mean—when you feel better couldn't we go away? I mean, by ourselves. Couldn't we find a way to go—
HORACE. Yes, I know what you mean. We'll try to find a way. I promise you, darling.
ADDIE (*moves to* BIRDIE). Rest a bit, Miss Birdie. You get talking like this you'll get a headache and—
BIRDIE (*sharply, turning to her*). I've never had a headache in my life. (*Begins to cry hysterically.*) You know it as well as I do. (*Turns to* ALEXANDRA.) I never had a headache, Zan. That's a lie they tell for me. I drink. All by myself, in my own room, by myself, I drink. Then, when they want to hide it, they say, "Birdie's got a headache again"—
ALEXANDRA (*comes to her quickly*). Aunt Birdie.
BIRDIE (*turning away*). Even you won't like me now. You won't like me any more.
ALEXANDRA. I love you. I'll always love you.
BIRDIE (*furiously*). Well, don't. Don't love me. Because in twenty years you'll just be like me. They'll do all the same things to you. (*Begins to laugh hysterically.*) You know what? In twenty-two years I haven't had a whole day of happiness. Oh, a little, like today with you all. But never a single, whole day. I say to myself, if only I had one more

*whole* day, then— (*The laugh stops.*) And that's the way you'll be. And you'll trail after them, just like me, hoping they won't be so mean that day or say something to make you feel so bad—only you'll be worse off because you haven't got my Mama to remember— (*Turns away, her head drops. She stands quietly, swaying a little, holding to the sofa.* ALEXANDRA *leans down, puts her cheek on* BIRDIE'S *arm.*)

ALEXANDRA (*to* BIRDIE). I guess we were all trying to make a happy day. You know, we sit around and try to pretend nothing's happened. We try to pretend we are not here. We make believe we are just by ourselves, some place else, and it doesn't seem to work. (*Kisses* BIRDIE'S *hand.*) Come now, Aunt Birdie, I'll walk you home. You and me. (*She takes* BIRDIE'S *arm. They move slowly out.*)

BIRDIE (*softly as they exit*). You and me.

ADDIE (*after a minute*). Well. First time I ever heard Miss Birdie say a word. (HORACE *looks at her.*) Maybe it's good for her. I'm just sorry Zan had to hear it. (HORACE *moves his head as if he were uncomfortable.*) You feel bad, don't you? (*He shrugs.*)

HORACE. So you didn't want Zan to hear? It would be nice to let her stay innocent, like Birdie at her age. Let her listen now. Let her see everything. How else is she going to know that she's got to get away? I'm trying to show her that. I'm trying, but I've only got a little time left. She can even hate me when I'm dead, if she'll only learn to hate and fear this.

ADDIE. Mr. Horace—

HORACE. Pretty soon there'll be nobody to help her but you.

ADDIE (*crossing to him*). What can I do?

HORACE. Take her away.

ADDIE. How can I do that? Do you think they'd let me just go away with her?

HORACE. I'll fix it so they can't stop you when you're ready to go. You'll go, Addie?

ADDIE (*after a second, softly*). Yes, sir, I promise. (*He touches her arm, nods.*)

HORACE (*quietly*). I'm going to have Sol Fowler make me a new will. They'll make trouble, but you make Zan stand firm and Fowler'll do the rest. Addie, I'd like to leave you something for yourself. I always wanted to.

ADDIE (*laughs*). Don't you do that, Mr. Horace. A nigger woman in a white man's will! I'd never get it nohow.

HORACE. I know. But upstairs in the armoire drawer there's seventeen hundred dollar bills. It's money left from my trip. It's in an envelope with your name. It's for you.

ADDIE. Seventeen hundred dollar bills! My God, Mr. Horace, I won't know how to count up that high. (*Shyly.*) It's mighty kind and good of you. I don't know what to say for thanks—

CAL (*appears in doorway*). I'm back. (*No answer.*) I'm back.

ADDIE. So we see.

HORACE. Well?

CAL. Nothing. I just went down and spoke my piece. Just like you told me. I say, "Mr. Horace he thank you mightily for the safe box arriving in good shape and he say you come right after supper to his house and bring Mr. Attorney-at-law Sol Fowler with you." Then I wipe my hands on my coat. Every time I ever told a lie in my whole life, I wipe my hands right after. Can't help doing it. Well, while I'm wiping my hands, Mr. Leo jump up and say to me, "What box? What you talking about?"

HORACE (*smiles*). Did he?

CAL. And Mr. Leo say he got to leave a little early cause he got something to do. And then Mr. Manders say Mr. Leo should sit right down and finish up his work and stop acting like somebody made him Mr. President. So he sit down. Now, just like I told you, Mr. Manders was mighty surprised with the message because he knows right well he brought the box— (*Points to box, sighs.*) But he took it all right. Some men take everything easy and some do not.

HORACE (*puts his head back, laughs*). Mr. Leo was telling the truth; he *has* got something to do. I hope Manders don't keep him too long. (*Outside there is the sound of voices.* CAL *exits.* ADDIE *crosses quickly to* HORACE, *puts basket on table, begins to wheel his chair toward the stairs. Sharply.*) No. Leave me where I am.

ADDIE. But that's Miss Regina coming back.

HORACE (*nods, looking at door*). Go away, Addie.

ADDIE (*hesitates*). Mr. Horace. Don't talk no more today. You don't feel well and it won't do no good —

HORACE (*as he hears footsteps in the hall*). Go on. (*She looks at him for a second, then picks up her sewing from table and exits as* REGINA *comes in from hall.* HORACE'S *chair is now so placed that he is in front of the table with the medicine.* REGINA *stands in the hall, shakes umbrella, stands it in the corner, takes off her cloak and throws it over the banister. She stares at* HORACE.)

REGINA (*as she takes off her gloves*). We had agreed that you were to stay in your part of this house and I in mine. This room is *my* part of the house. Please don't come down here again.

HORACE. I won't.

REGINA (*crosses toward bell-cord*). I'll get Cal to take you upstairs.

HORACE (*smiles*). Before you do I want to tell you that after all, we have invested our money in Hubbard Sons and Marshall, Cotton Manufacturers.

REGINA (*stops, turns, stares at him*). What are you talking about? You haven't seen Ben — When did you change your mind?

HORACE. I didn't change my mind. *I* didn't invest the money. (*Smiles.*) It was invested for me.

REGINA (*angrily*). What—?

HORACE. I had eighty-eight thousand dollars' worth of Union Pacific bonds in that safe-deposit box. They are not there now. Go and look. (*As she stares at him, he points to the box.*) Go and look, Regina. (*She crosses quickly to the box, opens it.*) Those bonds are as negotiable as money.

REGINA (*turns back to him*). What kind of joke are you playing now? Is this for my benefit?

HORACE. I don't look in that box very often, but three days ago, on Wednesday it was, because I had made a decision —

REGINA. I want to know what you are talking about.

HORACE (*sharply*). Don't interrupt me again. Because I had made a decision, I sent for the box. The bonds were gone. Eighty-eight thousand dollars gone. (*He smiles at her.*)
REGINA (*after a moment's silence, quietly*). Do you think I'm crazy enough to believe what you're saying?
HORACE (*shrugs*). Believe anything you like.
REGINA (*stares at him, slowly*). Where did they go to?
HORACE. They are in Chicago. With Mr. Marshall, I should guess.
REGINA. What did they do? Walk to Chicago? Have you really gone crazy?
HORACE. Leo took the bonds.
REGINA (*turns sharply then speaks softly, without conviction*). I don't believe it.
HORACE (*leans forward*). I wasn't there but I can guess what happened. This fine gentleman, to whom you were willing to marry your daughter, took the keys and opened the box. You remember that the day of the fight Oscar went to Chicago? Well, he went with my bonds that his son Leo had stolen for him. (*Pleasantly.*) And for Ben, of course, too.
REGINA (*slowly, nods*). When did you find out the bonds were gone?
HORACE. Wednesday night.
REGINA. I thought that's what you said. Why have you waited three days to do anything? (*Suddenly laughs.*) This *will* make a fine story.
HORACE (*nods*). Couldn't it?
REGINA (*still laughing*). A fine story to hold over their heads. How could they be such fools? (*Turns to him.*)
HORACE. But I'm not going to hold it over their heads.
REGINA (*the laugh stops*). What?
HORACE (*turns his chair to face her*). I'm going to let them keep the bonds—as a loan from you. An eighty-eight-thousand-dollar loan; they should be grateful to you. They will be, I think.
REGINA (*slowly, smiles*). I see. You are punishing me. But I won't let you punish me. If you won't do anything, I will. Now. (*She starts for door.*)

HORACE. You won't do anything. Because you can't. (REGINA *stops.*) It won't do you any good to make trouble because I shall simply say that I lent them the bonds.

REGINA (*slowly*). You would do that?

HORACE. Yes. For once in your life, I am tying your hands. There is nothing for you to do. (*There is silence. Then she sits down.*)

REGINA. I see. You are going to lend them the bonds and let them keep all the profit they make on them, and there is nothing I can do about it. Is that right?

HORACE. Yes.

REGINA (*softly*). Why did you say that I was making this gift?

HORACE. I was coming to that. I am going to make a new will, Regina, leaving you eighty-eight thousand dollars in Union Pacific bonds. The rest will go to Zan. It's true that your brothers have borrowed your share for a little while. After my death I advise you to talk to Ben and Oscar. They won't admit anything and Ben, I think, will be smart enough to see that he's safe. Because I knew about the theft and said nothing. Nor will I say anything as long as I live. Is that clear to you?

REGINA (*nods, softly, without looking at him*). You will not say anything as long as you live.

HORACE. That's right. And by that time they will probably have replaced your bonds, and then they'll belong to you and nobody but us will ever know what happened. (*Stops, smiles.*) They'll be around any minute to see what I am going to do. I took good care to see that word reached Leo. They'll be mighty relieved to know I'm going to do nothing and Ben will think it all a capital joke on you. And that will be the end of that. There's nothing you can do to them, nothing you can do to me.

REGINA. You hate me very much.

HORACE. No.

REGINA. Oh, I think you do. (*Puts her head back, sighs.*) Well, we haven't been very good together. Anyway, I don't hate you either. I have only contempt for you. I've always had.

HORACE. From the very first?

REGINA. I think so.
HORACE. I was in love with *you*. But why did *you* marry *me*?
REGINA. I was lonely when I was young.
HORACE. *You* were lonely?
REGINA. Not the way people usually mean. Lonely for all the things I wasn't going to get. Everybody in this house was so busy and there was so little place for what I wanted. I wanted the world. Then, and then—(*Smiles.*) Papa died and left the money to Ben and Oscar.
HORACE. And you married me?
REGINA. Yes, I thought— But I was wrong. You were a small-town clerk then. You haven't changed.
HORACE (*nods, smiles*). And that wasn't what you wanted.
REGINA. No. No, it wasn't what I wanted. (*Pauses, leans back, pleasantly.*) It took me a little while to find out I had made a mistake. As for you—I don't know. It was almost as if I couldn't stand the kind of man you were— (*Smiles, softly.*) I used to lie there at night, praying you wouldn't come near—
HORACE. Really? It was as bad as that?
REGINA (*nods*). Remember when I went to Doctor Sloan and I told you he said there was something the matter with me and that you shouldn't touch me any more?
HORACE. I remember.
REGINA. But you believed it. I couldn't understand that. I couldn't understand that anybody could be such a soft fool. That was when I began to despise you.
HORACE (*puts his hand to his throat, looks at the bottle of medicine on table*). Why didn't you leave me?
REGINA. I told you I married you for something. It turned out it was only for this. (*Carefully.*) This wasn't what I wanted, but it was something. I never thought about it much but if I had (HORACE *puts his hand to his throat.*) I'd have known that you would die before I would. But I couldn't have known that you would get heart trouble so early and so bad. I'm lucky, Horace. I've always been lucky. (HORACE *turns slowly to the medicine.*) I'll be lucky again. (HORACE *looks at her. Then he puts his hand to his throat. Because he cannot reach the bottle he moves*

*the chair closer. He reaches for the medicine, takes out the cork, picks up the spoon. The bottle slips and smashes on the table. He draws in his breath, gasps.)*

HORACE. Please. Tell Addie— The other bottle is upstairs. (REGINA *has not moved. She does not move now. He stares at her. Then, suddenly as if he understood, he raises his voice. It is a panic-stricken whisper, too small to be heard outside the room.)* Addie! Addie! Come— *(Stops as he hears the softness of his voice. He makes a sudden, furious spring from the chair to the stairs, taking the first few steps as if he were a desperate runner. On the fourth step he slips, gasps, grasps the rail, makes a great effort to reach the landing. When he reaches the landing, he is on his knees. His knees give way, he falls on the landing, out of view.* REGINA *has not turned during his climb up the stairs. Now she waits a second. Then she goes below the landing, speaks up.)*

REGINA. Horace. Horace. *(When there is no answer, she turns, calls.)* Addie! Cal! Come in here. *(She starts up the steps.* ADDIE *and* CAL *appear. Both run toward the stairs.)* He's had an attack. Come up here. *(They run up the steps quickly.)*

CAL. My God. Mr. Horace—

*(They cannot be seen now.)*

REGINA *(her voice comes from the head of the stairs).* Be still, Cal. Bring him in here.

*(Before the footsteps and the voices have completely died away,* ALEXANDRA *appears in the hall door, in her raincloak and hood. She comes into the room, begins to unfasten the cloak, suddenly looks around, sees the empty wheel chair, stares, begins to move swiftly as if to look in the dining room. At the same moment* ADDIE *runs down the stairs.* ALEXANDRA *turns and stares up at* ADDIE.*)*

ALEXANDRA. Addie! What?

ADDIE (*takes* ALEXANDRA *by the shoulders*). I'm going for the doctor. Go upstairs. (ALEXANDRA *looks at her, then quickly breaks away and runs up the steps.* ADDIE *exits. The stage is empty for a minute. Then the front door bell begins to ring. When there is no answer, it rings again. A second later* LEO *appears in the hall, talking as he comes in.*)

LEO (*very nervous*). Hello. (*Irritably.*) Never saw any use ringing a bell when a door was open. If you are going to ring a bell, then somebody should answer it. (*Gets in the room, looks around, puzzled, listens, hears no sound.*) Aunt Regina. (*He moves around restlessly.*) Addie. (*Waits.*) Where the hell— (*Crosses to the bell cord, rings it impatiently, waits, gets no answer, calls.*) Cal! Cal! (CAL *appears on the stair landing.*)

CAL (*his voice is soft, shaken*). Mr. Leo. Miss Regina says you stop that screaming noise.

LEO (*angrily*). Where is everybody?

CAL. Mr. Horace he got an attack. He's bad. Miss Regina says you stop that noise.

LEO. Uncle Horace— What— What happened? (CAL *starts down the stairs, shakes his head, begins to move swiftly off.* LEO *looks around wildly.*) But when— You seen Mr. Oscar or Mr. Ben? (CAL *shakes his head. Moves on.* LEO *grabs him by the arm.*) Answer me, will you?

CAL. No, I ain't seen 'em. I ain't got time to answer you. I got to get things. (CAL *runs off.*)

LEO. But what's the matter with him? When did this happen— (*Calling after* CAL.) You'd think Papa'd be some place where you could find him. I been chasing him all afternoon.

(OSCAR *and* BEN *come quickly into the room.*)

LEO. Papa, I've been looking all over town for you and Uncle Ben—

BEN. Where is he?

OSCAR. Addie just told us it was a sudden attack, and—

BEN (*to* LEO). Where is he? When did it happen?

LEO. Upstairs. Will you listen to me, please? I been looking for you for—
OSCAR (*to* BEN). You think we should go up? (BEN, *looking up the steps, shakes his head.*)
BEN. I don't know. I don't know.
OSCAR (*shakes his head*). But he was all right—
LEO (*yelling*). *Will you listen to me?*
OSCAR (*sharply*). What is the matter with you?
LEO. I been trying to tell you. I been trying to find you for an hour—
OSCAR. Tell me what?
LEO. Uncle Horace knows about the bonds. He knows about them. He's had the box since Wednesday—
BEN (*sharply*). Stop shouting! What the hell are you talking about?
LEO (*furiously*). I'm telling you he knows about the bonds. Ain't that clear enough—
OSCAR (*grabbing* LEO'S *arm*). You God-damn fool! Stop screaming!
BEN. Now what happened? Talk quietly.
LEO. You heard me. Uncle Horace knows about the bonds. He's known since Wednesday.
BEN (*after a second*). How do you know that?
LEO. Because Cal comes down to Manders and says the box came O.K. and—
OSCAR (*trembling*). That might not mean a thing—
LEO (*angrily*). No? It might not, huh? Then he says Manders should come here tonight and bring Sol Fowler with him. I guess that don't mean a thing either.
OSCAR (*to* BEN). Ben— What— Do you think he's seen the—
BEN (*motions to the box*). There's the box. (*Both* OSCAR *and* LEO *turn sharply.* LEO *makes a leap to the box.*) You ass. Put it down. What are you going to do with it, eat it?
LEO. I'm going to— (*Starts.*)
BEN (*furiously*). Put it down. Don't touch it again. Now sit down and shut up for a minute.
OSCAR. Since Wednesday. (*To* LEO.) You said he had it since Wednesday. Why didn't he say something— (*To* BEN.) I don't understand—

LEO (*taking a step*). I can put it back. I can put it back before anybody knows.
BEN (*who is standing at the table, softly*). He's had it since Wednesday. Yet he hasn't said a word to us.
OSCAR. Why? Why?
LEO. What's the difference why? He was getting ready to say plenty. He was going to say it to Fowler tonight—
OSCAR (*angrily*). Be still. (*Turns to* BEN, *looks at him, waits.*)
BEN (*after a minute*). I don't believe that.
LEO (*wildly*). *You* don't believe it? What do I care what *you* believe? I do the dirty work and then—
BEN (*turning his head sharply to* LEO). I'm remembering that. I'm remembering that, Leo.
OSCAR. What do you mean?
LEO. You—
BEN (*to* OSCAR). If you don't shut that little fool up, I'll show you what I mean. For some reason he knows, but he don't say a word.
OSCAR. Maybe he didn't know that *we*—
BEN (*quickly*). That *Leo*— He's no fool. Does Manders know the bonds are missing?
LEO. How could I tell? I was half crazy. I don't think so. Because Manders seemed kind of puzzled and—
OSCAR. But we got to find out— (*He breaks off as* CAL *comes into the room carrying a kettle of hot water.*)
BEN. How is he, Cal?
CAL. I don't know, Mr. Ben. He was bad. (*Going toward stairs.*)
OSCAR. But when did it happen?
CAL (*shrugs.*) He wasn't feeling bad early. (ADDIE *comes in quickly from the hall.*) Then there he is next thing on the landing, fallen over, his eyes tight—
ADDIE (*to* CAL). Dr. Sloan's over at the Ballongs. Hitch the buggy and go get him. (*She takes the kettle and cloths from him, pushes him, runs up the stairs.*) Go on. (*She disappears.* CAL *exits.*)
BEN. Never seen Sloan anywhere when you need him.
OSCAR (*softly*). Sounds bad.

LEO. He would have told *her* about it. Aunt Regina. He would have told his own wife—

BEN (*turning to* LEO). Yes, he might have told her. But they weren't on such pretty terms and maybe he didn't. Maybe he didn't. (*Goes quickly to* LEO.) Now, listen to me. If she doesn't know, it may work out all right. If she does know, you're to say he lent you the bonds.

LEO. Lent them to me! Who's going to believe that?

BEN. Nobody.

OSCAR (*to* LEO). Don't you understand? It can't do no harm to say it—

LEO. Why should I say he lent them to me? Why not to you? (*Carefully.*) Why not to Uncle Ben?

BEN (*smiles*). Just because he didn't lend them to me. Remember that.

LEO. But all he has to do is say he didn't lend them to me—

BEN (*furiously*). But for some reason, he doesn't seem to be talking, does he?

(*There are footsteps above. They all stand looking at the stairs.* REGINA *begins to come slowly down.*)

BEN. What happened?

REGINA. He's had a bad attack.

OSCAR. Too bad. I'm sorry we weren't here when—when Horace needed us.

BEN. When *you* needed us.

REGINA (*looks at him*). Yes.

BEN. How is he? Can we—can we go up?

REGINA (*shakes her head*). He's not conscious.

OSCAR (*pacing around*). It's that—it's that bad? Wouldn't you think Sloan could be found quickly, just once, just once?

REGINA. I don't think there is much for him to do.

BEN. Oh, don't talk like that. He's come through attacks before. He will now.

(REGINA *sits down. After a second she speaks softly.*)

REGINA. Well. We haven't seen each other since the day of our fight.

BEN (*tenderly*). That was nothing. Why, you and Oscar and I used to fight when we were kids.

OSCAR (*hurriedly*). Don't you think we should go up? Is there anything we can do for Horace—

BEN. You don't feel well. Ah—

REGINA (*without looking at them*). No, I don't. (*Slight pause.*) Horace told me about the bonds this afternoon. (*There is an immediate shocked silence.*)

LEO. The bonds. What do you mean? What bonds? What—

BEN (*looks at him furiously. Then to* REGINA). The Union Pacific bonds? *Horace's* Union Pacific bonds?

REGINA. Yes.

OSCAR (*steps to her, very nervously*). Well. Well what—what about them? What—what could he say?

REGINA. He said that Leo had stolen the bonds and given them to you.

OSCAR (*aghast, very loudly*). That's ridiculous, Regina, absolutely—

LEO. I don't know what you're talking about. What would I— Why—

REGINA (*wearily to* BEN). Isn't it enough that he stole them from me? Do I have to listen to this in the bargain?

OSCAR. You are talking—

LEO. I didn't steal anything. I don't know why—

REGINA (*to* BEN). Would you ask them to stop that, please? (*There is silence for a minute.* BEN *glowers at* OSCAR *and* LEO.)

BEN. Aren't we starting at the wrong end, Regina? What did Horace tell you?

REGINA (*smiles at him*). He told me that Leo had stolen the bonds.

LEO. I didn't steal—

REGINA. Please. Let me finish. Then he told me that he was going to pretend that he had lent them to you (LEO *turns sharply to* REGINA, *then looks at* OSCAR, *then looks back at* REGINA.) as a present from me—to my brothers. He said there was nothing I could do about it. He said the rest of his money would go to Alexandra. That is all. (*There is a silence.* OSCAR *coughs,* LEO *smiles slyly.*)

LEO (*taking a step to her*). I told you he had lent them— I could have told you—

REGINA (*ignores him, smiles sadly at* BEN). So I'm very badly off, you see. (*Carefully.*) But Horace said there was nothing I could do about it as long as he was alive to say he had lent you the bonds.

BEN. You shouldn't feel that way. It can all be explained, all be adjusted. It isn't as bad—

REGINA. So you, at least, are willing to admit that the bonds were stolen?

BEN (OSCAR *laughs nervously*). I admit no such thing. It's possible that Horace made up that part of the story to tease you— (*Looks at her.*) Or perhaps to punish you. Punish you.

REGINA (*sadly*). It's not a pleasant story. I feel bad, Ben, naturally. I hadn't thought—

BEN. Now you shall have the bonds safely back. That was the understanding, wasn't it, Oscar?

OSCAR. Yes.

REGINA. I'm glad to know that. (*Smiles.*) Ah, I had greater hopes—

BEN. Don't talk that way. That's foolish. (*Looks at his watch.*) I think we ought to drive out for Sloan ourselves. If we can't find him we'll go over to Senateville for Doctor Morris. And don't think I'm dismissing this other business. I'm not. We'll have it all out on a more appropriate day.

REGINA (*looks up, quietly*). I don't think you had better go yet. I think you had better stay and sit down.

BEN. We'll be back with Sloan.

REGINA. Cal has gone for him. I don't want you to go.

BEN. Now don't worry and—

REGINA. You will come back in this room and sit down. I have something more to say.

BEN (*turns, comes toward her*). Since when do I take orders from you?

REGINA (*smiles*). You don't—yet. (*Sharply.*) Come back, Oscar. You too, Leo.

OSCAR (*sure of himself, laughs*). My dear Regina—
BEN (*softly, pats her hand*). Horace has already clipped your wings and very wittily. Do I have to clip them, too? (*Smiles at her.*) You'd get farther with a smile, Regina. I'm a soft man for a woman's smile.
REGINA. I'm smiling, Ben. I'm smiling because you are quite safe while Horace lives. But I don't think Horace will live. And if he doesn't live I shall want seventy-five per cent in exchange for the bonds.
BEN (*steps back, whistles, laughs*). Greedy! What a greedy girl you are! You want so much of everything.
REGINA. Yes. And if I don't get what I want I am going to put all three of you in jail.
OSCAR (*furiously*). You're mighty crazy. Having just admitted—
BEN. And on what evidence would you put Oscar and Leo in jail?
REGINA (*laughs, gaily*). Oscar, listen to him. He's getting ready to swear that it was you and Leo! What do you say to that? (OSCAR *turns furiously toward* BEN.) Oh, don't be angry, Oscar. I'm going to see that he goes in with you.
BEN. Try anything you like, Regina. (*Sharply.*) And now we can stop all this and say good-bye to you. (ALEXANDRA *comes slowly down the steps.*) It's his money and he's obviously willing to let us borrow it. (*More pleasantly.*) Learn to make threats when you can carry them through. For how many years have I told you a good-looking woman gets more by being soft and appealing? Mama used to tell you that. (*Looks at his watch.*) Where the hell is Sloan? (*To* OSCAR.) Take the buggy and— (*As* BEN *turns to* OSCAR, *he sees* ALEXANDRA. *She walks stiffly. She goes slowly to the lower window, her head bent. They all turn to look at her.*)
OSCAR (*after a second, moving toward her*). What? Alexandra— (*She does not answer. After a second,* ADDIE *comes slowly down the stairs, moving as if she were very tired. At foot of steps, she looks at* ALEXANDRA, *then turns and slowly crosses to door and exits.* REGINA *rises.* BEN *looks nervously at* ALEXANDRA, *at* REGINA.)

OSCAR (*as* ADDIE *passes him, irritably to* ALEXANDRA). Well, what is— (*Turns into room—sees* ADDIE *at foot of steps.*) —what's? (BEN *puts up a hand, shakes his head.*) My God, I didn't know—who *could* have known—I didn't know he was that sick. Well, well—I— (REGINA *stands quietly, her back to them.*)

BEN (*softly, sincerely*). Seems like yesterday when he first came here.

OSCAR. (*sincerely, nervously*). Yes, that's true. (*Turns to* BEN.) The whole town loved him and respected him.

ALEXANDRA (*turns*). Did you love him, Uncle Oscar?

OSCAR. Certainly, I— What a strange thing to ask! I—

ALEXANDRA. Did you love him, Uncle Ben?

BEN (*simply*). He had—

ALEXANDRA (*suddenly starts to laugh very loudly*). And you, Mama, did you love him, too?

REGINA. I know what you feel, Alexandra, but please try to control yourself.

ALEXANDRA (*still laughing*). I'm trying, Mama. I'm trying very hard.

BEN. Grief makes some people laugh and some people cry. It's better to cry, Alexandra.

ALEXANDRA (*the laugh has stopped. Tensely moves toward* REGINA). What was Papa doing on the staircase?

(BEN *turns to look at* ALEXANDRA.)

REGINA. Please go and lie down, my dear. We all need time to get over shocks like this. (ALEXANDRA *does not move.* REGINA's *voice becomes softer, more insistent.*) Please go, Alexandra.

ALEXANDRA. No, Mama. I'll wait. I've got to talk to you.

REGINA. Later. Go and rest now.

ALEXANDRA (*quietly*). I'll wait, Mama. I've plenty of time.

REGINA (*hesitates, stares, makes a half shrug, turns back to* BEN). As I was saying. Tomorrow morning I am going up to Judge Simmes. I shall tell him about Leo.

BEN (*motioning toward* ALEXANDRA). Not in front of the child, Regina. I—

REGINA (*turns to him. Sharply*). I didn't ask her to stay. Tomorrow morning I go to Judge Simmes—
OSCAR. And what proof? What proof of all this—
REGINA (*turns sharply*). None. I won't need any. The bonds are missing and they are with Marshall. That will be enough. If it isn't, I'll add what's necessary.
BEN. I'm sure of that.
REGINA (*turns to* BEN). You can be quite sure.
OSCAR. We'll deny—
REGINA. Deny your heads off. You couldn't find a jury that wouldn't weep for a woman whose brothers steal from her. And you couldn't find twelve men in this state you haven't cheated and who hate you for it.
OSCAR. What kind of talk is this? You couldn't do anything like that! We're your own brothers. (*Points upstairs.*) How can you talk that way when upstairs not five minutes ago—
REGINA (*slowly*). There are people who can't go back, who must finish what they start. I am one of those people, Oscar. (*After a slight pause.*) Where was I? (*Smiles at* BEN.) Well, they'll convict you. But I won't care much if they don't. (*Leans forward, pleasantly.*) Because by that time you'll be ruined. I shall also tell my story to Mr. Marshall, who likes me, I think, and who will not want to be involved in your scandal. A respectable firm like Marshall and Company. The deal would be off in an hour. (*Turns to them angrily.*) And you know it. Now I don't want to hear any more from any of you. *You'll do no more bargaining in this house.* I'll take my seventy-five per cent and we'll forget the story forever. That's one way of doing it, and the way I prefer. You know me well enough to know that I don't mind taking the other way.
BEN (*after a second, slowly*). None of us has ever known you well enough, Regina.
REGINA. You're getting old, Ben. Your tricks aren't as smart as they used to be. (*There is no answer. She waits, then smiles.*) All right. I take it that's settled and I get what I asked for.
OSCAR (*furiously to* BEN). Are you going to let her do this—
BEN (*turns to look at him, slowly*). You have a suggestion?

REGINA (*puts her arms above her head, stretches, laughs*). No, he hasn't. All right. Now, Leo, I have forgotten that you ever saw the bonds. (*Archly, to* BEN *and* OSCAR.) And as long as you boys both behave yourselves, I've forgotten that we ever talked about them. You can draw up the necessary papers tomorrow. (BEN *laughs.* LEO *stares at him, starts for door. Exits.* OSCAR *moves toward door angrily.* REGINA *looks at* BEN, *nods, laughs with him. For a second,* OSCAR *stands in the door, looking back at them. Then he exits.*)

REGINA. You're a good loser, Ben. I like that.

BEN (*he picks up his coat, then turns to her*). Well, I say to myself, what's the good? You and I aren't like Oscar. We're not sour people. I think that comes from a good digestion. Then, too, one loses today and wins tomorrow. I say to myself, years of planning and I get what I want. Then I don't get it. But I'm not discouraged. The century's turning, the world is open. Open for people like you and me. Ready for us, waiting for us. After all this is just the beginning. There are hundreds of Hubbards sitting in rooms like this throughout the country. All their names aren't Hubbard, but they are all Hubbards and they will own this country some day. We'll get along.

REGINA (*smiles*). I think so.

BEN. Then, too, I say to myself, things may change. (*Looks at* ALEXANDRA.) I agree with Alexandra. What is a man in a wheel chair doing on a staircase? I ask myself that.

REGINA (*looks up at him*). And what do you answer?

BEN. I have no answer. But maybe some day I will. Maybe never, but maybe some day. (*Smiles. Pats her arm.*) When I do, I'll let you know. (*Goes toward hall.*)

REGINA. When you do, write me. I will be in Chicago. (*Gaily.*) Ah, Ben, if Papa had only left me his money.

BEN. I'll see you tomorrow.

REGINA. Oh, yes. Certainly. You'll be sort of working for me now.

BEN (*as he passes* ALEXANDRA, *smiles*). Alexandra, you're turning out to be a right interesting girl. (*Looks at* REGINA.) Well, good night all. (*He exits.*)

REGINA (*sits quietly for a second, stretches, turns to look at* ALEXANDRA). What do you want to talk to me about, Alexandra?

ALEXANDRA (*slowly*). I've changed my mind. I don't want to talk. There's nothing to talk about now.

REGINA. You're acting very strange. Not like yourself. You've had a bad shock today. I know that. And you loved Papa, but you must have expected this to come some day. You knew how sick he was.

ALEXANDRA. I knew. We all knew.

REGINA. It will be good for you to get away from here. Good for me, too. Time heals most wounds, Alexandra. You're young, you shall have all the things I wanted. I'll make the world for you the way I wanted it to be for me. (*Uncomfortably.*) Don't sit there staring. You've been around Birdie so much you're getting just like her.

ALEXANDRA (*nods*). Funny. That's what Aunt Birdie said today.

REGINA (*nods*). Be good for you to get away from all this.

(ADDIE *enters.*)

ADDIE. Cal is back, Miss Regina. He says Dr. Sloan will be coming in a few minutes.

REGINA. We'll go in a few weeks. A few weeks! That means two or three Saturdays, two or three Sundays. (*Sighs.*) Well, I'm very tired. I shall go to bed. I don't want any supper. Put the lights out and lock up. (ADDIE *moves to the piano lamp, turns it out.*) You go to your room, Alexandra. Addie will bring you something hot. You look very tired. (*Rises. To* ADDIE.) Call me when Dr. Sloan gets here. I don't want to see anybody else. I don't want any condolence calls tonight. The whole town will be over.

ALEXANDRA. Mama, I'm not coming with you. I'm not going to Chicago.

REGINA (*turns to her*). You're very upset, Alexandra.

ALEXANDRA (*quietly*). I mean what I say. With all my heart.

REGINA. We'll talk about it tomorrow. The morning will make a difference.

ALEXANDRA. It won't make any difference. And there isn't anything to talk about. I am going away from you. Because I want to. Because I know Papa would want me to.

REGINA (*puzzled, careful, polite*). You *know* your papa wanted you to go away from me?

ALEXANDRA. Yes.

REGINA (*softly*). And if I say no?

ALEXANDRA (*looks at her*). Say it Mama, say it. And see what happens.

REGINA (*softly, after a pause*). And if I make you stay?

ALEXANDRA. That would be foolish. It wouldn't work in the end.

REGINA. You're very serious about it, aren't you? (*Crosses to stairs.*) Well, you'll change your mind in a few days.

ALEXANDRA. You only change your mind when you want to. And I won't want to.

REGINA (*going up the steps*). Alexandra, I've come to the end of my rope. Somewhere there has to be what I want, too. Life goes too fast. Do what you want; think what you want; go where you want. I'd like to keep you with me, but I won't make you stay. Too many people used to make me do too many things. No, I won't make you stay.

ALEXANDRA. You couldn't, Mama, because I want to leave here. As I've never wanted anything in my life before. Because now I understand what Papa was trying to tell me. (*Pause.*) All in one day: Addie said there were people who ate the earth and other people who stood around and watched them do it. And just now Uncle Ben said the same thing. Really, he said the same thing. (*Tensely.*) Well, tell him for me, Mama, I'm not going to stand around and watch you do it. Tell him I'll be fighting as hard as he'll be fighting (*Rises.*) some place where people don't just stand around and watch.

REGINA. Well, you have spirit, after all. I used to think you were all sugar water. We don't have to be bad friends. I don't want us to be bad friends, Alexandra. (*Starts, stops, turns to* ALEXANDRA.) Would you like to come and talk to me, Alexandra? Would you—would you like to sleep in my room tonight?

ALEXANDRA *(takes a step toward her).* Are you afraid, Mama? (REGINA *does not answer. She moves slowly out of sight.* ADDIE *comes to* ALEXANDRA, *presses her arm.*)

*The Curtain Falls*

FOR DISCUSSION

# Act I

1. In the opening stage directions, Regina's house is described as having the very best and most expensive furniture but as revealing "no particular taste." What does this statement reveal about Regina?
2. What do their names suggest about Regina, Birdie, and Alexandra?
3. Birdie's seemingly rambling comments to Addie and Cal actually furnish important exposition or background information. What do these remarks convey about her family's traditions and history?
4. When Oscar appears, what kind of man does he seem to be? Which of his first actions conveys something of his character? What do you learn immediately about the relationship between Oscar and Birdie?
5. In Regina's discussion about moving to Chicago, what do you find out about her goals and attitudes? Do her values make her appear more, or less, sympathetic?
6. What does the conversation between Ben, Leo, and Oscar (page 11) suggest about their attitudes toward women? What do they agree is the "proper attitude"? To what extent does each of the women in the play fit such ideas?
7. Marshall seems to suspect that "good Southern families" would be uninterested in, or inept at, business. Ben's statement that "Southern aristocrats have *not* kept what belonged to them" (page 13) seems to substantiate such suspicions. How good at business matters are the Hubbards? What kind of family do their talents suggest they are?
8. Regina's speech (page 15) implies that ladies should never have anything to do with business. Accepting her rule, is she a lady?

9. For Birdie, workers on her family plantation were "our people." When Ben calls such workers *niggers*, what does he suggest about his own family background? What other things in his speeches suggest that he was reared in a different manner from Birdie?
10. When Oscar says to Marshall, "My brother always says that it's folks like us who have struggled and fought to bring to our land some of the prosperity of your land," what does he reveal about the Southern view of the North and about his own assumptions concerning "Southern" and "Northern" values?
11. What is the relationship between Leo and his uncle, Ben? Between Leo and his father? If Leo is as weak as his description implies, do these relationships explain his weakness in any way?
12. What do their daydreams and wishes for the future reveal about the Hubbards? About Birdie?
13. What does Act I tell you about the relationships between the three Hubbards — Ben, Oscar, and Regina? Are these ties and attitudes developed more through language or gesture?
14. Remembering the accepted view of ladylike behavior which is implied throughout the play, why is it so important to Regina that Alexandra travel to Baltimore alone — a somewhat unladylike act? What might happen if she took the expected chaperone?
15. Why might Birdie love Alexandra more than she loves her own son? What do the two women have in common?

## Act II

1. What does Oscar's attitude toward Addie and Cal tell you about the reasons for and sources of prejudice and repression?
2. What does Oscar mean by *outside women* and by *serious things* (page 34)? How does he view marriage?
3. What kind of man do you conclude Horace is from Leo's description of the safe-deposit box?
4. Horace says his homecoming is just like old times. What were the old times like?
5. Describe the relationship between Regina and Horace. What attitudes do they have toward each other?
6. How do the Hubbard men apparently make their money? What are their political ties? Social opinions? Whom do they control? What are their weapons? What are Horace's views of these methods and the social conditions they create?

7. Why do Ben and Oscar go to such elaborate lengths to maintain their pretenses while they discuss the bonds? Why is such pretense important to them?
8. What kind of person does Regina appear to be by the end of Act II? What is your attitude toward her at this point?

# Act III

1. What effects are added by the rain in Act III?
2. Act III gives you your clearest picture of Addie. Characterize her. Does she appear more, or less, sympathetic than her employers? Why?
3. Unlike Addie, Cal provides humor in this act. What stereotype does Miss Hellman use in portraying Cal?
4. When Horace, Alexandra, and Birdie sit together and enjoy the music and the tea party, they represent the music lovers allied against the nonlovers of music. What does Oscar's attitude toward music tell you about other attitudes of his?
5. What is Birdie's secret weakness? Is this weakness consistent with all the other aspects of her character which you have learned throughout the play? Explain.
6. Why does Birdie grow so angry with Alexandra? What makes Birdie think her own life will be repeated by Alexandra? Why has Birdie lived the kind of life she has? From what you know of Alexandra, do you feel this fear is well-founded?
7. What, according to Horace is the price of innocence? Why does he seek to rob Alexandra of her innocence? Does he seem to be properly "paternal" in his efforts?
8. To what extent does Miss Hellman manage to make you hope Regina wins the struggle at the end of the play? How does the playwright accomplish this feat?
9. What hint of a future reversal occurs at the end of the play? What appears to be Alexandra's fate?
10. What is the effect of Ben's statement that the Hubbards "will own this country some day"?
11. Regina suggests that her whole life has been shaped by resentment because their father left his money to her brothers. Do you find this explanation believable, or too simplistic?
12. What is the dramatic effect of the play's last line?

ON THE PLAY AS A WHOLE

1. Birdie tells you about herself directly when she reminisces about her family. How many other methods of characterization do you

find in the play; that is, in how many different ways does the playwright let you know what kind of people her characters are?
2. *The Little Foxes* is often called a "well-made play." In a well-made play every episode and conversation is essential to the plot. Assuming that an episode can be identified by the entrance or exit of a major character, test the play to see if all episodes are really so important. Can you find episodes which could be removed without harming the total play? Can you find lines that are unnecessary or repetitious?
3. The impact of this drama comes partially from the reversals of fortune affecting Regina. At what points do her prospects seem to change? Is each change brought about in some way by one of the characters, or are any imposed by forces operating apart from the relationships within the drama?
4. What purpose do you feel Miss Hellman had in mind when she wrote the play? What themes, or statements about life, does she explore in her drama? What do these themes let you know about her purposes?

## FOR COMPOSITION

1. Compare and contrast the Hubbard family's view of tradition to Birdie's view. Discuss the way in which Miss Hellman makes one attitude more appealing than the other.
2. Using this play alone to find your evidence, discuss Miss Hellman's view of the "New South" as opposed to the "Old South." Show how you can tell which she admires more.
3. Write a composition on the importance of the family in Southern society. Discuss the social implications of your conclusions.
4. For extra credit: Compare the view of Southern life in Miss Hellman's play with the facts you discover in such books as C. Vann Woodward's *The Origins of the New South*, W. J. Cash's *The Mind of the South*, or John Dollard's *Caste and Class in a Southern Town*. Then write a composition entitled "The Southern Way of Life: Fact and Myth."
5. Imagine that you are a drama critic reviewing the opening performance of *The Little Foxes*. Write a review of the play and comment on the effectiveness of the drama. Mention especially scenes that captured your imagination, or scenes you felt were inadequately developed.

# Thornton Wilder

In an interview printed in the *Paris Review*, Thornton Wilder said, "The comic spirit is given to us in order that we may analyze, weigh, and clarify things in us which nettle us, or which we are outgrowing, or trying to reshape." This spirit is evident in all his plays, dramas as well as comedies. Each play is concerned, in its own way, with the events of daily life. Each is an attempt to show that only when individual action is raised "into the realm of idea and type and universal" is it "able to evoke our belief."

In Shakespeare's time the theater had been "the greatest of all arts." By the end of the nineteenth century, it had been turned into "a minor art and an inconsequential diversion." As the middle classes had come into power, they had succeeded not only in taming it but also in squeezing the action into the box-set stage originally intended merely as a protection against the weather. The result, Wilder believed, was that the theater had become false.

Probably Wilder's dissatisfaction with the theater of the 1920's influenced not only his decision to write plays but also the original and unconventional form in which he wrote them. In the Preface to *Three Plays*, he stated that his purpose in writing *The Matchmaker* was to parody the stock company plays he had seen as a boy in Oakland, California. melodramas, sentimental dramas, and comedies "in which the characters were so represented that they always resembled someone else and not oneself." All "aimed to be *soothing*. The tragic had no heat; the comic no bite; the social criticism failed to indict us with responsibility." The middle-class audiences who attended these plays "were pious, law-abiding, and industrious. . . . They were benevolent within certain limits, but chose to ignore wide tracts of injustice and stupidity in the world about them; and they shrank from contemplating those elements within themselves that were ridiculous, shallow, and harmful." Above all, they "sought justification and reassurance in making money and displaying it."

In this play, through situations so exaggerated and broadly humorous as to be farcical, Wilder pokes fun at such people and their values and, at the same time, at old-fashioned playwriting. The effect is highly entertaining, but the "comic" *has* a "bite." There is social criticism, too, but it is conveyed so subtly that it takes the reader or theater audience by surprise. Wilder's parody goes beyond mere "poking fun," as he himself pointed out. "My play is about the aspirations of the young (and not only of the young) for a fuller, freer participation in life."

At the close of the Preface to *Three Plays*, Wilder commented, "I am not an innovator but a rediscoverer of forgotten goods and I hope a remover of obstructive bric-a-brac. And as I view the work of my contemporaries I seem to feel that I am exceptional in one thing—I give (don't I?) the impression of having enormously enjoyed it."[1]

---

[1] Except for the quotation from the *Paris Review*, all quoted material in this essay is from the Preface to *Three Plays*, by Thornton Wilder (New York: Harper & Row, Publishers, 1957), pp. vii-xiii.

# The Matchmaker

**CHARACTERS**

HORACE VANDERGELDER, *a merchant of Yonkers, New York*
ERMENGARDE, *his niece*
GERTRUDE, *his housekeeper*
AMBROSE KEMPER, *an artist*
MRS. DOLLY LEVI } *friends of Vandergelder's*
MISS FLORA VAN HUYSEN } *late wife*
JOE SCANLON, *a barber*
CORNELIUS HACKL }
BARNABY TUCKER } *clerks in Vandergelder's store*
MALACHI STACK }
MRS. IRENE MOLLOY, *a milliner*
MINNIE FAY, *her assistant*
RUDOLPH }
AUGUST } *waiters*
A CABMAN
MISS VAN HUYSEN'S *Cook*

SCENE: *Yonkers, and later New York City, in the early 1880's.*

# Act I

*Living room of* MR. VANDERGELDER'S *house, over his hay, feed and provision store in Yonkers, fifteen miles north of New York City. Articles from the store have overflowed into this room; it has not been cleaned for a long time and is in some disorder, but it is not sordid or gloomy.*

*There are three entrances. One at the center back leads into the principal rooms of the house. One on the back right (all the directions are from the point of view of the actors) opens on steps which descend to the street door. One on the left leads to* ERMENGARDE'S *room.*

*In the center of the room is a trap door; below it is a ladder descending to the store below.*

*Behind the trap door and to the left of it is a tall accountant's desk; to the left of it is an old-fashioned stove with a stovepipe going up into the ceiling. Before the desk is a tall stool. On the right of the stage is a table with some chairs about it.*

MR. VANDERGELDER'S *Gladstone bag, packed for a journey, is beside the desk.*

*It is early morning.*

VANDERGELDER, *sixty, choleric, vain and sly, wears a soiled dressing gown. He is seated with a towel about his neck, in a chair beside the desk, being shaved by* JOE SCANLON. VANDERGELDER *is smoking a cigar and holding a hand mirror.* AMBROSE KEMPER *is angrily striding about the room.*

VANDERGELDER (*loudly*). I tell you for the hundredth time you will never marry my niece.
AMBROSE (*thirty; dressed as an "artist"*). And I tell you for the thousandth time that I will marry your niece; and right soon, too.
VANDERGELDER. Never!

AMBROSE. Your niece is of age, Mr. Vandergelder. Your niece has consented to marry me. This is a free country, Mr. Vandergelder—not a private kingdom of your own.

VANDERGELDER. There are no free countries for fools, Mr. Kemper. Thank you for the honor of your visit—good morning.

JOE (*fifty; lanky, mass of gray hair falling into his eyes*). Mr. Vandergelder, will you please sit still one minute? If I cut your throat it'll be practically unintentional.

VANDERGELDER. Ermengarde is not for you, nor for anybody else who can't support her.

AMBROSE. I tell you I can support her. I make a very good living.

VANDERGELDER. No, sir! A living is made, Mr. Kemper, by selling something that everybody needs at least once a year. Yes, sir! And a million is made by producing something that everybody needs every day. You artists produce something that nobody needs at any time. You may sell a picture once in a while, but you'll make no living. Joe, go over there and stamp three times. I want to talk to Cornelius.

(JOE *crosses to trap door and stamps three times.*)

AMBROSE. Not only can I support her now, but I have considerable expectations.

VANDERGELDER. *Expectations!* We merchants don't do business with them. I don't keep accounts with people who promise somehow to pay something someday, and I don't allow my niece to marry such people.

AMBROSE. Very well, from now on you might as well know that I regard any way we can find to get married is right and fair. Ermengarde is of age, and there's no law . . .

(VANDERGELDER *rises and crosses toward* AMBROSE. JOE SCANLON *follows him complainingly and tries to find a chance to cut his hair even while he is standing.*)

VANDERGELDER. Law? Let me tell you something, Mr. Kemper: most of the people in the world are fools. The

law is there to prevent crime; we men of sense are there to prevent foolishness. It's I, and not the law, that will prevent Ermengarde from marrying you, and I've taken some steps already. I've sent her away to get this nonsense out of her head.
AMBROSE. Ermengarde's ... not here?
VANDERGELDER. She's gone—east, west, north, south. I thank you for the honor of your visit.

(*Enter* GERTRUDE—*eighty; deaf; half blind; and very pleased with herself.*)

*Vandergelder: Also, she smiles at you!*

GERTRUDE. Everything's ready, Mr. Vandergelder. Ermengarde and I have just finished packing the trunk.
VANDERGELDER. Hold your tongue! (JOE *is shaving* VANDERGELDER'S *throat, so he can only wave his hands vainly.*)
GERTRUDE. Yes, Mr. Vandergelder, Ermengarde's ready to leave. Her trunk's all marked. Care Miss Van Huysen, 8 Jackson Street, New York.
VANDERGELDER (*breaking away from* JOE). Hell and damnation! Didn't I tell you it was a secret?
AMBROSE (*picks up hat and coat—kisses* GERTRUDE). Care Miss Van Huysen, 8 Jackson Street, New York. Thank you very much. Good morning, Mr. Vandergelder. (*Exit* AMBROSE, *to the street.*)
VANDERGELDER. It won't help you, Mr. Kemper— (*To* GERTRUDE.) Deaf! And blind! At least you can do me the favor of being dumb!
GERTRUDE. Chk—chk! Such a temper! Lord save us!

(CORNELIUS *puts his head up through the trap door. He is thirty-three; mock-deferential—he wears a green apron and is in his shirt-sleeves.*)

CORNELIUS. Yes, Mr. Vandergelder?
VANDERGELDER. Go in and get my niece's trunk and carry it over to the station. Wait! Gertrude, has Mrs. Levi arrived yet?

(CORNELIUS *comes up the trap door, steps into the room and closes the trap door behind him.*)

GERTRUDE. Don't shout. I can hear perfectly well. Everything's clearly marked. (*Exit left.*)

VANDERGELDER. Have the buggy brought round to the front of the store in half an hour.

CORNELIUS. Yes, Mr. Vandergelder.

VANDERGELDER. This morning I'm joining my lodge parade and this afternoon I'm going to New York. Before I go, I have something important to say to you and Barnaby. Good news. Fact is — I'm going to promote you. How old are you?

CORNELIUS. Thirty-three, Mr. Vandergelder.

VANDERGELDER. What?

CORNELIUS. Thirty-three.

VANDERGELDER. That all? That's a foolish age to be at. I thought you were forty.

CORNELIUS. Thirty-three.

VANDERGELDER. A man's not worth a cent until he's forty. We just pay 'em wages to make mistakes — don't we, Joe?

JOE. You almost lost an ear on it, Mr. Vandergelder.

VANDERGELDER. I was thinking of promoting you to chief clerk.

CORNELIUS. What am I now, Mr. Vandergelder?

VANDERGELDER. You're an impertinent fool, that's what you are. Now, if you behave yourself, I'll promote you from impertinent fool to chief clerk, with a raise in your wages. And Barnaby may be promoted from idiot apprentice to incompetent clerk.

CORNELIUS. Thank you, Mr. Vandergelder.

VANDERGELDER. However, I want to see you again before I go. Go in and get my niece's trunk.

CORNELIUS. Yes, Mr. Vandergelder. (*Exit* CORNELIUS, *left.*)

VANDERGELDER. Joe — the world's getting crazier every minute. Like my father used to say: the horses'll be taking over the world soon.

JOE (*presenting mirror*). I did what I could, Mr. Vandergelder, what with you flying in and out of the chair. (*He wipes last of the soap from* VANDERGELDER'S *face.*)

VANDERGELDER.  Fine, fine. Joe, you do a fine job, the same fine job you've done me for twenty years. Joe . . . I've got special reasons for looking my best today . . . isn't there something a little extry you could do, something a little special? I'll pay you right up to fifty cents—see what I mean? Do some of those things you do to the young fellas. Touch me up; smarten me up a bit.

JOE.  All I know is fifteen cents' worth, like usual, Mr. Vandergelder; and that includes everything that's decent to do to a man.

VANDERGELDER.  Now hold your horses, Joe—all I meant was . . .

JOE.  I've shaved you for twenty years and you never asked me no such question before.

VANDERGELDER.  Hold your horses, I say, Joe! I'm going to tell you a secret. But I don't want you telling it to that riffraff down to the barbershop what I'm going to tell you now. All I ask of you is a little extry because I'm thinking of getting married again; and this very afternoon I'm going to New York to call on my intended, a very refined lady.

JOE.  Your gettin' married is none of my business, Mr. Vandergelder. I done everything to you I know, and the charge is fifteen cents like it always was, and . . .

(CORNELIUS *crosses, left to right, and exit, carrying a trunk on his shoulder.* ERMENGARDE *and* GERTRUDE *enter from left.*)

I don't dye no hair, not even for fifty cents I don't!

VANDERGELDER.  Joe Scanlon, get out!

JOE.  And lastly, it looks to me like you're pretty rash to judge which is fools and which isn't fools, Mr. Vandergelder. People that's et onions is bad judges of who's et onions and who ain't. Good morning, ladies; good morning, Mr. Vandergelder. (*Exit* JOE.)

VANDERGELDER.  Well, what do you want?

ERMENGARDE (*twenty-four; pretty, sentimental*). Uncle! You said you wanted to talk to us.

VANDERGELDER.  Oh yes. Gertrude, go and get my parade regalia—the uniform for my lodge parade.

GERTRUDE. What? Oh yes. Lord have mercy! (*Exit* GERTRUDE, *back center.*)
VANDERGELDER. I had a talk with that artist of yours. He's a fool. (ERMENGARDE *starts to cry.*) Weeping! Weeping! You can go down and weep for a while in New York where it won't be noticed. (*He sits on desk chair, puts tie round neck and calls her over to tie it for him.*) Ermengarde! I told him that when you were old enough to marry you'd marry someone who could support you. I've done you a good turn. You'll come and thank me when you're fifty.
ERMENGARDE. But Uncle, I love him!
VANDERGELDER. I tell you you don't.
ERMENGARDE. But I *do!*
VANDERGELDER. And I tell you you don't. Leave those things to me.
ERMENGARDE. If I don't marry Ambrose I know I'll die.
VANDERGELDER. What of?
ERMENGARDE. A broken heart.
VANDERGELDER. Never heard of it. Mrs. Levi is coming in a moment to take you to New York. You are going to stay two or three weeks with Miss Van Huysen, an old friend of your mother's.

(GERTRUDE *re-enters with coat, sash and sword. Enter from the street, right,* MALACHI STACK.)

You're not to receive any letters except from me. I'm coming to New York myself today and I'll call on you tomorrow. (*To* MALACHI.) Who are you?
MALACHI (*fifty. Sardonic. Apparently innocent smile; pretense of humility*). Malachi Stack, your honor. I heard you wanted an apprentice in the hay, feed, provision, and hardware business.
VANDERGELDER. An apprentice at your age?
MALACHI. Yes, your honor; I bring a lot of experience to it.
VANDERGELDER. Have you any letters of recommendation?
MALACHI (*extending a sheaf of soiled papers*). Yes, indeed, your honor! First-class recommendation.
VANDERGELDER. Ermengarde! Are you ready to start?

ERMENGARDE.  Yes.
VANDERGELDER.  Well, go and get ready some more. Ermengarde! Let me know the minute Mrs. Levi gets here.
ERMENGARDE.  Yes, Uncle Horace.

(ERMENGARDE *and* GERTRUDE *exit.* VANDERGELDER *examines the letters, putting them down one by one.*)

VANDERGELDER.  I don't want an able seaman. Nor a typesetter. And I don't want a hospital cook.
MALACHI.  No, your honor, but it's all experience. Excuse me! (*Selects a letter.*) This one is from your former partner, Joshua Van Tuyl, in Albany. (*He puts letters from table back into pocket.*)
VANDERGELDER.  ". . . for the most part honest and reliable . . . occasionally willing and diligent." There seems to be a certain amount of hesitation about these recommendations.
MALACHI.  Businessmen aren't writers, your honor. There's only one businessman in a thousand that can write a good letter of recommendation, your honor. Mr. Van Tuyl sends his best wishes and wants to know if you can use me in the provision and hardware business.
VANDERGELDER.  Not so fast, not so fast! What's this "your honor" you use so much?
MALACHI.  Mr. Van Tuyl says you're President of the Hudson River Provision Dealers' Recreational, Musical and Burial Society.
VANDERGELDER.  I am; but there's no "your honor" that goes with it. Why did you come to Yonkers?
MALACHI.  I heard that you'd had an apprentice that was a good-for-nothing, and that you were at your wit's end for another.
VANDERGELDER.  Wit's end, wit's end! There's no dearth of good-for-nothing apprentices.
MALACHI.  That's right, Mr. Vandergelder. It's employers there's a dearth of. Seems like you hear of a new one dying every day.
VANDERGELDER.  What's that? Hold your tongue. I see

you've been a barber, and valet too. Why have you changed your place so often?
MALACHI. Changed my place, Mr. Vandergelder? When a man's interested in experience . . .
VANDERGELDER. Do you drink?
MALACHI. No, thanks. I've just had breakfast.
VANDERGELDER. I didn't ask you whether—Idiot! I asked you if you were a drunkard.
MALACHI. No, sir! No! Why, looking at it from all sides I don't even like liquor.
VANDERGELDER. Well, if you keep on looking at it from all sides, out you go. Remember that. Here. (*Gives him remaining letters.*) With all your faults, I'm going to give you a try.
MALACHI. You'll never regret it, Mr. Vandergelder. You'll never regret it.
VANDERGELDER. Now today I want to use you in New York. I judge you know your way around New York?
MALACHI. Do I know New York? Mr. Vandergelder, I know every hole and corner in New York.
VANDERGELDER. Here's a dollar. A train leaves in a minute. Take that bag to the Central Hotel on Water Street, have them save me a room. Wait for me. I'll be there about four o'clock.
MALACHI. Yes, Mr. Vandergelder. (*Picks up the bag, starts out, then comes back.*) Oh, but first, I'd like to meet the other clerks I'm to work with.
VANDERGELDER. You haven't time. Hurry now. The station's across the street.
MALACHI. Yes, sir. (*Away—then back once more.*) You'll see, sir, you'll never regret it . . .
VANDERGELDER. I regret it already. Go on. Off with you.

(*Exit* MALACHI, *right. The following speech is addressed to the audience. During it* MR. VANDERGELDER *takes off his dressing gown, puts on his scarlet sash, his sword and his bright-colored coat. He is already wearing light blue trousers with a red stripe down the sides.*)

**VANDERGELDER.** Ninety-nine per cent of the people in the world are fools and the rest of us are in great danger of contagion. But I wasn't always free of foolishness as I am now. I was once young, which was foolish; I fell in love, which was foolish; and I got married, which was foolish; and for a while I was poor, which was more foolish than all the other things put together. Then my wife died, which was foolish of her; I grew older, which was sensible of me; then I became a rich man, which is as sensible as it is rare. Since you see I'm a man of sense, I guess you were surprised to hear that I'm planning to get married again. Well, I've two reasons for it. In the first place, I like my house run with order, comfort and economy. That's a woman's work; but even a woman can't do it well if she's merely being paid for it. In order to run a house well, a woman must have the feeling that she owns it. Marriage is a bribe to make a housekeeper think she's a householder. Did you ever watch an ant carry a burden twice its size? What excitement! What patience! What will! Well, that's what I think of when I see a woman running a house. What giant passions in those little bodies—what quarrels with the butcher for the best cut—what fury at discovering a moth in a cupboard! Believe me!—if women could harness their natures to something bigger than a house and a baby carriage— tck! tck!—they'd change the world. And the second reason, ladies and gentlemen? Well, I see by your faces you've guessed it already. There's nothing like mixing with women to bring out all the foolishness in a man of sense. And that's a risk I'm willing to take. I've just turned sixty, and I've just laid side by side the last dollar of my first half million. So if I should lose my head a little, I still have enough money to buy it back. After many years' caution and hard work, I have a right to a little risk and adventure, and I'm thinking of getting married. Yes, like all you other fools, I'm willing to risk a little security for a certain amount of adventure. Think it over. (*Exit back center.*)

(AMBROSE *enters from the street, crosses left, and whistles softly.* ERMENGARDE *enters from left.*)

ERMENGARDE. Ambrose! If my uncle saw you!
AMBROSE. Sh! Get your hat.
ERMENGARDE. My hat!
AMBROSE. Quick! Your trunk's at the station. Now quick! We're running away.
ERMENGARDE. Running away!
AMBROSE. Sh!
ERMENGARDE. Where?
AMBROSE. To New York. To get married.
ERMENGARDE. Oh, Ambrose, I can't do that. Ambrose dear — it wouldn't be proper!
AMBROSE. Listen. I'm taking you to my friend's house. His wife will take care of you.
ERMENGARDE. But, Ambrose, a girl can't go on a train with a man. I can see you don't know anything about girls.
AMBROSE. But I'm telling you we're going to get married!
ERMENGARDE. Married! But what would *Uncle* say?
AMBROSE. We don't care what Uncle'd say — we're eloping.
ERMENGARDE. Ambrose Kemper! How can you use such an awful word!
AMBROSE. Ermengarde, you have the soul of a field mouse.
ERMENGARDE (*crying*). Ambrose, why do you say such cruel things to me?

(*Enter* MRS. LEVI, *from the street, right. She stands listening.*)

AMBROSE. For the last time I beg you — get your hat and coat. The train leaves in a few minutes. Ermengarde, we'll get married tomorrow....
ERMENGARDE. Oh, Ambrose! I see you don't understand anything about weddings. Ambrose, don't you *respect* me?...
MRS. LEVI (*uncertain age; mass of sandy hair; impoverished elegance; large, shrewd but generous nature, an assumption of worldly cynicism conceals a tireless amused en-*

*joyment of life. She carries a handbag and a small brown paper bag).* Good morning, darling girl—how are you?

(*They kiss.*)

ERMENGARDE. Oh, good morning, Mrs. Levi.

MRS. LEVI. And who is this gentleman who is so devoted to you?

ERMENGARDE. This is Mr. Kemper, Mrs. Levi. Ambrose, this is . . . Mrs. Levi . . . she's an old friend. . . .

MRS. LEVI. Mrs. Levi, born Gallagher. Very happy to meet you, Mr. Kemper.

AMBROSE. Good morning, Mrs. Levi.

MRS. LEVI. Mr. Kemper, *the artist!* Delighted! Mr. Kemper, may I say something very frankly?

AMBROSE. Yes, Mrs. Levi.

MRS. LEVI. This thing you were planning to do is a very great mistake.

ERMENGARDE. Oh, Mrs. Levi, please explain to Ambrose— of course I want to marry him, but to *elope!* . . . How . . .

MRS. LEVI. Now, my dear girl, you go in and keep one eye on your uncle. I wish to talk to Mr. Kemper for a moment. You give us a warning when you hear your Uncle Horace coming. . . .

ERMENGARDE. Ye-es, Mrs. Levi. (*Exit* ERMENGARDE, *back center.*)

MRS. LEVI. Mr. Kemper, I was this dear girl's mother's oldest friend. Believe me, I am on your side. I hope you two will be married very soon, and I think I can be of real service to you. Mr. Kemper, I always go right to the point.

AMBROSE. What is the point, Mrs. Levi?

MRS. LEVI. Mr. Vandergelder is a very rich man, Mr. Kemper, and Ermengarde is his only relative.

AMBROSE. But I am not interested in Mr. Vandergelder's money. I have enough to support a wife and family.

MRS. LEVI. Enough? How much is enough when one is thinking about children and the future? The future is the most expensive luxury in the world, Mr. Kemper.

AMBROSE. Mrs. Levi, what is the point?

MRS. LEVI. Believe me, Mr. Vandergelder wishes to get rid of Ermengarde, and if you follow my suggestions he will even permit her to marry you. You see, Mr. Vandergelder is planning to get married himself.

AMBROSE. What? That monster!

MRS. LEVI. Mr. Kemper!

AMBROSE. Married! To you, Mrs. Levi?

MRS. LEVI (*taken aback*). Oh, no, no . . . NO! I am merely arranging it. I am helping him find a suitable bride.

AMBROSE. For Mr. Vandergelder there are no suitable brides.

MRS. LEVI. I think we can safely say that Mr. Vandergelder will be married to someone by the end of next week.

AMBROSE. What are you suggesting, Mrs. Levi?

MRS. LEVI. I am taking Ermengarde to New York on the next train. I shall not take her to Miss Van Huysen's, as is planned; I shall take her to my house. I wish you to call for her at my house at five thirty. Here is my card.

AMBROSE. "Mrs. Dolly Gallagher Levi. Varicose veins reduced."

MRS. LEVI (*trying to take back card*). I beg your pardon . . .

AMBROSE (*holding card*). I beg *your* pardon. "Consultations free."

MRS. LEVI. I meant to give you my other card. Here.

AMBROSE. "Mrs. Dolly Gallagher Levi. Aurora Hosiery. Instruction in the guitar and mandolin." You do all these things, Mrs. Levi?

MRS. LEVI. Two and two make four, Mr. Kemper—always did. So you will come to my house at five thirty. At about six I shall take you both with me to the Harmonia Gardens Restaurant on the Battery; Mr. Vandergelder will be there and everything will be arranged.

AMBROSE. How?

MRS. LEVI. Oh, I don't know. One thing will lead to another.

AMBROSE. How do I know that I can trust you, Mrs. Levi? You could easily make our situation worse.

MRS. LEVI. Mr. Kemper, your situation could not possibly be worse.

AMBROSE. I wish I knew what you get out of this, Mrs. Levi.

MRS. LEVI. That is a very proper question. I get two things: profit and pleasure.

AMBROSE. How?

MRS. LEVI. Mr. Kemper, I am a woman who arranges things. At present I am arranging Mr. Vandergelder's domestic affairs. Out of it I get—shall we call it: little pickings? I need little pickings, Mr. Kemper, and especially just now, when I haven't got my train fare back to New York. You see: I am frank with you.

AMBROSE. That's your profit, Mrs. Levi; but where do you get your pleasure?

MRS. LEVI. My pleasure? Mr. Kemper, when you artists paint a hillside or a river you change everything a little, you make thousands of little changes, don't you? Nature is never completely satisfactory and must be corrected. Well, I'm like you artists. Life as it is is never quite interesting enough for me—I'm bored, Mr. Kemper, with life as it is—and so I do things. I put my hand in here, and I put my hand in there, and I watch and I listen—and often I'm very much amused.

AMBROSE (*rises*). Not in my affairs, Mrs. Levi.

MRS. LEVI. Wait, I haven't finished. There's another thing. I'm very interested in this household here—in Mr. Vandergelder and all that idle, frozen money of his. I don't like the thought of it lying in great piles, useless, motionless, in the bank, Mr. Kemper. Money should circulate like rain water. It should be flowing down among the people, through dressmakers and restaurants and cabmen, setting up a little business here, and furnishing a good time there. Do you see what I mean?

AMBROSE. Yes, I do.

MRS. LEVI. New York should be a very happy city, Mr. Kemper, but it isn't. My late husband came from Vienna; now there's a city that understands this. I want New York to be more like Vienna and less like a collection of nervous and tired ants. And if you and Ermengarde get a good deal of Mr. Vandergelder's money, I want you to see that it starts flowing in and around a lot of people's lives. And for that reason I want you to come with me to the Harmonia Gardens Restaurant tonight.

(*Enter* ERMENGARDE.)

ERMENGARDE.   Mrs. Levi, Uncle Horace is coming.
MRS. LEVI.   Mr. Kemper, I think you'd better be going . . . (AMBROSE *crosses to trap door and disappears down the ladder, closing trap as he goes.*) Darling girl, Mr. Kemper and I have had a very good talk. You'll see: Mr. Vandergelder and I will be dancing at your wedding very soon — (*Enter* VANDERGELDER *at back. He has now added a splendid plumed hat to his costume and is carrying a standard or small flag bearing the initials of his lodge.*) Oh, Mr. Vandergelder, how handsome you look! You take my breath away. Yes, my dear girl, I'll see you soon. (*Exit* ERMENGARDE *back center.*) Oh, Mr. Vandergelder, I wish Irene Molloy could see you now. But then! I don't know what's come over you lately. You seem to be growing younger every day.
VANDERGELDER.   Allowing for exaggeration, Mrs. Levi. If a man eats careful there's no reason why he should look old.
MRS. LEVI.   You never said a truer word.
VANDERGELDER.   I'll never see fifty-five again.
MRS. LEVI.   Fifty-five! Why, I can see at a glance that you're the sort that will be stamping about at a hundred — and eating five meals a day, like my Uncle Harry. At fifty-five my Uncle Harry was a mere boy. I'm a judge of hands, Mr. Vandergelder — show me your hand. (*Looks at it.*) Lord in heaven! What a life line!
VANDERGELDER.   Where?
MRS. LEVI.   From *here* to *here*. It runs right off your hand. I don't know where it goes. They'll have to hit you on the head with a mallet. They'll have to stifle you with a sofa pillow. You'll bury us all! However, to return to our business — Mr. Vandergelder, I suppose you've changed your mind again. I suppose you've given up all idea of getting married.
VANDERGELDER (*complacently*).   Not at all, Mrs. Levi. I have news for you.
MRS. LEVI.   News?
VANDERGELDER.   Mrs. Levi, I've practically decided to ask Mrs. Molloy to be my wife.

MRS. LEVI (*taken aback*). You have?
VANDERGELDER Yes, I have.
MRS. LEVI. Oh, you have! Well, I guess that's just about the best news I ever heard. So there's nothing more for me to do but wish you every happiness under the sun and say good-by. (*Crosses as if to leave.*)
VANDERGELDER (*stopping her*). Well — Mrs. Levi — Surely I thought —
MRS. LEVI. Well, I did have a little suggestion to make — but I won't. You're going to marry Irene Molloy, and that closes the matter.
VANDERGELDER. What suggestion was that, Mrs. Levi?
MRS. LEVI. Well — I *had* found *another* girl for you.
VANDERGELDER. Another?
MRS. LEVI. The most wonderful girl, the ideal wife.
VANDERGELDER. Another, eh? What's her name?
MRS. LEVI. Her name?
VANDERGELDER. Yes!
MRS. LEVI (*groping for it*). Err . . . er . . . her *name?* — Ernestina — Simple. *Miss* Ernestina Simple. But now of course all that's too late. After all, you're engaged — you're practically engaged to marry Irene Molloy.
VANDERGELDER. Oh, I ain't engaged to Mrs. Molloy!
MRS. LEVI. Nonsense! You can't break poor Irene's heart now and change to another girl. . . . When a man at your time of life calls four times on an attractive widow like that — and sends her a pot of geraniums — that's practically an engagement!
VANDERGELDER. That ain't an engagement!
MRS. LEVI. And yet —! If only you were free! I've found this treasure of a girl. Every moment I felt like a traitor to Irene Molloy — but let me tell you: I couldn't help it. I told this girl all about you, just as though you were a free man. Isn't that dreadful? The fact is: she has fallen in love with you already.
VANDERGELDER. Ernestina?
MRS. LEVI. Ernestina Simple.
VANDERGELDER. Ernestina Simple.
MRS. LEVI. Of course she's a very different idea from Mrs.

Molloy, Ernestina is. Like her name—simple, domestic, practical.

VANDERGELDER. Can she cook?

MRS. LEVI. Cook, Mr. Vandergelder? I've had two meals from her hands, and—as I live—I don't know what I've done that God should reward me with such meals. Her duck! Her steak!

VANDERGELDER. Eh! Eh! In this house we don't eat duck and steak every day, Mrs. Levi.

MRS. LEVI. But didn't I tell you?—that's the wonderful part about it. Her duck—what was it? Pigeon! I'm alive to tell you. I don't know how she does it. It's a secret that's come down in her family. The greatest chefs would give their right hands to know it. And the steaks? Shoulder of beef—four cents a pound. Dogs wouldn't eat. But when Ernestina passes her hands over it—!!

VANDERGELDER. Allowing for exaggeration, Mrs. Levi.

MRS. LEVI. No exaggeration. I'm the best cook in the world myself, and I *know* what's good.

VANDERGELDER. Hm. How old is she, Mrs. Levi?

MRS. LEVI. Nineteen, well—say twenty.

VANDERGELDER. Twenty, Mrs. Levi? Girls of twenty are apt to favor young fellows of their own age.

MRS. LEVI. But you don't listen to me. And you don't know the girl. Mr. Vandergelder, she has a positive horror of flighty, brainless young men. A fine head of gray hair, she says, is worth twenty shined up with goose grease. No, sir. "I like a man that's *settled*"—in so many words she said it.

VANDERGELDER. That's . . . that's not usual, Mrs. Levi.

MRS. LEVI. Usual? I'm not wearing myself to the bone hunting up *usual* girls to interest you, Mr. Vandergelder. Usual, indeed. Listen to me. Do you know the sort of pictures she has on her wall? Is it any of these young Romeos and Lochinvars? No!—it's Moses on the Mountain—that's what she's got. If you want to make her happy, you give her a picture of Methuselah surrounded by his grandchildren. That's my advice to you.

VANDERGELDER. I hope ... hm ... that she has some means, Mrs. Levi. I have a large household to run.

MRS. LEVI. Ernestina? She'll bring you five thousand dollars a year.

VANDERGELDER. Eh! Eh!

MRS. LEVI. Listen to me, Mr. Vandergelder. You're a man of sense, I hope. A man that can reckon. In the first place, she's an orphan. She's been brought up with a great saving of food. What does she eat herself? Apples and lettuce. It's what she's been used to eat and what she likes best. She saves you two thousand a year right there. Secondly, she makes her own clothes—out of old tablecloths and window curtains. And she's the best-dressed woman in Brooklyn this minute. She saves you a thousand dollars right there. Thirdly, her health is of iron—

VANDERGELDER. But, Mrs. Levi, that's not money in the pocket.

MRS. LEVI. We're talking about marriage, aren't we, Mr. Vandergelder? The money she saves while she's in Brooklyn is none of your affair—but if she were your wife that would be *money*. Yes, sir, that's money.

VANDERGELDER. What's her family?

MRS. LEVI. Her father?—God be good to him! He was the best—what am I trying to say?—the best undertaker in Brooklyn, respected, esteemed. He knew all the best people—knew them well, even before they died. So—well, that's the way it is. (*Lowering her voice, intimately.*) Now let me tell you a little more of her appearance. Can you hear me: as I say, a beautiful girl, beautiful, I've seen her go down the street—you know what I mean?—the young men get dizzy. They have to lean against lampposts. And she? Modest, eyes on the ground—I'm not going to tell you any more. . . . Couldn't you come to New York today?

VANDERGELDER. I was thinking of coming to New York this afternoon. . . .

MRS. LEVI. You were? Well now, I wonder if something could be arranged—oh, she's so eager to see you! Let me see . . .

VANDERGELDER. Could I . . . Mrs. Levi, could I give you a little dinner, maybe?

MRS. LEVI. Really, come to think of it, I don't see where I could get the time. I'm so busy over that wretched lawsuit of mine. Yes, if I win it, I don't mind telling you, I'll be what's called a very rich woman. I'll own half of Long Island, that's a fact. But just now I'm at my wit's end for a little help, just enough money to finish it off. My wit's end! (*She looks in her handbag. In order not to hear this,* VANDERGELDER *has a series of coughs, sneezes and minor convulsions.*) But perhaps I could arrange a little dinner; I'll see. Yes, for that lawsuit all I need is fifty dollars, and Staten Island's as good as mine. I've been trotting all over New York for you, trying to find you a suitable wife.

VANDERGELDER. Fifty dollars!!

MRS. LEVI. Two whole months I've been . . .

VANDERGELDER. Fifty dollars, Mrs. Levi . . . is no joke. (*Producing purse.*) I don't know where money's gone to these days. It's in hiding. . . . There's twenty . . . well, there's twenty-five. I can't spare no more, not now I can't.

MRS. LEVI. Well, this will help—will help somewhat. Now let me tell you what we'll do. I'll bring Ernestina to that restaurant on the Battery. You know it: the Harmonia Gardens. It's good, but it's not flashy. Now, Mr. Vandergelder, I think it'd be nice if just this once you'd order a real nice dinner. I guess you can afford it.

VANDERGELDER. Well, just this once.

MRS. LEVI. A chicken wouldn't hurt.

VANDERGELDER. Chicken!!—Well, just this once.

MRS. LEVI. And a little wine.

VANDERGELDER. Wine? Well, just this once.

MRS. LEVI. Now about Mrs. Molloy—what do you think? Shall we call that subject closed?

VANDERGELDER. No, not at all, Mrs. Levi, I want to have dinner with Miss . . . with Miss . . .

MRS. LEVI. Simple.

VANDERGELDER. With Miss Simple; but first I want to make another call on Mrs. Molloy.

MRS. LEVI. Dear, dear, dear! And Miss Simple? What races you make me run! Very well; I'll meet you on one of those benches in front of Mrs. Molloy's hat store at four thirty, as usual.

(*Trap door rises, and* CORNELIUS' *head appears.*)

CORNELIUS. The buggy's here, ready for the parade, Mr. Vandergelder.

VANDERGELDER. Call Barnaby. I want to talk to both of you.

CORNELIUS. Yes, Mr. Vandergelder. (*Exit* CORNELIUS *down trap door. Leaves trap open.*)

MRS. LEVI. Now do put your thoughts in order, Mr. Vandergelder. I can't keep upsetting and disturbing the finest women in New York City unless you mean business.

VANDERGELDER. Oh, I mean business all right!

MRS. LEVI. I hope so. Because, you know, you're playing a very dangerous game.

VANDERGELDER. Dangerous?—Dangerous, Mrs. Levi?

MRS. LEVI. Of course, it's dangerous—and there's a name for it! You're tampering with these women's affections, aren't you? And the only way you can save yourself now is to be married to *someone* by the end of next week. So think that over! (*Exit center back.*)

(*Enter* CORNELIUS *and* BARNABY, *by the trap door.*)

VANDERGELDER. This morning I'm joining my lodge parade, and this afternoon I'm going to New York. When I come back, there are going to be some changes in the house here. I'll tell you what the change is, but I don't want you discussing it amongst yourselves: you're going to have a mistress.

BARNABY (*seventeen; round-faced, wide-eyed innocence; wearing a green apron*). I'm too young, Mr. Vandergelder!!

VANDERGELDER. Not yours! Death and damnation! Not yours, idiot—mine! (*Then, realizing:*) Hey! Hold your

tongue until you're spoken to! I'm thinking of getting married.
CORNELIUS (*crosses, hand outstretched*). Many congratulations, Mr. Vandergelder, and my compliments to the lady.
VANDERGELDER. That's none of your business. Now go back to the store. (*The boys start down the ladder,* BARNABY *first.*) Have you got any questions you want to ask before I go?
CORNELIUS. Mr. Vandergelder — er — Mr. Vandergelder, does the chief clerk get one evening off every week?
VANDERGELDER. So that's the way you begin being chief clerk, is it? When I was your age I got up at five; I didn't close the shop until ten at night, and then I put in a good hour at the account books. The world's going to pieces. You elegant laddies lie in bed until six and at nine o'clock at night you rush to close the door so fast the line of customers bark their noses. No, sir — you'll attend to the store as usual, and on Friday and Saturday nights you'll remain open until ten — now hear what I say! This is the first time I've been away from the store overnight. When I come back I want to hear that you've run the place perfectly in my absence. If I hear of any foolishness, I'll discharge you. An evening free! Do you suppose that *I* had evenings free? (*At the top of his complacency.*) If I'd had evenings free I wouldn't be what I am now! (*He marches out, right.*)
BARNABY (*watching him go*). The horses nearly ran away when they saw him. What's the matter, Cornelius?
CORNELIUS (*sits in dejected thought*). Chief clerk! Promoted from chief clerk to chief clerk.
BARNABY. Don't you like it?
CORNELIUS. Chief clerk! — and if I'm good, in ten years I'll be promoted to chief clerk again. Thirty-three years old and I still don't get an evening free? When am I going to begin to live?
BARNABY. Well — ah . . . you can begin to live on Sundays, Cornelius.
CORNELIUS. That's no living. Twice to church, and old Wolftrap's eyes on the back of my head the whole time. And

as for holidays! What did we do last Christmas? All those canned tomatoes went bad and exploded. We had to clean up the mess all afternoon. Was that living?

BARNABY (*holding his nose at the memory of the bad smell*). No!!!

CORNELIUS (*rising with sudden resolution*). Barnaby, how much money have you got—where you can get at it?

BARNABY. Oh—three dollars. Why, Cornelius?

CORNELIUS. You and I are going to New York.

BARNABY. Cornelius!!! We can't! Close the store?

CORNELIUS. Some more rotten-tomato cans are going to explode.

BARNABY. Holy cabooses! How do you know?

CORNELIUS. I know they're rotten. All you have to do is to light a match under them. They'll make such a smell that customers can't come into the place for twenty-four hours. That'll get us an evening free. We're going to New York too, Barnaby, we're going to live! I'm going to have enough adventures to last me until I'm *partner*. So go and get your Sunday clothes on.

BARNABY. Wha-a-a-t?

CORNELIUS. Yes, I mean it. We're going to have a good meal; and we're going to be in danger; and we're going to get almost arrested; and we're going to spend all our money.

BARNABY. Holy cabooses!!

CORNELIUS. And one more thing: we're not coming back to Yonkers until we've kissed a girl.

BARNABY. Kissed a girl! Cornelius, you can't do that. You don't know any girls.

CORNELIUS. I'm thirty-three. I've got to begin sometime.

BARNABY. I'm only seventeen, Cornelius. It isn't so urgent for me.

CORNELIUS. Don't start backing down now—if the worst comes to the worst and we get discharged from here we can always join the Army.

BARNABY. Uh—did I hear you say that you'd be old Wolf-trap's partner?

CORNELIUS. How can I help it? He's growing old. If you go to bed at nine and open the store at six, you get promoted upward whether you like it or not.

BARNABY. My! Partner.
CORNELIUS. Oh, there's no way of getting away from it. You and I will be Vandergelders.
BARNABY. I? Oh, no—I may rise a little, but I'll never be a Vandergelder.
CORNELIUS. Listen—everybody thinks when he gets rich he'll be a different kind of rich person from the rich people he sees around him; later on he finds out there's only one kind of rich person, and he's it.
BARNABY. Oh, but I'll—
CORNELIUS. No. The best of all would be a person who has all the good things a poor person has, and all the good meals a rich person has, but that's never been known. No, you and I are going to be Vandergelders; all the more reason, then, for us to try and get some living and some adventure into us now—will you come, Barnaby?
BARNABY (*in a struggle with his fears, a whirlwind of words*). But Wolf-trap—KRR-pt, Gertrude-KRR-pt—(*With a sudden cry of agreement.*) Yes, Cornelius!

(*Enter* MRS. LEVI, ERMENGARDE *and* GERTRUDE *from back center. The bous start down the ladder,* CORNELIUS *last.*)

MRS. LEVI. Mr. Hackl, is the trunk waiting at the station?
CORNELIUS. Yes, Mrs. Levi. (*Closes the trap door.*)
MRS. LEVI. Take a last look, Ermengarde.
ERMENGARDE. What?
MRS. LEVI. Take a last look at your girlhood home, dear. I remember when I left my home. I gave a whinny like a young colt, and off I went.

(ERMENGARDE *and* GERTRUDE *exit.*)

ERMENGARDE (*As they go*). Oh, Gertrude, do you think I ought to get married this way? A young girl has to be so careful!

(MRS. LEVI *is alone. She addresses the audience.*)

MRS. LEVI. You know, I think I'm going to have this room with *blue* wallpaper,—yes, in blue! (*Hurries out after the others.*)

(BARNABY *comes up trap door, looks off right, then lies on floor, gazing down through the trap door.*)

BARNABY. All clear up here, Cornelius! Cornelius—hold the candle steady a minute—the bottom row's all right—but try the top now . . . they're swelled up like they are ready to burst! (*BANG.*) Holy CABOOSES! (*BANG, BANG.*) Cornelius! I can smell it up here! (*Rises and dances about, holding his nose.*)

CORNELIUS (*rushing up the trap door*). Get into your Sunday clothes, Barnaby. We're going to New York!

(*As they run out . . . there is a big explosion. A shower of tomato cans comes up from below, as—*

*The Curtain Falls*

# Act II

MRS. MOLLOY'S *hat shop, New York City.*

*There are two entrances. One door at the extreme right of the back wall, to* MRS. MOLLOY'S *workroom; one at the back left corner, to the street. The whole left wall is taken up with the show windows, filled with hats. It is separated from the shop by a low brass rail, hung with net; during the act both* MRS. MOLLOY *and* BARNABY *stoop under the rail and go into the shop window. By the street door stands a large cheval glass. In the middle of the back wall is a large wardrobe or clothes cupboard, filled with ladies' coats, large enough for* CORNELIUS *to hide in. At the left, beginning at the back wall, between the wardrobe and the workroom door, a long counter extends toward the audience, almost to the footlights. In the center of the room is a large round table with a low-*

hanging red cloth. There are a small gilt chair by the wardrobe and two chairs in front of the counter. Over the street door and the workroom door are bells which ring when the doors are opened.

As the curtain rises, MRS. MOLLOY is in the window, standing on a box, reaching up to put hats on the stand. MINNIE FAY is sewing by the counter. MRS. MOLLOY has a pair of felt overshoes, to be removed later.

MRS. MOLLOY. Minnie, you're a fool. Of course I shall marry Horace Vandergelder.
MINNIE. Oh, Mrs. Molloy! I didn't ask you. I wouldn't dream of asking you such a personal question.
MRS. MOLLOY. Well, it's what you meant, isn't it? And there's your answer. I shall certainly marry Horace Vandergelder if he asks me. (*Crawls under window rail, into the room, singing loudly.*)
MINNIE. I know it's none of my business...
MRS. MOLLOY. Speak up, Minnie, I can't hear you.
MINNIE. ...but do you...do you...?
MRS. MOLLOY (*having crossed the room, is busy at the counter*). Minnie, you're a fool. Say it: Do I love him? Of course, I don't love him. But I have two good reasons for marrying him just the same. Minnie, put something on that hat. It's not ugly enough. (*Throws hat over counter.*)
MINNIE (*catching and taking hat to table*). Not ugly enough!
MRS. MOLLOY. I couldn't sell it. Put a...put a sponge on it.
MINNIE. Why, Mrs. Molloy, you're in such a *mood* today.
MRS. MOLLOY. In the first place I shall marry Mr. Vandergelder to get away from the millinery business. I've hated it from the first day I had anything to do with it. Minnie, I hate hats. (*Sings loudly again.*)
MINNIE. Why, what's the matter with the millinery business?
MRS. MOLLOY (*crossing to window with two hats*). I can no longer stand being suspected of being a wicked woman, while I have nothing to show for it. I can't stand it. (*She crawls under rail into window.*)
MINNIE. Why, no one would dream of suspecting you —

MRS. MOLLOY (*on her knees, she looks over the rail*). Minnie, you're a fool. All millineresses are suspected of being wicked women. Why, half the time all those women come into the shop merely to look at me.

MINNIE. Oh!

MRS. MOLLOY. They enjoy the suspicion. But they aren't certain. If they were *certain* I was a wicked woman, they wouldn't put foot in this place again. Do I go to restaurants? No, it would be bad for business. Do I go to balls, or theaters, or operas? No, it would be bad for business. The only men I ever meet are feather merchants. (*Crawls out of window, but gazes intently into the street.*) What are those two young men doing out there on that park bench? Take my word for it, Minnie, either I marry Horace Vandergelder, or I break out of this place like a fire engine. I'll go to every theater and ball and opera in New York City. (*Returns to counter, singing again.*)

MINNIE. But Mr. Vandergelder's not...

MRS. MOLLOY. Speak up, Minnie, I can't hear you.

MINNIE. ... I don't think he's attractive.

MRS. MOLLOY. But what I think he is—and it's very important—I think he'd make a good fighter.

MINNIE. Mrs. Molloy!

MRS. MOLLOY. Take my word for it, Minnie: the best part of married life is the fights. The rest is merely so-so.

MINNIE (*fingers in ears*). I won't listen.

MRS. MOLLOY. Peter Molloy—God rest him!—was a fine arguing man. I pity the woman whose husband slams the door and walks out of the house at the beginning of an argument. Peter Molloy would stand up and fight for hours on end. He'd even throw things, Minnie, and there's no pleasure to equal that. When I felt tired I'd start a good bloodwarming fight and it'd take ten years off my age; now Horace Vandergelder would put up a good fight; I know it. I've a mind to marry him.

MINNIE. I think they're just awful, the things you're saying today.

MRS. MOLLOY. Well, I'm enjoying them myself, too.

MINNIE (*at the window*). Mrs. Molloy, those two men out in the street—

MRS. MOLLOY. What?
MINNIE. Those men. It looks as if they meant to come in here.
MRS. MOLLOY. Well now, it's time some men came into this place. I give you the younger one, Minnie.
MINNIE. Aren't you terrible!

(MRS. MOLLOY *sits on center table, while* MINNIE *takes off her felt overshoes.*)

MRS. MOLLOY. Wait till I get my hands on that older one! Mark my words, Minnie, we'll get an adventure out of this yet. Adventure, adventure! Why does everybody have adventures except me, Minnie? Because I have no spirit, I have no gumption. Minnie, they're coming in here. Let's go into the workroom and make them wait for us for a minute.
MINNIE. Oh, but Mrs. Molloy . . . my work! . . .
MRS. MOLLOY (*running to workroom*). Hurry up, be quick now, Minnie!

(*They go out to workroom.* BARNABY *and* CORNELIUS *run in from street, leaving front door open. They are dressed in the stiff discomfort of their Sunday clothes.* CORNELIUS *wears a bowler hat,* BARNABY *a straw hat too large for him.*)

BARNABY. No one's here.
CORNELIUS. Some women were here a minute ago. I saw them. (*They jump back to the street door and peer down the street.*) That's Wolf-trap all right! (*Coming back.*) Well, we've got to hide here until he passes by.
BARNABY. He's sitting down on that bench. It may be quite a while.
CORNELIUS. When these women come in, we'll have to make conversation until he's gone away. We'll pretend we're buying a hat. How much money have you got now?
BARNABY (*counting his money*). Forty cents for the train—

seventy cents for dinner—twenty cents to see the whale—and a dollar I lost—I have seventy cents.

CORNELIUS. And I have a dollar seventy-five. I wish I knew how much hats cost!

BARNABY. Is this an adventure, Cornelius?

CORNELIUS. No, but it may be.

BARNABY. I think it is. There we wander around New York all day and nothing happens; and then we come to the quietest street in the whole city and suddenly Mr. Vandergelder turns the corner. (*Going to door.*) I think that's an adventure. I think . . . Cornelius! That Mrs. Levi is there now. She's sitting down on the bench with him.

CORNELIUS. What do you know about that! We know only one person in all New York City, and there she is!

BARNABY. Even if our adventure came along now I'd be too tired to enjoy it. Cornelius, why isn't this an adventure?

CORNELIUS. Don't be asking that. When you're in an adventure, you'll know it all right.

BARNABY. Maybe I wouldn't. Cornelius, let's arrange a signal for you to give me when an adventure's really going on. For instance, Cornelius, you say . . . uh . . . uh . . . *pudding;* you say *pudding* to me if it's an adventure we're in.

CORNELIUS. I wonder where the lady who runs this store is? What's her name again?

BARNABY. "Mrs. Molloy, hats for ladies."

CORNELIUS. Oh yes. I must think over what I'm going to say when she comes in. (*To counter.*) "Good afternoon, Mrs. Molloy, wonderful weather we're having. We've been looking everywhere for some beautiful hats."

BARNABY. That's fine, Cornelius!

CORNELIUS. "Good afternoon, Mrs. Molloy; wonderful weather . . ." We'll make her think we're very rich. (*One hand in trouser pocket, the other on back of chair.*) "Good afternoon, Mrs. Molloy . . ." You keep one eye on the door the whole time. "We've been looking everywhere for . . ."

(*Enter* MRS. MOLLOY *from the workroom.*)

MRS. MOLLOY *(behind the counter)*. Oh, I'm sorry. Have I kept you waiting? Good afternoon, gentlemen.
CORNELIUS *(hat off)*. Here, Cornelius Hackl.
BARNABY *(hat off)*. Here, Barnaby Tucker.
MRS. MOLLOY. I'm very happy to meet you. Perhaps I can help you. Won't you sit down?
CORNELIUS. Thank you, we will. *(The boys place their hats on the table, then sit down at the counter facing* MRS. MOLLOY.*)* You see, Mrs. Molloy, we're looking for hats. We've looked everywhere. Do you know what we heard? Go to Mrs. Molloy's, they said. So we came here. Only place we *could* go . . .
MRS. MOLLOY. Well now, that's *very* complimentary.
CORNELIUS. . . . and we were right. Everybody was right.
MRS. MOLLOY. You wish to choose some hats for a friend?
CORNELIUS. Yes, exactly. *(Kicks* BARNABY.*)*
BARNABY. Yes, exactly.
CORNELIUS. We were thinking of five or six, weren't we, Barnaby?
BARNABY. Er — five.
CORNELIUS. You see, Mrs. Molloy, money's no object with us. None at all.
MRS. MOLLOY. Why, Mr. Hackl . . .
CORNELIUS *(rises and goes toward street door)*. . . . I beg your pardon, what an interesting street! Something happening every minute. Passers-by, and . . .

*(*BARNABY *runs to join him.)*

MRS. MOLLOY. You're from out of town, Mr. Hackl?
CORNELIUS *(coming back)*. Yes, ma'am — Barnaby, just keep an eye on the street, will you? You won't see that in Yonkers every day. *(*BARNABY *remains kneeling at street door.)*
BARNABY. Oh yes, I will.
CORNELIUS. Not all of it.
MRS. MOLLOY. Now this friend of yours — couldn't she come in with you someday and choose her hats herself?
CORNELIUS *(sits at counter)*. No. Oh, no. It's a surprise for her.

MRS. MOLLOY. Indeed? That may be a little difficult, Mr. Hackl. It's not entirely customary.—Your friend's very interested in the street, Mr. Hackl.
CORNELIUS. Oh yes. Yes. He has reason to be.
MRS. MOLLOY. You said you were from out of town?
CORNELIUS. Yes, we're from Yonkers.
MRS. MOLLOY. Yonkers?
CORNELIUS. Yonkers . . . yes, Yonkers. (*He gazes rapt into her eyes.*) You should know Yonkers, Mrs. Molloy. Hudson River; Palisades; drives; some say it's the most beautiful town in the world; that's what they say.
MRS. MOLLOY. Is that so!
CORNELIUS (*rises*). Mrs. Molloy, if you ever had a Sunday free, I'd . . . we'd like to show you Yonkers. Y'know, it's very historic, too.
MRS. MOLLOY. That's very kind of you. Well, perhaps . . . now about those hats. (*Takes two hats from under counter, and crosses to back center of the room.*)
CORNELIUS (*following*). Is there . . . Have you a . . . Maybe Mr. Molloy would like to see Yonkers too?
MRS. MOLLOY. Oh, I'm a widow, Mr. Hackl.
CORNELIUS (*joyfully*). You are! (*With sudden gravity.*) Oh, that's too bad. Mr. Molloy would have enjoyed Yonkers.
MRS. MOLLOY. Very likely. Now about these hats. Is your friend dark or light?
CORNELIUS. Don't think about that for a minute. Any hat you'd like would be perfectly all right with her.
MRS. MOLLOY. Really! (*She puts one on.*) Do you like this one?
CORNELIUS (*in awe-struck admiration*). Barnaby! (*In sudden anger.*) Barnaby! Look! (BARNABY *turns; unimpressed, he laughs vaguely, and turns to door again.*) Mrs. Molloy, that's the most beautiful hat I ever saw.

(BARNABY *now crawls under the rail into the window.*)

MRS. MOLLOY. Your friend is acting very strangely, Mr. Hackl.
CORNELIUS. Barnaby, stop acting strangely. When the street's quiet and empty, come back and talk to us. What

was I saying? Oh yes: Mrs. Molloy, you should know Yonkers.

MRS. MOLLOY *(hat off).* The fact is, I have a friend in Yonkers. Perhaps you know him. It's always so foolish to ask in cases like that, isn't it? *(They both laugh over this with increasing congeniality.* MRS. MOLLOY *goes to counter with hats from table.* CORNELIUS *follows.)* It's a Mr. Vandergelder.

CORNELIUS *(stops abruptly).* What was that you said?

MRS. MOLLOY. Then you do know him?

CORNELIUS. Horace Vandergelder?

MRS. MOLLOY. Yes, that's right.

CORNELIUS. Know him! *(Looks to* BARNABY.*)* Why, no. No!

BARNABY. No! No!

CORNELIUS *(starting to glide about the room, in search of a hiding place).* I beg your pardon, Mrs. Molloy—what an attractive shop you have! *(Smiling fixedly at her he moves to the workshop door.)* And where does this door lead to? *(Opens it, and is alarmed by the bell which rings above it.)*

MRS. MOLLOY. Why, Mr. Hackl, that's my workroom.

CORNELIUS. Everything here is so interesting. *(Looks under counter.)* Every corner. Every door, Mrs. Molloy. Barnaby, notice the interesting doors and cupboards. *(He opens the cupboard door.)* Deeply interesting. Coats for ladies. *(Laughs.)* Barnaby, make a note of the table. Precious piece of furniture, with a low-hanging cloth, I see. *(Stretches his leg under table.)*

MRS. MOLLOY *(taking a hat from box left of wardrobe).* Perhaps your friend might like some of this new Italian straw. Mr. Vandergelder's a substantial man and very well liked, they tell me.

CORNELIUS. A lovely man, Mrs. Molloy.

MRS. MOLLOY. Oh yes—charming, charming!

CORNELIUS *(smiling sweetly).* Has only one fault, as far as I know; he's hard as nails; but apart from that, as you say, a charming nature, ma'am.

MRS. MOLLOY. And a large circle of friends—?

CORNELIUS. Yes, indeed, yes indeed—five or six.

BARNABY.  Five!
CORNELIUS.  He comes and calls on you here from time to time, I suppose.
MRS. MOLLOY (*turns from mirror where she has been putting a hat on*).  This summer we'll be wearing ribbons down our back. Yes, as a matter of fact I am expecting a call from him this afternoon. (*Hat off.*)
BARNABY.  I think . . . Cornelius! I think . . . !!
MRS. MOLLOY.  Now to show you some more hats—
BARNABY.  Look out! (*He takes a flying leap over the rail and flings himself under the table.*)
CORNELIUS.  Begging your pardon, Mrs. Molloy. (*He jumps into the cupboard.*)
MRS. MOLLOY.  Gentlemen! Mr. Hackl! Come right out of there this minute!
CORNELIUS (*sticking his head out of the wardrobe door*).  Help us just this once, Mrs. Molloy! We'll explain later!
MRS. MOLLOY.  Mr. Hackl!
BARNABY.  We're as innocent as can be, Mrs. Molloy.
MRS. MOLLOY.  But really! Gentlemen! I can't have this! What are you doing?
BARNABY.  Cornelius! Cornelius! Pudding?
CORNELIUS (*a shout*).  Pudding!

(*They disappear. Enter from the street* MRS. LEVI, *followed by* MR. VANDERGELDER. VANDERGELDER *is dressed in a too-bright checked suit, and wears a green derby—or bowler—hat. He is carrying a large ornate box of chocolates in one hand, and a cane in the other.*)

MRS. LEVI.  Irene, my darling child, how *are* you? Heaven be good to us, how well you look! (*They kiss.*)
MRS. MOLLOY.  But what a surprise! And Mr. Vandergelder in New York—what a pleasure!
VANDERGELDER (*swaying back and forth on his heels complacently*).  Good afternoon, Mrs. Molloy.

(*They shake hands.* MRS. MOLLOY *brings chair from counter for him. He sits at left of table.*)

MRS. LEVI. Yes, Mr. Vandergelder's in New York. Yonkers lies up there—*decimated* today. Irene, we thought we'd pay you a very short call. Now you'll tell us if it's inconvenient, won't you?

MRS. MOLLOY (*placing a chair for* MRS. LEVI *at right of table*). Inconvenient, Dolly! The idea! Why, it's sweet of you to come. (*She notices the boys' hats on the table—sticks a spray of flowers into crown of* CORNELIUS' *bowler and winds a piece of chiffon round* BARNABY'S *panama.*)

VANDERGELDER. We waited outside a moment.

MRS. LEVI. Mr. Vandergelder thought he saw two customers coming in—two men.

MRS. MOLLOY. Men! Men, Mr. Vandergelder? Why, what will you be saying next?

MRS. LEVI. Then we'll sit down for a minute or two. . . .

MRS. MOLLOY (*wishing to get them out of the shop into the workroom*). Before you sit down— (*She pushes them both.*) Before you sit down, there's something I want to show you. I want to show Mr. Vandergelder my workroom, too.

MRS. LEVI. I've seen the workroom a hundred times. I'll stay right here and try on some of these hats.

MRS. MOLLOY. No, Dolly, you come too. I have something for you. Come along, everybody. (*Exit* MRS. LEVI *to workroom*). Mr. Vandergelder, I want your advice. You don't know how helpless a woman in business is. Oh, I feel I need advice every minute from a fine business head like yours. (*Exit* VANDERGELDER *to workroom.* MRS. MOLLOY *shouts this line and then slams the workroom door.*) Now I shut the door!!

(*Exit* MRS. MOLLOY. CORNELIUS *puts his head out of the wardrobe door and gradually comes out into the room, leaving door open.*)

CORNELIUS. Hsst!

BARNABY (*pokes his head out from under the table*). Maybe she wants us to go, Cornelius?

CORNELIUS. Certainly I won't go. Mrs. Molloy would think we were just thoughtless fellows. No, all I want is to stretch a minute.
BARNABY. What are you going to do when he's gone, Cornelius? Are we just going to run away?
CORNELIUS. Well . . . I don't know yet. I like Mrs. Molloy a lot. I wouldn't like her to think badly of me. I think I'll buy a hat. We can walk home to Yonkers, even if it takes us all night. I wonder how much hats cost. Barnaby, give me all the money you've got. (*As he leans over to take the money, he sneezes. Both return to their hiding places in alarm; then emerge again.*) My, all those perfumes in that cupboard tickled my nose! But I like it in there . . . it's a woman's world, and very different.
BARNABY. I like it where I am, too; only I'd like it better if I had a pillow.
CORNELIUS (*taking coat from wardrobe*). Here, take one of these coats. I'll roll it up for you so it won't get mussed. Ladies don't like to have their coats mussed.
BARNABY. That's fine. Now I can just lie here and hear Mr. Vandergelder talk.

(CORNELIUS *goes slowly above table towards cheval mirror, repeating* MRS. MOLLOY'S *line dreamily.*)

CORNELIUS. This summer we'll be wearing ribbons down our back . . .
BARNABY. Can I take off my shoes, Cornelius?

(CORNELIUS *does not reply. He comes to the footlights and addresses the audience, in completely simple naïve sincerity:*)

CORNELIUS. Isn't the world full of wonderful things. There we sit cooped up in Yonkers for years and years and all the time wonderful people like Mrs. Molloy are walking around in New York and we don't know them at all. I don't know whether—from where you're sitting—you can see—well, for instance, the way (*he points to the edge of his right eye*) her eye and forehead and cheek come together, up here. Can you? And the kind of fireworks that shoot out of her eyes all the time. I tell you right now: a fine woman is the greatest work of God. You can talk all you like about Niagara Falls and the Pyramids; they aren't in it at all. Of course, up there at Yonkers they came into the store all the time, and bought this and that, and I said, "Yes, ma'am," and "That'll be seventy-five cents, ma'am"; and I *watched* them. But today I've talked to one, equal to equal, equal to equal, and to the finest one that ever existed, in my opinion. They're so different from men! Everything that they say and do is so different that you feel like laughing all the time. (*He laughs.*) Golly, they're different from men. And they're awfully mysterious, too. You never can be really sure what's going on in their heads. They have a kind of wall around them all the time—of pride and a sort of play-acting: I bet you could know a woman a hundred years without ever being really sure whether she liked you or not. This minute I'm in danger. I'm in danger of losing my job and my future and everything that people think is important; but I don't care. Even if I have to dig ditches for the rest of my life, I'll be a ditch digger who once had a wonderful day. Barnaby!

BARNABY. Oh, you woke me up!

CORNELIUS (*kneels*). Barnaby, we can't go back to Yonkers yet and you know why.

BARNABY. Why not?

CORNELIUS. We've had a good meal. We've had an adventure. We've been in danger of getting arrested. There's only one more thing we've got to do before we go back to be successes in Yonkers.

BARNABY. Cornelius! You're never going to kiss Mrs. Molloy!

CORNELIUS. Maybe.

BARNABY. But she'll scream.

CORNELIUS. Barnaby, you don't know anything at all. You might as well know right now that everybody except us

goes through life kissing right and left all the time.
BARNABY (*pauses for reflection: humbly*). Well, thanks for telling me, Cornelius. I often wondered.

(*Enter* MRS. LEVI *from workroom.*)

MRS. LEVI. Just a minute, Irene. I must find my handkerchief. (CORNELIUS, *caught by the arrival of* MRS. LEVI, *drops to his hands and knees, and starts very slowly to crawl back to the wardrobe, as though the slowness rendered him invisible.* MRS. LEVI, *leaning over the counter, watches him. From the cupboard he puts his head out of it and looks pleadingly at her.*) Why, Mr. Hackl, I thought you were up in Yonkers.
CORNELIUS. I almost always am, Mrs. Levi. Oh, Mrs. Levi, don't tell Mr. Vandergelder! I'll explain everything later.
BARNABY (*puts head out*). We're terribly innocent, Mrs. Levi.
MRS. LEVI. Why who's that?
BARNABY. Barnaby Tucker—just paying a call.
MRS. LEVI (*looking under counter and even shaking out her skirts.*) Well, who else is here?
CORNELIUS. Just the two of us, Mrs. Levi, that's all.
MRS. LEVI. Old friends of Mrs. Molloy's, is that it?
CORNELIUS. We never knew her before a few minutes ago, but we like her a lot—don't we, Barnaby? In fact, I think she's . . . I think she's the finest person in the world. I'm ready to tell that to anybody.
MRS. LEVI. And does she think *you're* the finest person in the world?
CORNELIUS. Oh, no. I don't suppose she even notices that I'm alive.
MRS. LEVI. Well, I think she must notice that you're alive in that cupboard, Mr. Hackl. Well, if I were you, I'd get back into it right away. Somebody could be coming in any minute.

(CORNELIUS *disappears. She sits unconcernedly in chair right. Enter* MRS. MOLLOY.)

MRS. MOLLOY (*leaving door open and looking about in concealed alarm*). Can I help you, Dolly?
MRS. LEVI. No, no, no. I was just blowing my nose.

(*Enter* VANDERGELDER *from workroom.*)

VANDERGELDER. Mrs. Molloy, I've got some advice to give you about your business.

(MRS. MOLLOY *comes to the center of the room and puts* BARNABY'S *hat on floor in window, then* CORNELIUS' *hat on the counter.*)

MRS. LEVI. Oh, advice from Mr. Vandergelder! The whole city should hear this.
VANDERGELDER (*standing in the workroom door, pompously*). In the first place, the aim of business is to make profit.
MRS. MOLLOY. Is that so?
MRS. LEVI. I never heard it put so clearly before. Did you hear it?
VANDERGELDER (*crossing the room to the left*). You pay those girls of yours too much. You pay them as much as men. Girls like that enjoy their work. Wages, Mrs. Molloy, are paid to make people do work they don't want to do.
MRS. LEVI. Mr. Vandergelder thinks so ably. And that's exactly the way his business is run up in Yonkers.
VANDERGELDER (*patting her hand*). Mrs. Molloy, I'd like for you to come up to Yonkers.
MRS. MOLLOY. That would be very nice. (*He hands her the box of chocolates.*) Oh, thank you. As a matter of fact, I know someone from Yonkers, someone else.
VANDERGELDER (*hangs hat on the cheval mirror*). Oh? Who's that?

(MRS. MOLLOY *puts chocolates on table and brings gilt chair forward and sits center at table facing the audience.*)

MRS. MOLLOY. Someone quite well-to-do, I believe, though

a little free and easy in his behavior. Mr. Vandergelder, do you know Mr. Cornelius Hackl in Yonkers?

VANDERGELDER. I know him like I know my own boot. He's my head clerk.

MRS. MOLLOY. Is that so?

VANDERGELDER. He's been in my store for ten years.

MRS. MOLLOY. Well, I never!

VANDERGELDER. Where would you have known him?

(MRS. MOLLOY *is in silent confusion. She looks for help to* MRS. LEVI, *seated at right end of table*.)

MRS. LEVI (*groping for means to help* MRS. MOLLOY). Err... blah... err... bl... er... Oh, just one of those chance meetings, I suppose.

MRS. MOLLOY. Yes, oh yes! One of those chance meetings.

VANDERGELDER. What? Chance meetings? Cornelius Hackl has no right to chance meetings. Where was it?

MRS. MOLLOY. Really, Mr. Vandergelder, it's very unlike you to question me in such a way. I think Mr. Hackl is better known than you think he is.

VANDERGELDER. Nonsense.

MRS. MOLLOY. He's in New York often, and he's very well liked.

MRS. LEVI (*having found her idea, with decision*). Well, the truth might as well come out now as later. Mr. Vandergelder, Irene is quite right. Your head clerk is often in New York. Goes everywhere; has an army of friends. Everybody knows Cornelius Hackl.

VANDERGELDER (*laughs blandly and sits in chair at left of table*). He never comes to New York. He works all day in my store and at nine o'clock at night he goes to sleep in the bran room.

MRS. LEVI. So you think. But it's not true.

VANDERGELDER. Dolly Gallagher, you're crazy.

MRS. LEVI. Listen to me. You keep your nose so deep in your account books you don't know what goes on. Yes, by day, Cornelius Hackl is your faithful trusted clerk—that's true; but by night! Well, he leads a double life, that's all! He's here at the opera; at the great restaurants; in all the fashionable homes . . . why, he's at the Harmonia Gardens Restaurant three nights a week. The fact is, he's the wittiest, gayest, naughtiest, most delightful man in New York. Well, he's just *the* famous Cornelius Hackl!

VANDERGELDER *(sure of himself).* It ain't the same man. If I ever thought Cornelius Hackl came to New York, I'd discharge him.

MRS. LEVI. Who took the horses out of Jenny Lind's carriage and pulled her through the streets?

MRS. MOLLOY. Who?

MRS. LEVI. Cornelius Hackl! Who dressed up as a waiter at the Fifth Avenue Hotel the other night and took an oyster and dropped it right down Mrs. . . . (*Rises.*) No, it's too wicked to tell you!

MRS. MOLLOY. Oh yes, Dolly, tell it! Go on!

MRS. LEVI. No. But it *was* Cornelius Hackl.

VANDERGELDER (*loud*). It ain't the same man. Where'd he get the money?

MRS. LEVI. But he's very rich.

VANDERGELDER (*rises*). Rich! I keep his money in my own safe. He has a hundred and forty-six dollars and thirty-five cents.

MRS. LEVI. Oh, Mr. Vandergelder, you're killing me! Do come to your senses. He's one of *the* Hackls.

(MRS. MOLLOY *sits at chair right of table where* MRS. LEVI *has been sitting.*)

VANDERGELDER. *The* Hackls?

MRS. LEVI. They built the Raritan Canal.

VANDERGELDER. Then why should he work in my store?

MRS. LEVI. Well, I'll tell you. (*Sits at the center of the table, facing the audience.*)

VANDERGELDER (*striding about*). I don't want to hear! I've got a headache! I'm going home. *It ain't the same man!!* He sleeps in my bran room. You can't get away from facts. I just made him my chief clerk.

MRS. LEVI. If you had any sense you'd make him partner.

(*Rises, crosses to* MRS. MOLLOY.) Now Irene, I can see you were as taken with him as everybody else is.

MRS. MOLLOY. Why, I only met him once, very hastily.

MRS. LEVI. Yes, but I can see that you were taken with him. Now don't you be thinking of marrying him!

MRS. MOLLOY (*her hands on her cheeks*). Dolly! What are you saying! Oh!

MRS. LEVI. Maybe it'd be fine. But think it over carefully. He breaks hearts like hickory nuts.

VANDERGELDER. Who?

MRS. LEVI. Cornelius Hackl!

VANDERGELDER. Mrs. Molloy, how often has he called on you?

MRS. MOLLOY. Oh, I'm telling the truth. I've only seen him once in my life. Dolly Levi's been exaggerating so. I don't know where to look!

(*Enter* MINNIE *from workroom and crosses to window.*)

MINNIE. Excuse me, Mrs. Molloy. I must get together that order for Mrs. Parkinson.

MRS. MOLLOY. Yes, we must get that off before closing.

MINNIE. I want to send it off by the errand girl. (*Having taken a hat from the window.*) Oh, I almost forgot the coat. (*She starts for the wardrobe.*)

MRS. MOLLOY (*running to the wardrobe to prevent her*). Oh, oh! I'll do that, Minnie!

(*But she is too late.* MINNIE *opens the right-hand cupboard door and falls back in terror, and screams.*)

MINNIE. Oh, Mrs. Molloy! Help! There's a man!

(MRS. MOLLOY *with the following speech pushes her to the workroom door.* MINNIE *walks with one arm pointing at the cupboard. At the end of each of* MRS. MOLLOY'S *sentences she repeats—at the same pitch and degree— the words:* "There's a man!")

MRS. MOLLOY (*slamming cupboard door*). Minnie, you imagined it. You're tired, dear. You go back in the workroom and lie down. Minnie, you're a fool; hold your tongue!

MINNIE. There's a man!

(*Exit* MINNIE *to workroom.* MRS. MOLLOY *returns to the front of the stage.* VANDERGELDER *raises his stick threateningly.*)

VANDERGELDER. If there's a man there, we'll get him out. Whoever you are, come out of there! (*Strikes table with his stick.*)

MRS. LEVI (*goes masterfully to the cupboard—sweeps her umbrella around among the coats and closes each door as she does so*). Nonsense! There's no man there. See! Miss Fay's nerves have been playing tricks on her. Come now, let's sit down again. What were you saying, Mr. Vandergelder? (*They sit,* MRS. MOLLOY *right,* MRS. LEVI *center,* VANDERGELDER *left. A sneeze is heard from the cupboard. They all rise, look towards cupboard, then sit again.*) Well now . . . (*Another tremendous sneeze. With a gesture that says, "I can do no more":*) God bless you!

(*They all rise.* MRS. MOLLOY *stands with her back to the cupboard.*)

MRS. MOLLOY (*to* VANDERGELDER). Yes, there is a man in there. I'll explain it all to you another time. Thank you very much for coming to see me. Good afternoon, Dolly. Good afternoon, Mr. Vandergelder.

VANDERGELDER. You're protecting a man in there!

MRS. MOLLOY (*with back to cupboard*). There's a very simple explanation, but for the present, good afternoon.

(BARNABY *now sneezes twice, lifting the table each time.* VANDERGELDER, *right of table jerks off the tablecloth.* BARNABY *pulls cloth under table and rolls himself up in it.* MRS. MOLLOY *picks up the box of chocolates which has rolled on to the floor.*)

MRS. LEVI.  Lord, the whole room's *crawling* with men! I'll never get over it.

VANDERGELDER.  The world is going to pieces! I can't believe my own eyes!

MRS. LEVI.  Come, Mr. Vandergelder. Ernestina Simple is waiting for us.

VANDERGELDER (*finds his hat and puts it on*).  Mrs. Molloy, I shan't trouble you again, and *vice versa.*

(MRS. MOLLOY *is standing transfixed in front of cupboard, clasping the box of chocolates.* VANDERGELDER *snatches the box from her and goes out.*)

MRS. LEVI (*crosses to her*).  Irene, when I think of all the interesting things you have in this room! (*Kisses her.*) Make the most of it, dear. (*Raps cupboard.*) Good-by! (*Raps on table with umbrella.*) Good-by!

(*Exit* MRS. LEVI. MRS. MOLLOY *opens door of cupboard.* CORNELIUS *steps out.*)

MRS. MOLLOY.  So that was one of your practical jokes, Mr. Hackl?

CORNELIUS.  No, no, Mrs. Molloy!

MRS. MOLLOY.  Come out from under that, Barnaby Tucker, you troublemaker! (*She snatches the cloth and spreads it back on table.* MINNIE *enters.*) There's nothing to be afraid of, Minnie, I know all about these gentlemen.

CORNELIUS.  Mrs. Molloy, we realize that what happened here —

MRS. MOLLOY.  You think because you're rich you can make up for all the harm you do, is that it?

CORNELIUS.  No, no!

BARNABY (*on the floor putting shoes on*).  No, no!

MRS. MOLLOY.  Minnie, this is the famous Cornelius Hackl

who goes round New York tying people into knots; and that's Barnaby Tucker, another troublemaker.

BARNABY. How d'you do?

MRS. MOLLOY. Minnie, choose yourself any hat and coat in the store. We're going out to dinner. If this Mr. Hackl is so rich and gay and charming, he's going to be rich and gay and charming to us. He dines three nights a week at the Harmonia Gardens Restaurant, does he? Well, he's taking us there now.

MINNIE. Mrs. Molloy, are you sure it's safe?

MRS. MOLLOY. Minnie, hold your tongue. We're in a position to put these men into jail if they so much as squeak.

CORNELIUS. Jail, Mrs. Molloy?

MRS. MOLLOY. Jail, Mr. Hackl. Officer Cogarty does everything I tell him to do. Minnie, you and I have been respectable for years; now we're in disgrace, we might as well make the most of it. Come into the workroom with me; I know some ways we can perk up our appearances. Gentlemen, we'll be back in a minute.

CORNELIUS. Uh—Mrs. Molloy, I hear there's an awfully good restaurant at the railway station.

MRS. MOLLOY (*high indignation*). Railway station? Railway station? Certainly not! No, sir! You're going to give us a good dinner in the heart of the fashionable world. Go on in, Minnie! Don't you boys forget that you've made us lose our reputations, and now the fashionable world's the only place we *can* eat. (MRS. MOLLOY *exits to workroom.*)

BARNABY. She's angry at us, Cornelius. Maybe we'd better run away now.

CORNELIUS. No, I'm going to go through with this if it kills me. Barnaby, for a woman like that a man could consent to go back to Yonkers and be a success.

BARNABY. All I know is no woman's going to make a success out of me.

CORNELIUS. Jail or no jail, we're going to take those ladies out to dinner. So grit your teeth.

(*Enter* MRS. MOLLOY *and* MINNIE *from workroom dressed for the street.*)

MRS. MOLLOY. Gentlemen, the cabs are at the corner, so forward march! (*She takes a hat—which will be* BARNABY'S *at the end of Act III—and gives it to* MINNIE.)
CORNELIUS. Yes, ma'am. (BARNABY *stands shaking his empty pockets warningly.*) Oh, Mrs. Molloy . . . is it far to the restaurant? Couldn't we walk?
MRS. MOLLOY (*pauses a moment, then*). Minnie, take off your things. We're not going.
OTHERS. Mrs. Molloy!
MRS. MOLLOY. Mr. Hackl, I don't go anywhere I'm not wanted. Good night. I'm not very happy to have met you. (*She crosses the stage as though going to the workroom door.*)
OTHERS. Mrs. Molloy!
MRS. MOLLOY. I suppose you think we're not fashionable enough for you? Well, I won't be a burden to you. Good night, Mr. Tucker.

(*The others follow her behind counter:* CORNELIUS, BARNABY, *then* MINNIE.)

CORNELIUS. We want you to come with us more than anything in the world, Mrs. Molloy.

(MRS. MOLLOY *turns and pushes the three back. They are now near the center of the stage, to the right of the table,* MRS. MOLLOY *facing the audience.*)

MRS. MOLLOY. No, you don't! Look at you! Look at the pair of them, Minnie! Scowling, both of them!
CORNELIUS. Please, Mrs. Molloy!
MRS. MOLLOY. Then smile. (*To* BARNABY.) Go on, smile! No, that's not enough. Minnie, you come with me and we'll get our own supper.
CORNELIUS. Smile, Barnaby, you lout!
BARNABY. My face can't smile any stronger than that.
MRS. MOLLOY. Then do something! Show some interest. Do something lively: sing!
CORNELIUS. I can't sing, really I can't.

MRS. MOLLOY. We're wasting our time, Minnie. They don't want us.
CORNELIUS. Barnaby, what can you sing? Mrs. Molloy, all we know are sad songs.
MRS. MOLLOY. That doesn't matter. If you want us to go out with you, you've got to sing something.

(*All this has been very rapid; the boys turn up to counter, put heads together, confer and abruptly turn, stand stiffly and sing "Tenting tonight; tenting tonight; tenting on the old camp ground." The four of them now repeat the refrain, softly harmonizing. At the end of the song, after a pause,* MRS. MOLLOY, *moved, says:*)

MRS. MOLLOY. We'll come! (*The boys shout joyfully.*) You boys go ahead. (CORNELIUS *gets his hat from counter; as he puts it on he discovers the flowers on it.* BARNABY *gets his hat from window. They go out whistling.* MINNIE *turns and puts her hat on at the mirror.*) Minnie, get the front door key—I'll lock the workroom.

(MRS. MOLLOY *goes to workroom.* MINNIE *takes key from hook left of wardrobe and goes to* MRS. MOLLOY, *at the workroom door. She turns her around.*)

MINNIE. Why, Mrs. Molloy, you're crying! (MRS. MOLLOY *flings her arms round* MINNIE.)
MRS. MOLLOY. Oh, Minnie, the world is full of wonderful things. Watch me, dear, and tell me if my petticoat's showing. (*She crosses to door, followed by* MINNIE, *as—*

The Curtain Falls

# Act III

*Veranda at the Harmonia Gardens Restaurant on the Battery, New York.*

*This room is informal and rustic. The main restaurant is indicated to be off stage back right.*

*There are three entrances: swinging double doors at the center of the back wall leading to the kitchen; one on the right wall (perhaps up a few steps and flanked by potted palms) to the street; one on the left wall to the staircase leading to the rooms above.*

*On the stage are two tables, left and right, each with four chairs. It is now afternoon and they are not yet set for dinner.*

*Against the back wall is a large folding screen. Also against the back wall are hat and coat racks.*

*As the curtain rises,* VANDERGELDER *is standing, giving orders to* RUDOLPH, *a waiter.* MALACHI STACK *sits at table left.*

VANDERGELDER. Now, hear what I say. I don't want you to make any mistakes. I want a table for three.
RUDOLPH (*tall "snob" waiter, alternating between cold superiority and rage. German accent*). For three.
VANDERGELDER. There'll be two ladies and myself.
MALACHI. It's a bad combination, Mr. Vandergelder. You'll regret it.
VANDERGELDER. And I want a chicken.
MALACHI. A chicken! You'll regret it.
VANDERGELDER. Hold your tongue. Write it down: chicken.
RUDOLPH. Yes, sir. Chicken Esterhazy? Chicken cacciatore? Chicken à la crème—?
VANDERGELDER (*exploding*). A chicken! A chicken like everybody else has. And with the chicken I want a bottle of wine.
RUDOLPH. Moselle? Chablis? Vouvray?
MALACHI. He doesn't understand you, Mr. Vandergelder. You'd better speak louder.
VANDERGELDER (*spelling*). W-I-N-E.
RUDOLPH. Wine.
VANDERGELDER. Wine! And I want this table removed. We'll eat at that table alone.

(*Exit* RUDOLPH *through service door at back.*)

MALACHI. There are some people coming in here now, Mr. Vandergelder.

(VANDERGELDER *goes to back right to look at the newcomers.*)

VANDERGELDER. What! Thunder and damnation! It's my niece Ermengarde! What's she doing here?!—Wait till I get my hands on her.

MALACHI (*running up to him*). Mr. Vandergelder! You must keep your temper!

VANDERGELDER. And there's that rascal artist with her. Why, it's a plot. I'll throw them in jail.

MALACHI. Mr. Vandergelder! They're old enough to come to New York. You can't throw people into jail for coming to New York.

VANDERGELDER. And there's Mrs. Levi! What's she doing with them? It's a plot. It's a conspiracy! What's she saying to the cabman? Go up and hear what she's saying.

MALACHI (*listening at entrance, right*). She's telling the cabman to wait, Mr. Vandergelder. She's telling the young people to come in and have a good dinner, Mr. Vandergelder.

VANDERGELDER. I'll put an end to this.

MALACHI. Now, Mr. Vandergelder, if you lose your temper, you'll make matters worse. Mr. Vandergelder, come here and take my advice.

VANDERGELDER. Stop pulling my coat. What's your advice?

MALACHI. Hide, Mr. Vandergelder. Hide behind this screen, and listen to what they're saying.

VANDERGELDER (*being pulled behind the screen*). Stop pulling at me.

(*They hide behind the screen as* MRS. LEVI, ERMENGARDE *and* AMBROSE *enter from the right.* AMBROSE *is carrying* ERMENGARDE'S *luggage.*)

ERMENGARDE. But I don't want to eat in a restaurant. It's not proper.
MRS. LEVI. Now, Ermengarde, dear, there's nothing wicked about eating in a restaurant. There's nothing wicked, even, about being in New York. Clergymen just make those things up to fill out their sermons.
ERMENGARDE. Oh, I wish I were in Yonkers, where *nothing* ever happens!
MRS. LEVI. Ermengarde, you're hungry. That's what's troubling you.
ERMENGARDE. Anyway, after dinner you must promise to take me to Aunt Flora's. She's been waiting for me all day and she must be half dead of fright.
MRS. LEVI. All right, but of course you know at Miss Van Huysen's you'll be back in your uncle's hands.
AMBROSE (*hands raised to heaven*). I can't stand it.
MRS. LEVI (*to* AMBROSE). Just keep telling yourself how pretty she is. Pretty girls have very little opportunity to improve their other advantages.
AMBROSE. Listen, Ermengarde! You don't want to go back to your uncle. Stop and think! That old man with one foot in the grave!
MRS. LEVI. And the other three in the cashbox.
AMBROSE. Smelling of oats —
MRS. LEVI. And axle grease.
MALACHI. That's not true. It's only partly true.
VANDERGELDER (*loudly*). Hold your tongue! I'm going to teach them a lesson.
MALACHI (*whisper*). Keep your temper, Mr. Vandergelder. Listen to what they say.
MRS. LEVI (*hears this; throws a quick glance toward the screen; her whole manner changes*). Oh dear, what was I saying? The Lord be praised, how glad I am that I found you two dreadful children just as you were about to break poor dear Mr. Vandergelder's heart.
AMBROSE. He's got no heart to break!
MRS. LEVI (*vainly signaling*). Mr. Vandergelder's a much kinder man than you think.
AMBROSE. Kinder? He's a wolf.

MRS. LEVI. Remember that he leads a very lonely life. Now you're going to have dinner upstairs. There are some private rooms up there,—just meant for shy timid girls like Ermengarde. Come with me. (*She pushes the young people out left,* AMBROSE *carrying the luggage.*)

VANDERGELDER (*coming forward*). I'll show them! (*He sits at table right.*)

MALACHI. Everybody should eavesdrop once in a while, I always say. There's nothing like eavesdropping to show you that the world outside your head is different from the world inside your head.

VANDERGELDER (*producing a pencil and paper*). I want to write a note. Go and call that cabman in here. I want to talk to him.

MALACHI. No one asks advice of a cabman, Mr. Vandergelder. They see so much of life that they have no ideas left.

VANDERGELDER. Do as I tell you.

MALACHI. Yes, sir. Advice of a cabman! (*Exit right.*)

(VANDERGELDER *writes his letter.*)

VANDERGELDER. "My dear Miss Van Huysen"—(*To audience:*) Everybody's dear in a letter. It's enough to make you give up writing 'em. "My dear Miss Van Huysen. This is Ermengarde and that rascal Ambrose Kemper. They are trying to run away. Keep them in your house until I come."

(MALACHI *returns with an enormous Cabman in a high hat and a long coat. He carries a whip.*)

CABMAN (*entering*). What's he want?

VANDERGELDER. I want to talk to you.

CABMAN. I'm engaged. I'm waiting for my parties.

VANDERGELDER (*folding letter and writing address*). I know you are. Do you want to earn five dollars?

CABMAN. Eh?

VANDERGELDER. I asked you, do you want to earn five dollars?
CABMAN. I don't know. I never tried.
VANDERGELDER. When those parties of yours come downstairs, I want you to drive them to this address. Never mind what they say, drive them to this address. Ring the bell: give this letter to the lady of the house: see that they get in the door and keep them there.
CABMAN. I can't make people go into a house if they don't want to.
VANDERGELDER (*producing purse*). Can you for ten dollars?
CABMAN. Even for ten dollars, I can't do it alone.
VANDERGELDER. This fellow here will help you.
MALACHI (*sitting at table left*). Now I'm pushing people into houses.
VANDERGELDER. There's the address: Miss Flora Van Huysen, 8 Jackson Street.
CABMAN. Even if I get them in the door I can't be sure they'll stay there.
VANDERGELDER. For fifteen dollars you can.
MALACHI. Murder begins at twenty-five.
VANDERGELDER. Hold your tongue! (*To* Cabman.) The lady of the house will help you. All you have to do is to sit in the front hall and see that the man doesn't run off with the girl. I'll be at Miss Van Huysen's in an hour or two and I'll pay you then.
CABMAN. If they call the police, I can't do anything.
VANDERGELDER. It's perfectly honest business. Perfectly honest.
MALACHI. Every man's the best judge of his own honesty.
VANDERGELDER. The young lady is my niece. (*The* Cabman *laughs, skeptically.*) The young lady is my niece!! (*The* Cabman *looks at* MALACHI *and shrugs.*) She's trying to run away with a good-for-nothing and we're preventing it.
CABMAN. Oh, I know them, sir. They'll win in the end. Rivers don't run uphill.
MALACHI. What did I tell you, Mr. Vandergelder? Advice of a cabman.

VANDERGELDER (*hits table with his stick*). Stack! I'll be back in half an hour. See that the table's set for three. See that nobody else eats here. Then go and join the cabman on the box.
MALACHI. Yes, sir.

(*Exit* VANDERGELDER *right*.)

CABMAN. Who's your friend?
MALACHI. Friend!! That's not a friend; that's an employer I'm trying out for a few days.
CABMAN. You won't like him.
MALACHI. I can see you're in business for yourself because you talk about liking employers. No one's ever liked an employer since business began.
CABMAN. AW—!
MALACHI. No sir. I suppose you think *your horse* likes you?
CABMAN. My old Clementine? She'd give her right feet for me.
MALACHI. That's what all employers think. You imagine it. The streets of New York are full of cab horses winking at one another. Let's go in the kitchen and get some whisky. I can't push people into houses when I'm sober. No, I've had about fifty employers in my life, but this is the most employer of them all. He talks to everybody as though he were paying them.
CABMAN. I had an employer once. He watched me from eight in the morning until six at night—just sat there and watched me. Oh, dear! Even my mother didn't think I was as interesting as that.

(Cabman *exits through service door*.)

MALACHI (*following him off*). Yes, being employed is like being loved: you know that somebody's thinking about you the whole time. (*Exits*.)

(*Enter right*, MRS. MOLLOY, MINNIE, BARNABY *and* CORNELIUS.)

MRS. MOLLOY.  See! Here's the place I meant! Isn't it fine? Minnie, take off your things; we'll be here for hours.
CORNELIUS (*stopping at door*).  Mrs. Molloy, are you sure you'll like it here? I think I feel a draught.
MRS. MOLLOY.  Indeed, I do like it. We're going to have a fine dinner right in this room; it's private, and it's elegant. Now we're all going to forget our troubles and call each other by our first names. Cornelius! Call the waiter.
CORNELIUS.  Wait—wait—I can't make a sound. I must have caught a cold on that ride. Wai—No! It won't come.
MRS. MOLLOY.  I don't believe you. Barnaby, you call him.
BARNABY (*boldly*).  Waiter! Waiter! (CORNELIUS *threatens him*. BARNABY *runs left*.)
MINNIE.  I never thought I'd be in such a place in my whole life. Mrs. Molloy, is this what they call a "café"?
MRS. MOLLOY (*sits at table left, facing audience*).  Yes, this is a café. Sit down, Minnie. Cornelius, Mrs. Levi gave us to understand that every waiter in New York knew you.
CORNELIUS.  They will.

(BARNABY *sits at chair left;* MINNIE *in chair back to audience. Enter* RUDOLPH *from service door*.)

RUDOLPH.  Good evening, ladies and gentlemen.
CORNELIUS (*shaking his hand*).  How are you, Fritz? How are you, my friend?
RUDOLPH.  I am Rudolph.
CORNELIUS.  Of course. Rudolph, of course. Well, Rudolph, these ladies want a little something to eat—you know what I mean? Just if you can find the time—we know how busy you are.
MRS. MOLLOY.  Cornelius, there's no need to be so familiar with the waiter. (*Takes menu from* RUDOLPH.)
CORNELIUS.  Oh, yes, there is.
MRS. MOLLOY (*passing menu across*).  Minnie, what do you want to eat?
MINNIE.  Just anything, Irene.
MRS. MOLLOY.  No, speak up, Minnie. What do you want?
MINNIE.  No, really, I have no appetite at all. (*Swings round in her chair and studies the menu, horrified at the prices.*)

Oh . . . Oh . . . I'd like some sardines on toast and a glass of milk.

CORNELIUS (*takes menu from her*). Great grindstones! What a sensible girl. Barnaby, shake Minnie's hand. She's the most sensible girl in the world. Rudolph, bring us gentlemen two glasses of beer, a loaf of bread and some cheese.

MRS. MOLLOY (*takes menu*). I never heard such nonsense. Cornelius, we've come here for a good dinner and a good time. Minnie, have you ever eaten pheasant?

MINNIE. Pheasant? No-o-o-o!

MRS. MOLLOY. Rudolph, have you any pheasant?

RUDOLPH. Yes, ma'am. Just in from New Jersey today.

MRS. MOLLOY. Even the pheasants are leaving New Jersey. (*She laughs loudly, pushing* CORNELIUS, *then* RUDOLPH; *not from menu.*) Now, Rudolph, write this down: mock turtle soup; pheasant; mashed chestnuts; green salad; and some nice red wine.

(RUDOLPH *repeats each item after her.*)

CORNELIUS (*losing all his fears, boldly*). All right, Barnaby, you watch me. (*He reads from the bill of fare.*) Rudolph, write this down: Neapolitan ice cream; hothouse peaches; champagne . . .

ALL. Champagne!

(BARNABY *spins round in his chair.*)

CORNELIUS (*holds up a finger*). . . . and a German band. Have you got a German band?

MRS. MOLLOY. No, Cornelius, I won't let you be extravagant. Champagne, but no band. Now, Rudolph, be quick about this. We're hungry. (*Exit* RUDOLPH *to kitchen.* MRS. MOLLOY *crosses to right.*) Minnie, come upstairs. I have an idea about your hair. I think it'd be nice in two wee horns —

MINNIE (*hurrying after her, turns and looks at the boys*). Oh! Horns!

(*They go out right. There is a long pause.* CORNELIUS *sits staring after them.*)

BARNABY. Cornelius, in the Army, you have to peel potatoes all the time.
CORNELIUS (*not turning*). Oh, that doesn't matter. By the time we get out of jail we can move right over to the Old Men's Home.

(*Another waiter,* AUGUST, *enters from service door bearing a bottle of champagne in cooler, and five glasses.* MRS. MOLLOY *re-enters right, followed by* MINNIE, *and stops* AUGUST.)

MRS. MOLLOY. Waiter! What's that? What's that you have?
AUGUST (*young waiter; baby face; is continually bursting into tears*). It's some champagne, ma'am.
MRS. MOLLOY. Cornelius; it's our champagne.

(ALL *gather round* AUGUST.)

AUGUST. No, no. It's for His Honor the Mayor of New York and he's very impatient.
MRS. MOLLOY. Shame on him! The Mayor of New York has more important things to be impatient about. Cornelius, open it.

(CORNELIUS *takes the bottle, opens it and fills the glasses.*)

AUGUST. Ma'am, he'll kill me.
MRS. MOLLOY. Well, have a glass first and die happy.
AUGUST (*sits at table right, weeping*). He'll kill me.

(RUDOLPH *lays the cloth on the table, left.*)

MRS. MOLLOY. I go to a public restaurant for the first time in ten years and all the waiters burst into tears. There, take that and stop crying, love. (*She takes a glass to* AUGUST *and pats his head, then comes back.*) Barnaby, make a toast!

BARNABY (*center of the group, with naive sincerity*). I? ... uh ... To all the ladies in the world ... may I get to know more of them ... and ... may I get to know them better.

(*There is a hushed pause.*)

CORNELIUS (*softly*). To the ladies!

MRS. MOLLOY. That's very sweet and very refined. Minnie, for that I'm going to give Barnaby a kiss.

MINNIE. Oh!

MRS. MOLLOY. Hold your tongue, Minnie. I'm old enough to be his mother, and—(*indicating a height three feet from the floor*) a dear wee mother I would have been too. Barnaby, this is for you from all the ladies in the world.

(*She kisses him.* BARNABY *is at first silent and dazed, then:*)

BARNABY. Now I can go back to Yonkers, Cornelius. Pudding. Pudding. Pudding! (*He spins round and falls on his knees.*)

MRS. MOLLOY. Look at Barnaby. He's not strong enough for a kiss. His head can't stand it. (*Exit* AUGUST, *right service door, with tray and cooler. The sound of "Les Patineurs" waltz comes from off left.* CORNELIUS *sits in chair facing audience, top of table.* MINNIE *at left.* BARNABY *at right and* MRS. MOLLOY *back to audience.*) Minnie, I'm enjoying myself. To think that this goes on in hundreds of places every night, while I sit at home darning my stockings. (MRS. MOLLOY *rises and dances, alone, slowly about the stage.*) Cornelius, dance with me.

CORNELIUS (*rises*). Irene, the Hackls don't dance. We're Presbyterian.

MRS. MOLLOY. Minnie, you dance with me.

(MINNIE *joins her.* CORNELIUS *sits again.*)

MINNIE. Lovely music.

MRS. MOLLOY.  Why, Minnie, you dance beautifully.

MINNIE.  We girls dance in the workroom when you're not looking, Irene.

MRS. MOLLOY.  You thought I'd be angry! Oh dear, no one in the world understands anyone else in the world. (*The girls separate.* MINNIE *dances off to her place at the table.* MRS. MOLLOY *sits thoughtfully at table right. The music fades away.*) Cornelius! Jenny Lind and all those other ladies — do you see them all the time?

CORNELIUS (*rises and joins her at table right*).  Irene, I've put them right out of my head. I'm interested in . . .

(RUDOLPH *has entered by the service door. He now flings a tablecloth between them on table.*)

MRS. MOLLOY.  Rudolph, what are you doing?

RUDOLPH.  A table's been reserved here. Special orders.

MRS. MOLLOY.  Stop right where you are. That party can eat inside. This veranda's ours.

RUDOLPH.  I'm very sorry. This veranda is open to anybody who wants it. Ah, there comes the man who brought the order.

(*Enter* MALACHI *from the kitchen, drunk.*)

MRS. MOLLOY (*to* MALACHI).  Take your table away from here. We got here first. Cornelius, throw him out.

MALACHI.  Ma'am, my employer reserved this room at four o'clock this afternoon. You can go and eat in the restaurant. My employer said it was very important that he have a table alone.

MRS. MOLLOY.  No, sir. We got here first and we're going to stay here — alone, too.

(MINNIE *and* BARNABY *come forward.*)

RUDOLPH.  Ladies and gentlemen!

MRS. MOLLOY.  Shut up, you! (*To* MALACHI.) You're an impertinent, idiotic kill-joy.

MALACHI (*very pleased*). That's an insult!
MRS. MOLLOY. All the facts about you are insults. (*To* CORNELIUS.) Cornelius, do something. Knock it over! The table.
CORNELIUS. Knock it over.

(*After a shocked struggle with himself* CORNELIUS *calmly overturns the table.* AUGUST *rights the table and picks up cutlery, weeping copiously.*)

RUDOLPH (*in cold fury*). I'm sorry, but this room can't be reserved for anyone. If you want to eat alone, you must go upstairs. I'm sorry, but that's the rule.
MRS. MOLLOY. We're having a nice dinner alone and we're going to stay here. Cornelius, knock it over.

(CORNELIUS *overturns the table again. The girls squeal with pleasure. The waiter* AUGUST *again scrambles for the silver.*)

MALACHI. Wait till you see my employer!
RUDOLPH (*bringing screen down*). Ladies and gentlemen! I tell you what we'll do. There's a big screen here. We'll put the screen up between the tables. August, come and help me.
MRS. MOLLOY. I won't eat behind a screen. I won't. Minnie, make a noise. We're not animals in a menagerie. Cornelius, no screen. Minnie, there's a fight. I feel ten years younger. No screen! No screen!

(*During the struggle with the screen all talk at once.*)

MALACHI (*loud and clear and pointing to entrance right*). Now you'll learn something. There comes my employer now, getting out of that cab.
CORNELIUS (*coming to him, taking off his coat*). Where? I'll knock him down too.

(BARNABY *has gone up to right entrance. He turns and shouts clearly:*)

BARNABY. Cornelius, it's Wolf-trap. Yes, it is!
CORNELIUS. Wolf-trap! Listen, everybody. I think the screen's a good idea. Have you got any more screens, Rudolph? We could use three or four. (*He pulls the screen forward again.*)
MRS. MOLLOY. Quiet down, Cornelius, and stop changing your mind. Hurry up, Rudolph, we're ready for the soup.

(*During the following scene* RUDOLPH *serves the meal at the table left, as unobtrusively as possible. The stage is now divided in half. The quartet's table is at the left. Enter* VANDERGELDER *from the right. Now wears overcoat and carries the box of chocolates.*)

VANDERGELDER. Stack! What's the meaning of this? I told you I wanted a table alone. What's that?

(VANDERGELDER *hits the screen twice with his stick.* MRS. MOLLOY *hits back twice with a spoon. The four young people sit:* BARNABY *facing audience;* MRS. MOLLOY *right,* MINNIE *left, and* CORNELIUS *back to audience.*)

MALACHI. Mr. Vandergelder, I did what I could. Mr. Vandergelder, you wouldn't believe what wild savages the people of New York are. There's a woman over there, Mr. Vandergelder—civilization hasn't touched her.
VANDERGELDER. Everything's wrong. You can't even manage a thing like that. Help me off with my coat. Don't kill me. Don't kill me.

(*During the struggle with the overcoat* MR. VANDERGELDER's *purse flies out of his pocket and falls by the screen.* VANDERGELDER *goes to the coat tree and hangs his coat up.*)

MRS. MOLLOY. Speak up! I can't hear you.
CORNELIUS. My voice again. Barnaby, how's your throat? Can you speak?
BARNABY. Can't make a sound.

MRS. MOLLOY. Oh, all right. Bring your heads together, and we'll whisper.

VANDERGELDER. Who are those people over there?

MALACHI. Some city sparks and their girls, Mr. Vandergelder. What goes on in big cities, Mr. Vandergelder — best not think of it.

VANDERGELDER. Has that couple come down from upstairs yet? I hope they haven't gone off without your seeing them.

MALACHI. No, sir. Myself and the cabman have kept our eyes on everything.

VANDERGELDER (*sits at right of table right, profile to the audience*). I'll sit here and wait for my guests. You go out to the cab.

MALACHI. Yes, sir. (VANDERGELDER *unfurls newspaper and starts to read.* MALACHI *sees purse on the floor and picks it up.*) Eh? What's that? A purse. Did you drop something, Mr. Vandergelder?

VANDERGELDER. No. Don't bother me any more. Do as I tell you.

MALACHI (*stooping over. Coming center*). A purse. That fellow over there must have let it fall during the misunderstanding about the screen. No, I won't look inside. Twenty-dollar bills, dozens of them. I'll go over and give it to him. (*Starts towards* CORNELIUS, *then turns and says to audience:*) You're surprised? You're surprised to see me getting rid of this money so quickly, eh? I'll explain it to you. There was a time in my life when my chief interest was picking up money that didn't belong to me. The law is there to protect property, but — sure, the law doesn't care whether a property owner deserves his property or not, and the law has to be corrected. There are several thousands of people in this country engaged in correcting the law. For a while, I too was engaged in the redistribution of superfluities. A man works all his life and leaves a million to his widow. She sits in hotels and eats great meals and plays cards all afternoon and evening, with ten diamonds on her fingers. Call in the robbers! Call in the robbers! Or a man leaves it to his son who stands leaning against bars all night boring a bartender. Call in the robbers! Stealing's a weakness. There are some people who say you shouldn't have any weaknesses at all—no vices. But if a man has no vices, he's in great danger of making vices out of his virtues, and there's a spectacle. We've all seen them: men who were monsters of philanthropy and women who were dragons of purity. We've seen people who told the truth, though the Heavens fall,—and the Heavens fell. No, no—nurse one vice in your bosom. Give it the attention it deserves and let your virtues spring up modestly around it. Then you'll have the miser who's no liar; and the drunkard who's the benefactor of a whole city. Well, after I'd had that weakness of stealing for a while, I found another: I took to whisky— whisky took to me. And then I discovered an important rule that I'm going to pass on to you: Never support two weaknesses at the same time. It's your combination sinners—your lecherous liars and your miserly drunkards— who dishonor the vices and bring them into bad repute. So now you see why I want to get rid of this money: I want to keep my mind free to do the credit to whisky that it deserves. And my last word to you, ladies and gentlemen, is this: one vice at a time. (*Goes over to* CORNELIUS.) Can I speak to you for a minute?

CORNELIUS (*rises*). You certainly can. We all want to apologize to you about that screen—that little misunderstanding. (*They all rise, with exclamations of apology.*) What's your name, sir?

MALACHI. Stack, sir. Malachi Stack. If the ladies will excuse you, I'd like to speak to you for a minute. (*Draws* CORNELIUS *down to front of stage.*) Listen, boy, have you lost . . . ? Come here . . . (*Leads him further down, out of* VANDERGELDER's *hearing.*) Have you lost something?

CORNELIUS. Mr. Stack, in this one day I've lost everything I own.

MALACHI. There it is. (*Gives him purse.*) Don't mention it.

CORNELIUS. Why, Mr. Stack . . . you know what it is? It's a miracle. (*Looks toward the ceiling.*)

MALACHI. Don't mention it.

CORNELIUS. Barnaby, come here a minute. I want you to shake hands with Mr. Stack. (BARNABY, *napkin tucked into his collar, joins them.*) Mr. Stack's just found the purse I lost, Barnaby. You know—the purse full of money.

BARNABY (*shaking his hand vigorously*). You're a wonderful man, Mr. Stack.

MALACHI. Oh, it's nothing—nothing.

CORNELIUS. I'm certainly glad I went to church all these years. You're a good person to know, Mr. Stack. In a way. Mr. Stack, where do you work?

MALACHI. Well, I've just begun. I work for a Mr. Vandergelder in Yonkers.

(CORNELIUS *is thunderstruck. He glances at* BARNABY *and turns to* MALACHI *with awe. All three are swaying slightly, back and forth.*)

CORNELIUS. You do? It's a miracle. (*He points to the ceiling.*) Mr. Stack, I know you don't need it—but can I give you something for . . . for the good work?

MALACHI (*putting out his hand*). Don't mention it. It's nothing. (*Starts to go left.*)

CORNELIUS. Take that. (*Hands him a note.*)

MALACHI (*taking note*). Don't mention it.

CORNELIUS. And that. (*Another note.*)

MALACHI (*takes it and moves away*). I'd better be going.

CORNELIUS. Oh, here. And that.

MALACHI (*hands third note back*). No . . . I might get to like them. (*Exit left.*)

(CORNELIUS *bounds exultantly back to table.*)

CORNELIUS. Irene, I feel a lot better about everything. Irene, I feel so well that I'm going to tell the truth.

MRS. MOLLOY. I'd forgotten that, Minnie. Men get drunk so differently from women. All right, what is the truth?

CORNELIUS. If I tell the truth, will you let me . . . will you let me put my arm around your waist?

(MINNIE *screams and flings her napkin over her face.*)

MRS. MOLLOY. Hold your tongue, Minnie. All right, you put your arm around my waist just to show it can be done in a gentlemanly way; but I might as well warn you: a corset is a corset.
CORNELIUS (*his arm around her; softly*). You're a wonderful person, Mrs. Molloy.
MRS. MOLLOY. Thank you. (*She removes his hand from around her waist.*) All right, now that's enough. What is the truth?
CORNELIUS. Irene, I'm not as rich as Mrs. Levi said I was.
MRS. MOLLOY. Not rich!
CORNELIUS. I almost never came to New York. And I'm not like she said I was, — bad. And I think you ought to know that at this very minute Mr. Vandergelder's sitting on the other side of that screen.
MRS. MOLLOY. What!! Well, he's not going to spoil any party of mine. So *that's* why we've been whispering? Let's forget all about Mr. Vandergelder and have some more wine.

(*They start to sing softly: "The Sidewalks of New York." Enter* MRS. LEVI, *from the street, in an elaborate dress.* VANDERGELDER *rises.*)

MRS. LEVI. Good evening, Mr. Vandergelder.
VANDERGELDER. Where's — where's Miss Simple?
MRS. LEVI. Mr. Vandergelder, I'll never trust a woman again as long as I live.
VANDERGELDER. Well? What is it?
MRS. LEVI. She ran away this afternoon and got married!
VANDERGELDER. She did?
MRS. LEVI. Married, Mr. Vandergelder, to a young boy of fifty.
VANDERGELDER. She did?
MRS. LEVI. Oh, I'm as disappointed as you are. I-can't-eat-a-thing-what-have-you-ordered?
VANDERGELDER. I ordered what you told me to, a chicken.

(*Enter* AUGUST. *He goes to* VANDERGELDER'S *table.*)

MRS. LEVI.  I don't think I could face a chicken. Oh, waiter. How do you do? What's your name?
AUGUST.  August, ma'am.
MRS. LEVI.  August, this is Mr. Vandergelder of Yonkers — Yonkers' most influential citizen, in fact. I want you to see that he's served with the best you have and served promptly. And there'll only be the two of us. (MRS. LEVI *gives one set of cutlery to* AUGUST. VANDERGELDER *puts chocolate box under table.*) Mr. Vandergelder's been through some trying experiences today — what with men hidden all over Mrs. Molloy's store — like Indians in ambush.
VANDERGELDER (*between his teeth*).  Mrs. Levi, you don't have to tell him everything about me.

(*The quartet commences singing again very softly.*)

MRS. LEVI.  Mr. Vandergelder, if you're thinking about getting married, you might as well learn right now you have to let women be women. Now, August, we want excellent service.
AUGUST.  Yes, ma'am. (*Exits to kitchen.*)
VANDERGELDER.  You've managed things very badly. When I plan a thing it takes place. (MRS. LEVI *rises.*) Where are you going?
MRS. LEVI.  Oh, I'd just like to see who's on the other side of that screen.

(MRS. LEVI *crosses to the other side of the stage and sees the quartet. They are frightened and fall silent.*)

CORNELIUS (*rising*).  Good evening, Mrs. Levi.

(MRS. LEVI *takes no notice, but, taking up the refrain where they left off, returns to her place at the table right.*)

VANDERGELDER.  Well, who was it?
MRS. LEVI.  Oh, just some city sparks entertaining their girls, I guess.

VANDERGELDER. Always wanting to know everything; always curious about everything; always putting your nose into other people's affairs. Anybody who lived with you would get as nervous as a cat.

MRS. LEVI. What? What's that you're saying?

VANDERGELDER. I said anybody who lived with you would—

MRS. LEVI. Horace Vandergelder, get that idea right out of your head this minute. I'm surprised that you even mentioned such a thing. Understand once and for all that I have no intention of marrying you.

VANDERGELDER. I didn't mean that.

MRS. LEVI. You've been hinting around at such a thing for some time, but from now on put such ideas right out of your head.

VANDERGELDER. Stop talking that way. That's not what I meant at all.

MRS. LEVI. I hope not. I should hope not. Horace Vandergelder, you go your way (*Points a finger.*) and I'll go mine. (*Points again in same direction.*) I'm not some Irene Molloy, whose head can be turned by a pot of geraniums. Why, the idea of your even suggesting such a thing.

VANDERGELDER. Mrs. Levi, you misunderstood me.

MRS. LEVI. I certainly hope I did. If I had any intention of marrying again it would be to a far more pleasure-loving man than you. Why I'd marry Cornelius Hackl before I'd marry you. (CORNELIUS *raises his head in alarm. The others stop eating and listen.*) However, we won't discuss it any more. (*Enter* AUGUST *with a tray.*) Here's August with our food. I'll serve it, August.

AUGUST. Yes, ma'am. (*Exit* AUGUST.)

MRS. LEVI. Here's some white meat for you, and some giblets, very tender and very good for you. No, as I said before, you go your way and I'll go mine.—Start right in on the wine. I think you'll feel better at once. However, since you brought the matter up, there's one more thing I think I ought to say.

VANDERGELDER (*rising in rage*). I didn't bring the matter up at all.

MRS. LEVI. We'll have forgotten all about it in a moment, but

—sit down, sit down, we'll close the matter forever in just a moment, but there's one more thing I ought to say: (VANDERGELDER *sits down.*) It's true, I'm a woman who likes to know everything that's going on; who likes to manage things, you're perfectly right about that. But I wouldn't like to manage anything as disorderly as your household, as out of control, as untidy. You'll have to do that yourself, God helping you.

VANDERGELDER. It's not out of control.

MRS. LEVI. Very well, let's not say another word about it. Take some more of that squash, it's good. No, Horace, a complaining, quarrelsome, friendless soul like you is no sort of companion for me. You go your way (*Peppers her own plate.*) and I'll go mine. (*Peppers his plate.*)

VANDERGELDER. Stop saying that.

MRS. LEVI. I won't say another word.

VANDERGELDER. Besides . . . I'm not those things you said I am.

MRS. LEVI. What?—Well, I guess you're friendless, aren't you? Ermengarde told me this morning you'd even quarreled with your barber—a man who's held a razor to your throat for twenty years! Seems to me that that's sinking pretty low.

VANDERGELDER. Well, . . . but . . . my clerks, they . . .

MRS. LEVI. They like you? Cornelius Hackl and that Barnaby? Behind your back they call you Wolf-trap.

(*Quietly the quartet at the other table have moved up to the screen—bringing chairs for* MRS. MOLLOY *and* MINNIE. *Wine glasses in hand, they overhear this conversation.*)

VANDERGELDER (*blanching*). They don't.

MRS. LEVI. No, Horace. It looks to me as though I were the last person in the world that liked you, and even I'm just so-so. No, for the rest of my life I intend to have a good time. You'll be able to find some housekeeper who can prepare you three meals for a dollar a day—it can be done, you know, if you like cold baked beans. You'll spend your last days listening at keyholes, for fear someone's cheating you. Take some more of that.

VANDERGELDER. Dolly, you're a damned exasperating woman.
MRS. LEVI. There! You see? That's the difference between us. I'd be nagging you all day to get some spirit into you. You could be a perfectly charming, witty, amiable man, if you wanted to.
VANDERGELDER (*rising, bellowing*). I don't want to be charming.
MRS. LEVI. But you are. Look at you now. You can't hide it.
VANDERGELDER (*sits*). Listening at keyholes! Dolly, you have no right to say such things to me.
MRS. LEVI. At your age you ought to enjoy hearing the honest truth.
VANDERGELDER. My age! My age! You're always talking about my age.
MRS. LEVI. I don't know what your age is, but I do know that up at Yonkers with bad food and bad temper you'll double it in six months. Let's talk of something else; but before we leave the subject there's one more thing I *am* going to say.
VANDERGELDER. Don't!
MRS. LEVI. Sometimes, just sometimes, I think I'd be tempted to marry you out of sheer pity; and if the confusion in your house gets any worse I may *have* to.
VANDERGELDER. I haven't asked you to marry me.
MRS. LEVI. Well, *please don't*.
VANDERGELDER. And my house is not in confusion.
MRS. LEVI. What? With your niece upstairs in the restaurant right now?
VANDERGELDER. I've fixed that better than you know.
MRS. LEVI. And your clerks skipping around New York behind your back?
VANDERGELDER. They're in Yonkers where they always are.
MRS. LEVI. Nonsense!
VANDERGELDER. What do you mean, nonsense?
MRS. LEVI. Cornelius Hackl's the other side of that screen this very minute.
VANDERGELDER. It ain't the same man!
MRS. LEVI. All right. Go on. Push it, knock it down. Go and see.

VANDERGELDER (*goes to screen, pauses in doubt, then returns to his chair again*). I don't believe it.
MRS. LEVI. All right. All right. Eat your chicken. Of course, Horace, if your affairs went from bad to worse and you became actually miserable, I might feel that it was my duty to come up to Yonkers and be of some assistance to you. After all, I was your wife's oldest friend.
VANDERGELDER. I don't know how you ever got any such notion. Now understand, once and for all, I have *no intention of marrying anybody*. Now, I'm tired and I don't want to talk.

(CORNELIUS *crosses to extreme left*, MRS. MOLLOY *following him.*)

MRS. LEVI. I won't say another word, either.
CORNELIUS. Irene, I think we'd better go. You take this money and pay the bill. Oh, don't worry, it's not mine.
MRS. MOLLOY. No, no, I'll tell you what we'll do. You boys put on our coats and veils, and if he comes stamping over here, he'll think you're girls.
CORNELIUS. What! Those things!
MRS. MOLLOY. Yes. Come on. (*She and* MINNIE *take the clothes from the stand.*)
VANDERGELDER (*rises*). I've got a headache. I've had a bad day. I'm going to Flora Van Huysen's, and then I'm going back to my hotel. (*Reaches for his purse.*) So, here's the money to pay for the dinner. (*Searching another pocket.*) Here's the money to pay for the . . . (*Going through all his pockets.*) Here's the money . . . I've lost my purse!!
MRS. LEVI. Impossible! I can't imagine you without your purse.
VANDERGELDER. It's been stolen. (*Searching overcoat.*) Or I left it in the cab. What am I going to do? I'm new at the hotel; they don't know me. I've never been here before. . . . Stop eating the chicken, I can't pay for it!
MRS. LEVI (*laughing gaily*). Horace, I'll be able to find some money. Sit down and calm yourself.
VANDERGELDER. Dolly Gallagher, I gave you twenty-five dollars this morning.

MRS. LEVI.  I haven't a cent. I gave it to my lawyer. We can borrow it from Ambrose Kemper, upstairs.
VANDERGELDER.  I wouldn't take it.
MRS. LEVI.  Cornelius Hackl will lend it to us.
VANDERGELDER.  He's in Yonkers.—Waiter!

(CORNELIUS *comes forward dressed in* MRS. MOLLOY'S *coat, thrown over his shoulder like a cape.* MRS. LEVI *is enjoying herself immensely.* VANDERGELDER *again goes to back wall to examine the pockets of his overcoat.*)

MRS. MOLLOY.  Cornelius, is that Mr. Vandergelder's purse?
CORNELIUS.  I didn't know it myself. I thought it was money just wandering around loose that didn't belong to anybody.
MRS. MOLLOY.  Goodness! That's what politicians think!
VANDERGELDER.  Waiter!

(*A band off left starts playing a polka.* BARNABY *comes forward dressed in* MINNIE'S *hat, coat and veil.*)

MINNIE.  Irene, doesn't Barnaby make a lovely girl? He just ought to stay that way.

(MRS. LEVI *and* VANDERGELDER *move their table upstage while searching for the purse.*)

MRS. MOLLOY.  Why should we have our evening spoiled? Cornelius, I can teach you to dance in a few minutes. Oh, he won't recognize you.
MINNIE.  Barnaby, it's the easiest thing in the world.

(*They move their table up against the back wall.*)

MRS. LEVI.  Horace, you danced with me at your wedding and you danced with me at mine. Do you remember?
VANDERGELDER.  No. Yes.
MRS. LEVI.  Horace, you were a good dancer then. Don't confess to me that you're too old to dance.
VANDERGELDER.  I'm not too old. I just don't want to dance.

MRS. LEVI. Listen to that music. Horace, do you remember the dances in the firehouse at Yonkers on Saturday nights? You gave me a fan. Come, come on!

(VANDERGELDER *and* MRS. LEVI *start to dance.* CORNELIUS, *dancing with* MRS. MOLLOY, *bumps into* VANDERGELDER, *back to back.* VANDERGELDER, *turning, fails at first to recognize him, then does and roars:*)

VANDERGELDER. You're discharged! Not a word! You're fired! Where's that idiot, Barnaby Tucker? He's fired, too. (*The four young people, laughing, start rushing out the door to the street.* VANDERGELDER, *pointing at* MRS. MOLLOY, *shouts:*) You're discharged!
MRS. MOLLOY (*pointing at him*). You're discharged! (*Exit.*)
VANDERGELDER. You're discharged! (*Enter from left,* AMBROSE *and* ERMENGARDE. *To* ERMENGARDE.) I'll lock you up for the rest of your life, young lady.
ERMENGARDE. Uncle! (*She faints in* AMBROSE'S *arms.*)
VANDERGELDER (*to* AMBROSE). I'll have you arrested. Get out of my sight. I never want to see you again.
AMBROSE (*carrying* ERMENGARDE *across to exit right*). You can't do anything to me, Mr. Vandergelder.

(*Exit* AMBROSE *and* ERMENGARDE.)

MRS. LEVI (*who has been laughing heartily, follows the distraught* VANDERGELDER *about the stage as he continues to hunt for his purse*). Well, there's your life, Mr. Vandergelder! Without niece—without clerks—without bride—and without your purse. *Will you marry me now?*
VANDERGELDER. No!

(*To get away from her, he dashes into the kitchen.* MRS. LEVI, *still laughing, exclaims to the audience:*)

MRS. LEVI. Damn!! (*And rushes off right.*)

*The Curtain Falls*

## Act IV

MISS FLORA VAN HUYSEN'S *house.*
*This is a prosperous spinster's living room and is filled with knick-knacks, all in bright colors, and hung with family portraits, bird cages, shawls, etc.*
*There is only one entrance—a large double door in the center of the back wall. Beyond it one sees the hall which leads left to the street door and right to the kitchen and the rest of the house. On the left are big windows hung with lace curtains on heavy draperies. Front left is* MISS VAN HUYSEN'S *sofa, covered with bright-colored cushions, and behind it a table. On the right is another smaller sofa.* MISS VAN HUYSEN *is lying on the sofa. The* Cook *is at the window, left.* MISS VAN HUYSEN, *fifty, florid, stout and sentimental, is sniffing at smelling salts.* Cook (*enormous*) *holds a china mixing bowl.*

COOK. No, ma'am. I could swear I heard a cab drawing up to the door.
MISS VAN HUYSEN. You imagined it. Imagination. Everything in life . . . like that . . . disappointment . . . illusion. Our plans . . . our hopes . . . what becomes of them? Nothing. The story of my life. (*She sings for a moment.*)
COOK. Pray God nothing's happened to the dear girl. Is it a long journey from Yonkers?
MISS VAN HUYSEN. No; but long enough for a thousand things to happen.
COOK. Well, we've been waiting all day. Don't you think we ought to call the police about it?
MISS VAN HUYSEN. The police! If it's God's will, the police can't prevent it. Oh, in three days, in a week, in a year, we'll know what's happened. . . . And if anything *has* happened to Ermengarde, it'll be a lesson to *him*—that's what it'll be.
COOK. To who?
MISS VAN HUYSEN. To that cruel uncle of hers, of course,— to Horace Vandergelder, and to everyone else who tries

to separate young lovers. Young lovers have enough to contend with as it is. Who should know that better than I? No one. The story of my life. (*Sings for a moment, then:*) There! Now I hear a cab. Quick!

COOK.  No. No, ma'am. I don't see anything.

MISS VAN HUYSEN.  There! What did I tell you? Everything's imagination—illusion.

COOK.  But surely, if they'd changed their plans Mr. Vandergelder would have sent you a message.

MISS VAN HUYSEN.  Oh, I know what's the matter. That poor child probably thought she was coming to another prison—to another tyrant. If she'd known that I was her friend, and a friend of all young lovers, she'd be here by now. Oh, yes, she would. Her life shall not be crossed with obstacles and disappointments as . . . Cook, a minute ago my smelling salts were on this table. Now they've completely disappeared.

COOK.  Why, there they are, ma'am, right there in your hand.

MISS VAN HUYSEN.  Goodness! How did they get there? I won't inquire. Stranger things have happened!

COOK.  I suppose Mr. Vandergelder was sending her down with someone?

MISS VAN HUYSEN.  Two can go astray as easily as . . . (*She sneezes.*)

COOK.  God bless you! (*Runs to window.*) Now, here's a carriage stopping.

(*The doorbell rings.*)

MISS VAN HUYSEN.  Well, open the door, Cook. (*Cook exits.*) It's probably some mistake . . . (*sneezes again*). God bless you! (*Sounds of altercation off in hall.*) It almost sounds as though I heard voices.

CORNELIUS (*off*).  I don't want to come in. This is a free country, I tell you.

CABMAN (*off*).  Forward march!

MALACHI (*off*).  In you go. We have orders.

CORNELIUS (*off*).  You can't make a person go where he doesn't want to go.

(*Enter* MALACHI, *followed by* COOK. *The* CABMAN *bundles* BARNABY *and* CORNELIUS *into the room, but they fight their way back into the hall.* CORNELIUS *has lost* MRS. MOLLOY'S *coat, but* BARNABY *is wearing* MINNIE'S *clothes.*)

MALACHI. Begging your pardon, ma'am, are you Miss Van Huysen?

MISS VAN HUYSEN. Yes, I am, unfortunately. What's all this noise about?

MALACHI. There are two people here that Mr. Vandergelder said must be brought to this house and kept here until he comes. And here's his letter to you.

MISS VAN HUYSEN. No one has any right to tell me whom I'm to keep in my house if they don't want to stay.

MALACHI. You're right, ma'am. Everybody's always talking about people breaking into houses, ma'am; but there are more people in the world who want to break out of houses, that's what I always say. — Bring them in, Joe.

(*Enter* CORNELIUS *and* BARNABY *being pushed by the* Cabman.)

CORNELIUS. This young lady and I have no business here. We jumped into a cab and asked to be driven to the station and these men brought us to the house and forced us to come inside. There's been a mistake.

CABMAN. Is your name Miss Van Huysen?

MISS VAN HUYSEN. Everybody's asking me if my name's Miss Van Huysen. I think that's a matter I can decide for myself. Now will you all be quiet while I read this letter? . . . "This is Ermengarde and that rascal Ambrose Kemper . . ." Now I know who you two are, anyway. "They are trying to run away . . ." Story of my life. "Keep them in your house until I come." Mr. Kemper, you have nothing to fear. (*To* Cabman.) Who are you?

CABMAN. I'm Joe. I stay here until the old man comes. He owes me fifteen dollars.

MALACHI. That's right, Miss Van Huysen, we must stay here to see they don't escape.

MISS VAN HUYSEN (*to* BARNABY). My dear child, take off your things. We'll all have some coffee. (*To* MALACHI *and* Cabman.) You two go out and wait in the hall. I'll send coffee out to you. Cook, take them.

(Cook *pushes* MALACHI *and* Cabman *into the hall*.)

CORNELIUS. Ma'am, we're not the people you're expecting, and there's no reason . . .
MISS VAN HUYSEN. Mr. Kemper, I'm not the tyrant you think I am. . . . You don't have to be afraid of me. . . . I know you're trying to run away with this innocent girl. . . . All my life I have suffered from the interference of others. You shall not suffer as I did. So put yourself entirely in my hands. (*She lifts* BARNABY'*s veil*.) Ermengarde! (*Kisses him on both cheeks*.) Where's your luggage?
BARNABY. It's—uh—uh—it's . . .
CORNELIUS. Oh, I'll find it in the morning. It's been mislaid.
MISS VAN HUYSEN. Mislaid! How like life! Well, Ermengarde; you shall put on some of my clothes.
BARNABY. Oh, I know I wouldn't be happy, really.
MISS VAN HUYSEN. She's a shy little thing, isn't she? Timid little darling! . . . Cook! Put some gingerbread in the oven and get the coffee ready . . .
COOK. Yes, ma'am. (*Exits to kitchen*.)
MISS VAN HUYSEN. . . . while I go and draw a good hot bath for Ermengarde.
CORNELIUS. Oh, no—Miss Van Huysen . . .
MISS VAN HUYSEN. Believe me, Ermengarde, your troubles are at an end. You two will be married tomorrow. (*To* BARNABY.) My dear, you look just like I did at your age, and your sufferings have been as mine. While you're bathing, I'll come and tell you the story of my life.
BARNABY. Oh, I don't want to take a bath. I always catch cold.
MISS VAN HUYSEN. No, dear, you won't catch cold. I'll slap you all over. I'll be back in a minute. (*Exit*.)
CORNELIUS (*looking out of window*). Barnaby, do you think we could jump down from this window?
BARNABY. Yes—we'd kill ourselves.

CORNELIUS. We'll just have to stay here and watch for something to happen. Barnaby, the situation's desperate.
BARNABY. It began getting desperate about half-past four and it's been getting worse ever since. Now I have to take a bath and get slapped all over.

(*Enter* MISS VAN HUYSEN *from kitchen.*)

MISS VAN HUYSEN. Ermengarde, you've still got those wet things on. Your bath's nearly ready. Mr. Kemper, you come into the kitchen and put your feet in the oven. (*The doorbell rings. Enter* Cook.) What's that? It's the doorbell. I expect it's your uncle.
COOK. There's the doorbell. (*At window.*) It's *another* man and a girl in a cab!
MISS VAN HUYSEN. Well, go and let them in, Cook. Now, come with me, you two. Come, Ermengarde.

(*Exit* Cook. MISS VAN HUYSEN *drags* CORNELIUS *and the protesting* BARNABY *off into the kitchen.*)

COOK (*off*). No, that's impossible. Come in, anyway. (*Enter* ERMENGARDE, *followed by* AMBROSE, *carrying the two pieces of luggage.*) There's some mistake. I'll tell Miss Van Huysen, but there's some mistake.
ERMENGARDE. But, I tell you, I *am* Mr. Vandergelder's niece; I'm Ermengarde.
COOK. Beg your pardon, Miss, but you *can't* be *Miss Ermengarde.*
ERMENGARDE. But—but—here I *am*. And that's my baggage.
COOK. Well, I'll tell Miss Van Huysen who you *think* you are, but she won't like it. (*Exits.*)
AMBROSE. You'll be all right now, Ermengarde. I'd better go before she sees me.
ERMENGARDE. Oh, no. You must stay. I feel so strange here.
AMBROSE. I know, but Mr. Vandergelder will be here in a minute. . . .
ERMENGARDE. Ambrose, you can't go. You can't leave me in this crazy house with those drunken men in the hall. Ambrose . . . Ambrose, let's say you're someone else that

my uncle sent down to take care of me. Let's say you're —
you're Cornelius Hackl!

AMBROSE.   Who's Cornelius Hackl?

ERMENGARDE.   You know. He's chief clerk in Uncle's store.

AMBROSE.   I don't want to be Cornelius Hackl. No, no, Ermengarde, come away with me now. I'll take you to my friend's house. Or I'll take you to Mrs. Levi's house.

ERMENGARDE.   Why it was Mrs. Levi who threw us right at Uncle Horace's face. Oh, I wish I were back in Yonkers where nothing ever happens.

(*Enter* MISS VAN HUYSEN.)

MISS VAN HUYSEN.   What's all this I hear? Who do you say you are?

ERMENGARDE.   Aunt Flora . . . don't you remember me? I'm Ermengarde.

MISS VAN HUYSEN.   And you're Mr. Vandergelder's niece?

ERMENGARDE.   Yes, I am.

MISS VAN HUYSEN.   Well, that's very strange indeed, because he has just sent me another niece named Ermengarde. She came with a letter from him, explaining everything. Have you got a letter from him?

ERMENGARDE.   No . . .

MISS VAN HUYSEN.   Really! — And who is this?

ERMENGARDE.   This is Cornelius Hackl, Aunt Flora.

MISS VAN HUYSEN.   Never heard of him.

ERMENGARDE.   He's chief clerk in Uncle's store.

MISS VAN HUYSEN.   Never heard of him. The other Ermengarde came with the man she's in love with, and that *proves* it. She came with Mr. Ambrose Kemper.

AMBROSE (*shouts*).   Ambrose Kemper!

MISS VAN HUYSEN.   Yes, Mr. Hackl, and Mr. Ambrose Kemper is in the kitchen there now *with his feet in the oven.* (ERMENGARDE *starts to cry.* MISS VAN HUYSEN *takes her to the sofa. They both sit.*) Dear child, what is your trouble?

ERMENGARDE.   Oh, dear. I don't know what to do.

MISS VAN HUYSEN (*in a low voice*). Are you in love with this man?

ERMENGARDE. Yes, I am.

MISS VAN HUYSEN. I could see it—and are people trying to separate you?

ERMENGARDE. Yes, they are.

MISS VAN HUYSEN. I could see it—who? Horace Vandergelder?

ERMENGARDE. Yes.

MISS VAN HUYSEN. That's enough for me. I'll put a stop to Horace Vandergelder's goings on. (MISS VAN HUYSEN *draws* AMBROSE *down to sit on her other side*.) Mr. Hackl, think of me as your friend. Come in the kitchen and get warm. . . . (*She rises and starts to go out*.) We can decide later who everybody is. My dear, would you like a good hot bath?

ERMENGARDE. Yes, I would.

MISS VAN HUYSEN. Well, when Ermengarde comes out you can go in. (*Enter* CORNELIUS *from the kitchen*.)

CORNELIUS. Oh, Miss Van Huysen . . .

ERMENGARDE. Why, Mr. Hack—!!

CORNELIUS (*sliding up to her, urgently*). Not yet! I'll explain. I'll explain everything.

MISS VAN HUYSEN. Mr. Kemper!—Mr. Kemper! This is Mr. Cornelius Hackl. (*To* AMBROSE.) Mr. Hackl, this is Mr. Ambrose Kemper. (*Pause, while the men glare at one another*.) Perhaps you two know one another?

AMBROSE. No!

CORNELIUS. No, we don't.

AMBROSE (*hotly*). Miss Van Huysen, I know that man is not Ambrose Kemper.

CORNELIUS (*ditto*). And he's not Cornelius Hackl.

MISS VAN HUYSEN. My dear young men, what does it matter what your names are? The important thing is that you are you. (*To* AMBROSE.) You are alive and breathing, aren't you, Mr. Hackl? (*Pinches* AMBROSE'S *left arm*.)

AMBROSE. Ouch, Miss Van Huysen.

MISS VAN HUYSEN. This dear child imagines she is Horace Vandergelder's niece Ermengarde.

ERMENGARDE. But I am.
MISS VAN HUYSEN. The important thing is that you're all in love. Everything else is illusion. (*She pinches* CORNELIUS' *arm.*)
CORNELIUS. Ouch! Miss Van Huysen!
MISS VAN HUYSEN (*comes down and addresses the audience*). Everybody keeps asking me if I'm Miss Van Huys ... (*She seems suddenly to be stricken with doubt as to who she is; her face shows bewildered alarm. She pinches herself on the upper arm and is abruptly and happily relieved.*) Now, you two gentlemen sit down and have a nice chat while this dear child has a good hot bath.

(*The doorbell rings.* ERMENGARDE *exits,* MISS VAN HUYSEN *about to follow her, but stops. Enter* Cook.)

COOK. There's the doorbell again.
MISS VAN HUYSEN. Well, answer it. (*She and* ERMENGARDE *exit to kitchen.*)
COOK (*at window, very happy about all these guests*). It's a cab and three ladies. I never saw such a night. (*Exit to front door.*)
MISS VAN HUYSEN. Gentlemen, you can rest easy. I'll see that Mr. Vandergelder lets his nieces marry you both.

(*Enter* MRS. LEVI.)

MRS. LEVI. Flora, how are you?
MISS VAN HUYSEN. Dolly Gallagher! What brings you here?
MRS. LEVI. Great Heavens, Flora, what are those two drunken men doing in your hall?
MISS VAN HUYSEN. I don't know. Horace Vandergelder sent them to me.
MRS. LEVI. Well, I've brought you two girls in much the same condition. Otherwise they're the finest girls in the world. (*She goes up to the door and leads in* MRS. MOLLOY. MINNIE *follows.*) I want you to meet Irene Molloy and Minnie Fay.
MISS VAN HUYSEN. Delighted to know you.

MRS. LEVI. Oh, I see you two gentlemen are here, too. Mr. Hackl, I was about to look for you (*pointing about the room*) *somewhere* here.
CORNELIUS. No, Mrs. Levi. I'm ready to face anything now.
MRS. LEVI. Mr. Vandergelder will be here in a minute. He's downstairs trying to pay for a cab without any money.
MRS. MOLLOY (*holding* VANDERGELDER'S *purse*). Oh, I'll help him.
MRS. LEVI. Yes, will you, dear? You had to pay the restaurant bills. You must have hundreds of dollars there it seems.
MRS. MOLLOY. This is his own purse he lost. I can't give it back to him without seeming . . .
MRS. LEVI. I'll give it back to him. — There, you help him with this now. (*She gives* MRS. MOLLOY *a bill and puts the purse airily under her arm.*)
VANDERGELDER (*off*). Will somebody please pay for this cab?

(MRS. MOLLOY *exits to front door.*)

MRS. MOLLOY (*off stage*). I'll take care of that, Mr. Vandergelder. (*As* MR. VANDERGELDER *enters,* MALACHI *and the* Cabman *follow him in.* VANDERGELDER *carries overcoat, stick and box of chocolates.*)
CABMAN. Fifteen dollars, Mr. Vandergelder.
MALACHI. Hello, Mr. Vandergelder.
VANDERGELDER (*to* MALACHI). You're discharged! (*To* Cabman.) You too! (MALACHI *and* Cabman *go out and wait in the hall.*) So I've caught up with you at last! (*To* AMBROSE.) I never want to see you again! (*To* CORNELIUS.) You're discharged! Get out of the house, both of you.

(*He strikes sofa with his stick; a second after,* MISS VAN HUYSEN *strikes him on the shoulder with a folded newspaper or magazine.*)

MISS VAN HUYSEN (*forcefully*). Now then you. Stop ordering people out of my house. You can shout and carry on in Yonkers, but when you're in my house you'll behave yourself.

VANDERGELDER. They're both dishonest scoundrels.
MISS VAN HUYSEN. Take your hat off. Gentlemen, you stay right where you are.
CORNELIUS. Mr. Vandergelder, I can explain—
MISS VAN HUYSEN. There aren't going to be any explanations. Horace, stop scowling at Mr. Kemper and forgive him.
VANDERGELDER. That's not Kemper, that's a dishonest rogue named Cornelius Hackl.
MISS VAN HUYSEN. You're crazy. (*Points to* AMBROSE.) That's Cornelius Hackl.
VANDERGELDER. I guess I know my own chief clerk.
MISS VAN HUYSEN. I don't care what their names are. You shake hands with them both, or out you go.
VANDERGELDER. Shake hands with those dogs and scoundrels!
MRS. LEVI. Mr. Vandergelder, you've had a hard day. You don't want to go out in the rain now. Just for form's sake, you shake hands with them. You can start quarreling with them tomorrow.
VANDERGELDER (*gives* CORNELIUS *one finger to shake*). There! Don't regard that as a handshake. (*He turns to* AMBROSE, *who mockingly offers him one finger.*) Hey! I never want to see you again.

(MRS. MOLLOY *enters from front door.*)

MRS. MOLLOY. Miss Van Huysen.
MISS VAN HUYSEN. Yes, dear?
MRS. MOLLOY. Do I smell coffee?
MISS VAN HUYSEN. Yes, dear.
MRS. MOLLOY. Can I have some, good and black?
MISS VAN HUYSEN. Come along, everybody. We'll all go into the kitchen and have some coffee. (*As they all go:*) Horace, you'll be interested to know there are two Ermengardes in there....
VANDERGELDER. Two!!

(*Last to go is* MINNIE, *who revolves about the room dreamily waltzing, a finger on her forehead.* MRS. LEVI has been standing at one side. She now comes forward, in thoughtful mood. MINNIE continues her waltz round the left sofa and out to the kitchen. MRS. LEVI, left alone, comes to front, addressing an imaginary Ephraim.)

MRS. LEVI. Ephraim Levi, I'm going to get married again. Ephraim, I'm marrying Horace Vandergelder for his money. I'm going to send his money out doing all the things you taught me. Oh, it won't be a marriage in the sense that we had one—but I shall certainly make him happy, and Ephraim—I'm tired. I'm tired of living from hand to mouth, and I'm asking your permission. Ephraim —will you give me away? (*Now addressing the audience, she holds up the purse.*) Money! Money!—it's like the sun we walk under; it can kill or cure.—Mr. Vandergelder's money! Vandergelder's never tired of saying most of the people in the world are fools, and in a way he's right, isn't he? Himself, Irene, Cornelius, myself! But there comes a moment in everybody's life when he must decide whether he'll live among human beings or not—a fool among fools or a fool alone.

As for me, I've decided to live among them.

I wasn't always so. After my husband's death I retired into myself. Yes, in the evenings, I'd put out the cat, and I'd lock the door, and I'd make myself a little rum toddy; and before I went to bed I'd say a little prayer, thanking God that I was independent—that no one else's life was mixed up with mine. And when ten o'clock sounded from Trinity Church tower, I fell off to sleep and I was a perfectly contented woman. And one night, after two years of this, an oak leaf fell out of my Bible. I had placed it there on the day my husband asked me to marry him; a perfectly good oak leaf—but without color and without life. And suddenly I realized that for a long time I had not shed one tear; nor had I been filled with the wonderful hope that something or other would turn out well. I saw that I was like that oak leaf, and on that night I decided to rejoin the human race.

Yes, we're all fools and we're all in danger of destroying the world with our folly. But the surest way to keep us out of harm is to give us the four or five human pleasures that are our right in the world,—and that takes a little *money!*

The difference between a little money and no money at all is enormous—and can shatter the world. And the difference between a little money and an enormous amount of money is very slight—and that, also, can shatter the world.

Money, I've always felt, money—pardon my expression—is like manure; it's not worth a thing unless it's spread about encouraging young things to grow.

Anyway,—that's the opinion of the second Mrs. Vandergelder.

(VANDERGELDER *enters with two cups of coffee. With his back, he closes both doors.*)

VANDERGELDER. Miss Van Huysen asked me to bring you this.

MRS. LEVI. Thank you both. Sit down and rest yourself. What's been going on in the kitchen?

VANDERGELDER. A lot of foolishness. Everybody falling in love with everybody. I forgave 'em, Ermengarde and that artist.

MRS. LEVI. I knew you would.

VANDERGELDER. I made Cornelius Hackl my partner.

MRS. LEVI. You won't regret it.

VANDERGELDER. Dolly, you said some mighty unpleasant things to me in the restaurant tonight . . . all that about my house . . . and everything.

MRS. LEVI. Let's not say another word about it.

VANDERGELDER. Dolly, you have a lot of faults—

MRS. LEVI. Oh, I know what you mean.

VANDERGELDER. You're bossy, scheming, inquisitive . . .

MRS. LEVI. Go on.

VANDERGELDER. But you're a wonderful woman. Dolly, marry me.

MRS. LEVI. Horace! (*Rises.*) Stop right there.
VANDERGELDER. I know I've been a fool about Mrs. Molloy, and that other woman. But, Dolly, forgive me and marry me. (*He goes on his knees.*)
MRS. LEVI. Horace, I don't dare. No, I don't dare.
VANDERGELDER. What do you mean?
MRS. LEVI. You know as well as I do that you're the first citizen of Yonkers. Naturally, you'd expect your wife to keep open house, to have scores of friends in and out all the time. Any wife of yours should be used to that kind of thing.
VANDERGELDER (*after a brief struggle with himself*). Dolly, you can live any way you like.
MRS. LEVI. Horace, you can't deny it, your wife would have to be a *somebody*. Answer me: am I a somebody?
VANDERGELDER. You are . . . you are. Wonderful woman.
MRS. LEVI. Oh, you're partial. (*She crosses, giving a big wink at the audience, and sits on sofa right.* VANDERGELDER *follows her on his knees.*) Horace, it won't be enough for you to load your wife with money and jewels; to insist that she be a benefactress to half the town. (*He rises and, still struggling with himself, coughs so as not to hear this.*) No, she must be a somebody. Do you really think I have it in me to be a credit to you?
VANDERGELDER. Dolly, everybody knows that you could do anything you wanted to do.
MRS. LEVI. I'll try. With your help, I'll try — and by the way, I found your purse. (*Holds it up.*)
VANDERGELDER. Where did you — ! Wonderful woman!
MRS. LEVI. It just walked into my hand. I don't know how I do it. Sometimes I frighten myself. Horace, take it. Money walks out of my hand, too.
VANDERGELDER. Keep it. Keep it.
MRS. LEVI. Horace! (*Half laughing, half weeping, and with an air of real affection for him.*) I never thought . . . I'd ever . . . hear you say a thing like that!

(BARNABY *dashes in from the kitchen in great excitement. He has discarded* MINNIE'S *clothes.*)

BARNABY. Oh! Excuse me. I didn't know anybody was here.
VANDERGELDER (*bellowing*). Didn't know anybody was here. Idiot!
MRS. LEVI (*putting her hand on* VANDERGELDER'S *arm; amiably:*). Come in Barnaby. Come in.

(VANDERGELDER *looks at her a minute; then says, imitating her tone:*)

VANDERGELDER. Come in, Barnaby. Come in.
BARNABY. Cornelius is going to marry Mrs. Molloy!!
MRS. LEVI. Isn't that fine! Horace! . . . (MRS. LEVI *rises, and indicates that he has an announcement to make.*)
VANDERGELDER. Barnaby, go in and tell the rest of them that Mrs. Levi has consented—
MRS. LEVI. *Finally* consented!
VANDERGELDER. Finally consented to become my wife.
BARNABY. Holy cabooses. (*Dashes back to the doorway.*) Hey! Listen, everybody! Wolf-trap—I mean—Mr. Vandergelder is going to marry Mrs. Levi.

(MISS VAN HUYSEN *enters followed by all the people in this act. She is now carrying the box of chocolates.*)

MISS VAN HUYSEN. Dolly, that's the best news I ever heard. (*She addresses the audience.*) There isn't any more coffee; there isn't any more gingerbread; but there are three couples in my house and they're all going to get married. And do you know, one of those Ermengardes wasn't a dear little girl at all—she was a boy! Well, that's what life is: disappointment, illusion.
MRS. LEVI (*to audience*). There isn't any more coffee; there isn't any more gingerbread, and there isn't any more play—but there is one more thing we have to do . . . Barnaby, come here. (*She whispers to him, pointing to the audience. Then she says to the audience:*) I think the youngest person here ought to tell us what the moral of the play is.

(BARNABY *is reluctantly pushed forward to the footlights.*)

BARNABY. Oh, I think it's about . . . I think it's about adventure. The test of an adventure is that when you're in the middle of it, you say to yourself, "Oh, now I've got myself into an awful mess; I wish I were sitting quietly at home." And the sign that something's wrong with you is when you sit quietly at home wishing you were out having lots of adventure. What we would like for you is that you have just the right amount of sitting quietly at home, and just the right amount of—adventure! So that now we all want to thank you for coming tonight, and we all hope that in your lives you have just the right amount of—adventure!

*The Curtain Falls*

FOR DISCUSSION

# Act I

1. From the opening dialogue between Ambrose and Vandergelder, what do you learn about the reason for conflict, the attitude of each toward what constitutes success, and the chance which Ambrose might have to outwit Vandergelder?
2. What information is brought out through Vandergelder's conversations with Gertrude, Cornelius, Joe Scanlon, and Ermengarde? Why does Joe refuse to carry out Vandergelder's request? What reason do you have for believing that Ermengarde will, or will not, obey her uncle's orders?
3. The arrival of Malachi Stack is typical of the use of coincidence in old-fashioned plays and modern soap operas. Why is he essential to the action at this moment? Do you think that the purpose of his conversation with Vandergelder is to make his arrival and employment believable, to reveal his character, to contribute to the humor, or all three? Support your opinion.
4. If you were viewing a performance of this play, how would you react to Vandergelder's speech to the audience? Does he give you essential information about himself and about his plans and the reasons for carrying them out? Do you think this speech is included primarily to allow Wilder to poke fun at the ideas approved by the middle-class audiences of the 1920's? In your opinion, which lines clearly indicate the purpose of this speech? Which do you find especially amusing?

5. As soon as Mrs. Levi appears, she begins to "arrange things." What reason does she have for believing that she can arrange the marriage of Ambrose and Ermengarde? What instructions does she give Ambrose that make him wonder if she can be trusted? From her explanation of the "profit and pleasure" derived from arranging things, and especially from her statements about money, what impression do you gain of her as a person?
6. What tricks of flattery and persuasion does Mrs. Levi use on Vandergelder? What do you think she is up to when she raises doubts in his mind about Irene Molloy, to whom Mrs. Levi undoubtedly introduced him? Why is he taken in by the hypothetical Ernestina Simple? During the conversation about Ernestina, what shallow, pretentious, and smugly "proper" values does Wilder subtly ridicule? What part of the humor and satire is due to Mrs. Levi's exaggeration?
7. In return for "arranging things" for Vandergelder, what "little pickings" does Mrs. Levi wheedle out of him? What possible events are foreshadowed by her instructions to Vandergelder, and by Cornelius' decision that he and Barnaby will also go to New York and have adventures? What do you think of Cornelius' comments about rich people? How does he make certain that the store won't need clerks? What is implied by Mrs. Levi's final comments to the audience?

## Act II

1. The playwright must depend almost entirely on dialogue to portray his characters and to inform the audience about past, present, and future events. From the dialogue between Mrs. Molloy and Minnie, what impression do you gain of each lady? What reasons does Mrs. Molloy give for marrying Vandergelder? Why is Minnie shocked by them? What values and attitudes do you think Wilder wants to make appear foolish or ridiculous?
2. Why is the presence of Cornelius and Barnaby in Mrs. Molloy's millinery shop especially nonsensical? Do their explanations and behavior and their plans for handling the situation make the coincidence seem more believable or less so? What possibilities does Mrs. Molloy see in their presence?
3. Before the entrance of Vandergelder and Mrs. Levi, what does Cornelius lead Mrs. Molloy to believe (a) about him and Barnaby and their acquaintance with Vandergelder, and (b) about his own interest in her? Is her response to their behavior—especially when they hide—equally far-fetched? Cite evidence from the play to support your answers.

4. Vandergelder's call on Mrs. Molloy has many of the characteristics of slapstick comedy. Why are he and Mrs. Levi suspicious from the very start? How does Mrs. Molloy attempt to remedy the situation? What do you find especially amusing in Cornelius' speech to the audience (page 121)?
5. Why is it important for Mrs. Levi to learn about Cornelius and Barnaby before Vandergelder comes back into the shop? When she makes up all those "tales" about Cornelius, is she (a) just being "the artist" and making life more interesting, (b) having fun by amazing and baffling Vandergelder, or (c) coming to Mrs. Molloy's rescue? Explain.
6. In view of Mrs. Levi's earlier decision about Mrs. Molloy, why is it necessary for Vandergelder to see with his own eyes that at least one man is hidden in the shop? What special touches does Mrs. Levi add?
7. When Mrs. Molloy demands reparations, why can't Cornelius admit the truth and run away, as Barnaby suggests? What complications seem inevitable? Point out the humorous satire in the remarks and actions of the characters in the closing scene of this act.

## Act III

1. You already know whom to expect at the Harmonia Gardens Restaurant. Whom is Vandergelder expecting? When the "unexpected" arrives, Malachi proves *almost* as good at arranging things as Mrs. Levi. Why is his eavesdropping scheme only partly successful? What brilliant—and expensive—plan does Vandergelder initiate to put an end to the "conspiracy"? What comments does this plan lead Malachi and the Cabman to make about life, people, and Vandergelder? Point out the comments you find most amusing and tell why.
2. After the arrival of Mrs. Molloy and her friends, what actions and situations give the comedy a slapstick quality? Is Malachi justified in referring to Cornelius and Barnaby as "wild savages" and to Mrs. Molloy as a woman whom "civilization hasn't touched"? Or is Wilder indirectly poking fun at so-called "civilized" behavior? Explain.
3. The coincidence of Vandergelder's dropping his purse is important in several ways. First, it provides a good excuse for Malachi to share with the audience the lessons he has learned from life. What is the "moral" of his speech? Second, it changes both the situation in which Cornelius finds himself and his entire attitude. How is this fact brought out?

4. When Mrs. Levi returns, she begins at once to "arrange things," this time to her own advantage. Discuss the steps in her method to get Vandergelder to propose marriage *on her terms*. What "honest truth" doesn't he want to hear? Why won't he believe her when she tells him that Cornelius is on the other side of the screen?
5. At the end of Act III, what does Mrs. Levi mean by the remark "Well, there's your life, Mr. Vandergelder"? What has happened to his power and pious self-confidence? Is Mrs. Levi admitting defeat in her final unladylike remark? At this point in the play, has she made things better or worse by "arranging" them? Has she succeeded in her other goals: to make life more interesting and to make money "circulate like rain water"? Cite evidence to support your opinions.

## Act IV

1. The comic device of mistaken identities (humorously exaggerated in the opening scenes of this act) depends upon the gullibility of Miss Van Huysen and her cook. What impression do you gain of these ladies? What do you learn about Miss Van Huysen's attitude toward Vandergelder and his opposition to Ermengarde's marriage?
2. How do you account for the complete mix-up that results from Vandergelder's plans to put an end to Ermengarde's romance? Why are Cornelius and Barnaby so desperate and Malachi and Joe so determined? How does Ermengarde make matters worse by persuading Ambrose to pose as Cornelius? What are her reasons?
3. What is Miss Van Huysen's reaction to the conflicting statements of her guests? What does she mean by "Everything else is illusion"? Why is she so confident that all will end happily?
4. What mysteries are left unexplained — such as why Mrs. Levi arrived with Mrs. Molloy and Minnie, and why Vandergelder arrived last and in a cab he couldn't pay for? How and when are they cleared up? How does Miss Van Huysen prove herself more than a match for the irate Vandergelder?
5. As the person who arranges things, Mrs. Levi is certainly the person to speak not only for herself but also for the playwright. In her speech to the audience, does she express in different words what Wilder had said this play was about? Support your own opinion by evaluating the opinions of "the second Mrs. Vandergelder."

6. In the proposal scene between Vandergelder and Mrs. Levi, does she use her feminine wiles to get her own way, or is she being completely honest because she considers her marriage to him a responsibility as well as an advantage? Are her remarks and actions consistent with her preceding speech to the audience? Explain.
7. The play could very well have ended with Miss Van Huysen's remark, "Well, that's what life is: disappointment and illusion." What reasons—dramatic and comic—can you see for having Barnaby "tell us what the moral of the play is"? Does he state a moral? Is Wilder still poking fun at old-fashioned playwriting and the people who want their plays "soothing"? Why is the ending an effective way of drawing all the far-fetched and ridiculous incidents together? If you think another way would have been equally effective, explain why.

## ON THE PLAY AS A WHOLE

1. When a writer parodies a poem or play, he imitates it in such a way as to poke fun at it. Therefore, from this parody you ought to be able to discover quite a little about the plays of the 1920's. What impressed you most about (a) the characters, (b) the kind of situations and events in which they are involved, (c) the values which influence their actions and decisions, and (d) the kind of dramatic performances—plays and acting—which the theater-going audience of that period expected? Support your comments by referring to specific incidents, lines of dialogue, and speeches addressed to the audience.
2. How important to the play is the romance between Ambrose and Ermengarde? Who, in your opinion, is the main character? Are there several main characters? If so, who are they? Which characters do you consider minor? What purposes do they serve? Discuss.
3. In a typical farce, the characters are often stereotypes. In this play which do you consider stereotypes? Do some characters seem stereotypes at first and then become individuals? Were some of the minor characters more than just representatives of a type; for example, a waiter or a cabman? If so, in what ways? Which of the main characters do you consider dynamic? Were any of them static? Support your opinions.
4. Identify the characters you think are motivated by a desire for "adventure." Does the word have a similar or different meaning

for each of them? Considering the nature of the adventures and the reactions of the characters to them, do you think Wilder is poking fun at, or subtly criticizing, the injustices and stupidities for which the money-making middle-class employers were responsible? Discuss.

5. Three basic elements in drama—as in fiction—are setting, character, and plot. In this play, what holds your interest: what the characters do—the series of incidents and events that make up the plot—or the characters themselves? How important is the setting for each act? When does it affect what happens or make those happenings possible? If you think the settings contribute to the humor of the play, explain how and why.

6. Full-length plays often have one or more subplots that are related to the main plot. Each subplot is made up of a series of incidents concerned with the solving of a problem. Sometimes a subplot ends fairly early in the play; sometimes it parallels the main plot and does not merge with it until the last scene. In this play is there at least one subplot in addition to the main plot? Before answering this question, point out the main plot and the incidents that make up this plot. Then decide whether the remaining incidents—if any—go together to make up one or more subplots. If they do, point out the characters involved and the problems they are trying to solve.

7. The basis of all drama—even farcical comedy—is some kind of conflict: a struggle between two opposing forces. Until one of the forces overcomes the other—or gives up trying—the conflict is not resolved. Who or what are the opposing forces in this play? How is the conflict resolved? Does the action reach a climax? If so, where does it occur in the play? Is this the point of highest dramatic intensity? Does it mark a turning point in the action? What part of the ending would you call the denouement? Discuss.

8. If you decided earlier that this play has a subplot—perhaps two—what is the conflict that the main character in the subplot must try to resolve? How is it resolved and at what point in the play?

9. Only a few American authors have mastered the difficult art of conveying in words that intangible quality called humor. It is something that happens when everything is in balance—exaggeration and understatement, the obvious and the unexpected, the believable and the fantastic, the commonplace and the witty. Point out examples of each of these and of any other qualities and dramatic techniques which contribute to the humor.

## FOR COMPOSITION

1. Suppose you were a talent scout looking for a leading lady and a leading man for *The Matchmaker*. In several paragraphs, describe the kind of person you think each one should be. Give a general picture of the physical appearance of each, but focus major attention on those qualities of personality and character which you feel each actor should be able to portray through his actions and through the way he speaks his lines.
2. Imagine that you had been an eyewitness to the strange events that took place in Mrs. Molloy's hat shop after the arrival of Cornelius and Barnaby. Write an account of what you saw and heard, and your opinion of it. Try to convey the mood of this scene as well as the hilarious confusion.
3. Mrs. Levi seemed never to run out of wise sayings, for even the ones that sounded a little silly had a pinch of truth in them. Write a personal essay in which you put down what you think and feel about Mrs. Levi's sayings. You might select the sayings in the play that you liked best or thought most amusing and tell why. You might comment on Mrs. Levi's ideas about people and life and her advice about enjoying both of them more. Or you might prefer to share with your reader how you felt about the way Mrs. Levi "arranged things," how well she succeeded, and what she contributed to "the aspirations of the young for a fuller, freer participation in life."
4. At the beginning of the play you are not sure whether Mrs. Levi is even interested in Vandergelder or he in her. Point out the incidents you think were especially important in bringing Vandergelder to think of Mrs. Levi as a possible bride and in furthering her plans to become the second Mrs. Vandergelder.
5. Choose a character in the play who intrigued you or whom you found especially entertaining. Write a sketch that will convey to your reader the kind of person you picture this character to be. In your sketch, you might cite examples of what he or she said and did that you consider especially revealing.
6. Your enjoyment of this play might have been greater if you had seen it rather than read it. This would certainly be true if you have difficulty creating the make-believe world of the theater in which the characters are literally "brought to life" by the actors who impersonate them. It would *not* be true if you enjoy producing the play "in your head" as you would like to see it performed. In a composition of several paragraphs, point out the advantages and disadvantages — as you see them — of reading this play and of seeing it performed.

# Frank D. Gilroy

The modern American theater has a strong tradition of plays that explore the emotions and behavior of apparently "ordinary" situations. The task of the playwright attempting such a theme is to show in ways that are psychologically credible, socially realistic, and dramatically compelling how these people react to critical situations in their lives. If a play of this genre is successful, the characters transcend their "ordinariness" because they express ideas and emotions of broad human validity.

Such a play is the one we are now about to read—Frank Gilroy's *The Subject Was Roses*. What could be more ordinary, more normal, more wholesome—and in a sense, more dull—than the situation that unfolds in the first scene. A young man has just come home from the army. He has made a creditable record and has survived the dangers of combat without a scratch. His parents are relatively young, fairly prosperous. They have a "nice home" in a middle class section of the Bronx, a borough of New York City. They are naturally overjoyed to have their only son—their only child—with them again. Everything seems just about as it should be, and "as American as apple pie." We seem to have the makings of an unusually bland soap opera or TV situation comedy.

But almost immediately we sense that there is something wrong. In tightly written scenes, with three subtly developed characters, and dialogue that has the authentic ring of life, the playwright tells us what that "something" is. The members of this family love each other, but the emotions have gone sour. The how and why are conveyed by the play with remarkable conviction.

As one critic put it: "The play is the drama of the inarticulate, the drama of people who have emotions but are uncertain how to convey them." It has something to say to everyone who has ever experienced a bitter family quarrel . . . who has loved a mate, a parent, or a child, but has found that love somehow tinged with conflict and bitterness. The Clearys, in their very ordinariness, embody universal aspects of human experience and provide a memorable insight into the human spirit.

*The Subject Was Roses* proved to be both a popular and critical success. It won drama's "triple crown" for 1965—the Pulitzer Prize, the New York Drama Critics' Award for the Best Play, and the "Tony" (Antoinette Perry) Award for the Best Play. It was made into an imperfect but generally effective film. (If you have a chance to catch it in a TV revival, don't miss it.)

# The Subject Was Roses

**CHARACTERS**

JOHN CLEARY
NETTIE CLEARY
TIMMY CLEARY

## Act I scene 1

SCENE: *The kitchen and living room of a middle-class apartment in the West Bronx. A doorway links the two rooms; an invisible wall divides them. The living room is furnished with the heavy upholstered pieces (replete with antimacassars) considered fashionable in the late twenties and early thirties. There is evidence of a party given the night before: a beer keg, a stack of camp chairs, a sagging banner that is hand lettered—"Welcome Home, Timmy."*
TIME: *A Saturday morning in May of 1946.*

AT RISE: *A man stands alone in the kitchen, lost in contemplation of an army jacket hanging from the door. The man,* JOHN CLEARY, *is fifty. The army jacket bears an infantry division patch, corporal chevrons, service ribbons (including the ETO with two battle stars, and a presidential unit citation), four "Hershey Bars" marking two years of overseas duty, and the "Ruptured Duck" signifying recent discharge.* JOHN CLEARY's *expression as he regards the jacket is one of almost reverent curiosity. He touches the jacket, feels the material, traces the outline of the chevrons inquiringly. Now, on an impulse, he takes the jacket from the hanger, dons it furtively, is enjoying what is obviously a secret moment when he hears a key turn in the front door. Quickly returning the jacket to the hanger, he takes a seat at the kitchen table and appears engrossed in a newspaper as the door opens and his wife,* NETTIE, *forty-five, enters with a bundle of groceries.*

NETTIE. It's a lovely day . . . Timmy still asleep?
JOHN. Haven't heard him . . . Better give me mine.
NETTIE. I thought we'd all have breakfast together.
JOHN. I have to go downtown.
NETTIE. Today?
JOHN. Ruskin wants to see me. (*She regards him a moment, then begins to set the food before him.*) I'm going to stop at Saint Francis on the way . . . to offer a prayer of thanks.
NETTIE. Toast?
JOHN. Yes . . . All those casualties and he never got a scratch. We're very lucky.
NETTIE. What do you want on it?
JOHN. Marmalade . . . The Freeman boy dead. The Mullin boy crippled for life . . . Makes you wonder . . . Think he enjoyed the party?

NETTIE. He seemed to.
JOHN. First time I ever saw him take a drink.
NETTIE. He drank too much.
JOHN. You don't get out of the army every day.
NETTIE. He was sick during the night.
JOHN. Probably the excitement.
NETTIE. It was the whiskey. You should have stopped him.
JOHN. For three years he's gotten along fine without anyone telling him what to do.
NETTIE. I had to hold his head.
JOHN. No one held his head in the army.
NETTIE. That's what *he* said.
JOHN. But that didn't stop *you*.
NETTIE. He's not in the army any more.
JOHN. It was a boy that walked out of this house three years ago. It's a man that's come back in.
NETTIE. You sound like a recruiting poster.
JOHN. *You* sound ready to repeat the old mistakes.
NETTIE. Mistakes?
JOHN. Pardon me.
NETTIE. You said mistakes.
JOHN. Slip of the tongue.
NETTIE. I'd like to know what mistakes you're referring to.
JOHN. The coffee's excellent.
NETTIE. I'd really like to know.
JOHN. He was eighteen when he went away. Until that time, he showed no special skill at anything, but you treated him like he was a protégé.
NETTIE. I think you mean prodigy.
JOHN. What I really mean is baby.
NETTIE. For a baby he certainly did well in the army.
JOHN. I didn't say he *was* a baby. I said you treated him like one.
NETTIE. You were surprised he did well. You didn't think he'd last a week.
JOHN. Bless us and save us, said Mrs. O'Davis.

NETTIE.  Do you know why you were surprised?
JOHN.  Joy, joy, said Mrs. Malloy.
NETTIE.  Because you never understood him.
JOHN.  Mercy, mercy, said old Mrs. Percy.
NETTIE.  I never doubted that he'd do as well as anyone else.
JOHN.  Where he's concerned you never doubted, period. If he came in here right now and said he could fly, you'd help him out the window.
NETTIE.  If you're saying I have confidence in him, you're right. And why not? Who knows him better?
JOHN.  Is there more coffee?
NETTIE.  He's exceptional.
JOHN.  Here we go again.
NETTIE.  Yes—exceptional!
JOHN.  In what way?
NETTIE.  I refuse to discuss it.
JOHN.  A person who's going to be famous usually drops a *few* clues by the time they're twenty-one.
NETTIE.  I didn't say famous—I said exceptional.
JOHN.  What's the difference?
NETTIE.  You wouldn't understand.
JOHN.  Here's something you better understand—you can't treat him as though he'd never been away. He's not a kid.
NETTIE.  If you had stopped him from drinking too much that would have been treating him like a kid?
JOHN.  This is where I came in.
NETTIE.  He was trying to keep up with you and you knew it.
JOHN.  You sound like you're jealous.
NETTIE.  The two of you so busy drinking you hardly paid attention to anyone else.
JOHN.  You *are* jealous!
NETTIE.  Don't be absurd.
JOHN.  He and I got along better yesterday than we ever did before and you're jealous. (*She turns away.*) Well, well, well.

(*He finishes the last of his coffee. Rises to leave.*)

NETTIE.  Can't Ruskin wait till Monday?
JOHN.  No. And don't pretend you're disappointed. What a charming little breakfast you and he will have together.
NETTIE.  You're welcome to stay.
JOHN.  My ears are burning already.
NETTIE.  I've never said a word against you and you know it.
JOHN.  Don't forget my excursion to Montreal.
NETTIE.  It was always your own actions that turned him against you.
JOHN.  And the convention—don't leave that out.

(*He starts from the room.*)

NETTIE.  The curtains. (*He regards her.*) The curtains for Timmy's room. They're coming today.
JOHN.  I don't know anything about curtains.
NETTIE.  Yes, you do.
JOHN.  I do not.
NETTIE.  They'll be ten dollars.
JOHN.  What's the matter with the old ones?

(TIMMY CLEARY, *twenty-one, wearing army suntans, open at the neck, emerges from his room, starts toward the kitchen, is arrested by their voices. He stops, listens.*)

NETTIE.  They're worn out.
JOHN.  They look all right to me.
NETTIE.  They aren't all right.

JOHN.   Ten dollars for curtains.
NETTIE.   Timmy will want to bring friends home.
JOHN.   The old squeeze play.

(TIMMY *puts his hands over his ears.*)

NETTIE.   Are you going to give me the money?

(JOHN *extracts a bill from his wallet, slaps it on the table.*)

JOHN.   Here!
NETTIE.   I need five dollars for the house.
JOHN.   I gave you fifteen yesterday.
NETTIE.   That went for the party.
JOHN.   That party cost close to a hundred dollars.
NETTIE.   It was worth it.
JOHN.   Did I say it wasn't? (*He takes another bill from his wallet and puts it down.*) There.

(TIMMY *goes back, slams the door of his room to alert them, then approaches the kitchen.* NETTIE *and* JOHN *compose themselves cheerfully as* TIMMY, *equally cheerful, enters.*)

TIMMY.   Good morning.
JOHN.   Champ.
NETTIE.   Morning, son.

(TIMMY *shakes hands with his father; kisses his mother on the cheek.*)

JOHN.  We thought you were going to sleep all day.
TIMMY.  I smelled the coffee.
JOHN.  Mother said you were sick during the night.
TIMMY.  I'm fine now.
JOHN.  I was a little rocky myself.
TIMMY.  I wonder why.

(*They both laugh.*)

NETTIE (*to* JOHN).  What time is your appointment?
JOHN.  Eleven-fifteen.
NETTIE.  It's twenty-five of.
JOHN (*to* TIMMY).  Mr. Ruskin wants to see me.
TIMMY.  That's too bad.
JOHN.  Why?
TIMMY.  Thought we might take in the Giant game.
NETTIE (*to* JOHN).  Why don't you?
JOHN.  You know I can't. (*To* TIMMY.) This thing with Ruskin means a sure sale.
TIMMY.  I understand.
JOHN.  We'll go tomorrow.
NETTIE.  My mother expects us for dinner tomorrow.

(JOHN *looks at* NETTIE *as though he might say something, thinks better of it, turns to* TIMMY.)

JOHN.  How about *next* Saturday?
TIMMY.  All right.
JOHN.  We'll get box seats—the works.
TIMMY.  Sounds fine.
JOHN.  Swell.
NETTIE.  What time will you be home?

JOHN.   I'll call you.
NETTIE.   I'll be at my mother's.
JOHN (*appraising* TIMMY). I understand none of your old clothes fit.
TIMMY.   That's right.
JOHN.   Meet me downtown on Monday and we'll get you some new ones.
TIMMY.   Okay.

(JOHN *feints a jab.* TIMMY *covers up. They spar good-naturedly until* TIMMY *drops his hands.*)

JOHN.   I still think I can take you.
TIMMY.   I wouldn't be surprised.
JOHN.   See you later.
TIMMY.   Right.

(JOHN *moves toward the door, stops before the army jacket, indicates one of the ribbons.*)

JOHN.   What did you say this one was for?
TIMMY.   It's a combat infantry badge.
JOHN.   How about that?
TIMMY.   It's not as important as it sounds.
JOHN.   We'll have to sit down and have a real talk. I want to hear all about it.
TIMMY.   All right.
JOHN.   It's great to have you home.
TIMMY.   It's great to be home.
JOHN.   The Mullin boy crippled. The Freeman boy dead. We're very lucky.
TIMMY.   I know.

JOHN. I'm stopping off at St. Francis this morning to offer a prayer of thanks ... See you later.
TIMMY. Right.

(JOHN *exits from the apartment.* TIMMY *looks after him.*)

NETTIE. How did you sleep?
TIMMY. Fine ... How's he feeling?
NETTIE. All right.
TIMMY. He looks a lot older.
NETTIE. It's been two years ... It must have seemed strange. (*He glances at her.*) Sleeping in your own bed.
TIMMY (*turning away again*). Yes ... How's his business?
NETTIE. Who knows?
TIMMY. The coffee market's off.
NETTIE. I hope you're hungry.
TIMMY. I can't get over the change in him.
NETTIE. Guess what we're having for breakfast.
TIMMY. It's not just the way he looks.
NETTIE. *Guess what we're having for breakfast.* (*He turns to her.*) Guess what we're having.
TIMMY. What?
NETTIE. Guess.
TIMMY. I don't know.
NETTIE. Yes, you do.
TIMMY. No.
NETTIE. Sure you do.
TIMMY. What is it?
NETTIE. You're fooling.
TIMMY. What is it?
NETTIE. What's your favorite?
TIMMY. Bacon and eggs?
NETTIE. Now I know you're fooling.
TIMMY. No.

NETTIE. I forgot what a tease you were.
TIMMY. I'm not teasing.
NETTIE. Waffles. We're having waffles.
TIMMY. Fine.
NETTIE. You used to be crazy about waffles.
TIMMY. I still am.
NETTIE. I've got the waffle batter ready.
TIMMY. Swell.
NETTIE. Your first morning home, you're entitled to whatever you want.
TIMMY. I want waffles.
NETTIE. I used the last egg in the batter.
TIMMY. *I want waffles.*
NETTIE. Really?
TIMMY. Cross my heart.
NETTIE. All right.

(*While she prepares things, he goes to a window, gazes out.*)

TIMMY. I see a new butcher.
NETTIE. Quite a few new stores.
TIMMY. Pop said the Bremens moved.
NETTIE. And the Costellos . . . Remember old Zimmer the tailor?
TIMMY. Sure.
NETTIE. A few weeks ago a woman brought him a coat she wanted altered. Zimmer started to fix it, then very politely excused himself, went up to the roof and jumped. No one knows why.
TIMMY. Who was the woman?
NETTIE. Mrs. Levin.
TIMMY. That explains it.

NETTIE. That's not funny.
TIMMY. Sorry.
NETTIE. What a thing to say.
TIMMY. I said I'm sorry.
NETTIE. I'm surprised at you.
TIMMY. Bless us and save us.
NETTIE. *What?*
TIMMY. Bless us and save us. As in "Bless us and save us, said Mrs. O'Davis; Joy, joy, said Mrs. Malloy . . ." (*She regards him incredulously.*) What's the matter?
NETTIE. I never expected to hear that nonsense from *you!*
TIMMY. It beats swearing.
NETTIE. You used to cover your ears when your father said it.
TIMMY (*with mock solemnity*). I'll never say it again.
NETTIE. *Don't talk to me like that!* . . . I'm sorry. I don't know what's wrong with me this morning. I don't think I slept well . . . Too much excitement—the party and all. (*She resumes the preparation of breakfast: pours batter on the waffle iron while he, still not recovered from her outburst, studies her.*) Will you have bacon with it?
TIMMY. Just the waffles will be fine.
NETTIE. Did you like the party?
TIMMY. Yes.
NETTIE. I wish the house had looked better.
TIMMY. What's wrong with it?
NETTIE. It needs painting. The sofa's on its last legs. And the rugs . . . Well, now that you're here I'll get it all fixed up.
TIMMY. It looks fine to me.
NETTIE. I still can't believe you're here.
TIMMY. I find it a little hard to believe myself.
NETTIE. You *are* here?
TIMMY. Want to pinch me? . . . Go ahead. (*She hesitates. He holds out his hand.*) Go on. (*She takes his hand.*) Believe it now? (*She continues to hold his hand. He be-*

*comes uneasy.*) Hey. (*Oblivious to his resistance, she still clings to his hand.*) What are you doing? (*She persists. His agitation mounts.*) Cut it out . . . *Cut it out!* (*He jerks free of her; immediately tries to make light of it.*) One pinch to a customer . . . House rule. (*She regards him mutely.*) The waffles must be ready; the light on the iron went out. (*She just looks at him.*) Isn't that what it means when that little light goes out? (*She looks at him a moment more, then goes to the waffle iron, lifts the cover, starts to remove the waffles, stops, moves to a chair, sits, folds her hands in her lap and begins to cry.*) What's the matter? . . . What's wrong? . . . What is it? . . . *What is it?*

NETTIE (*continuing to cry*). They stuck.
TIMMY. What?
NETTIE. Why did they have to stick today?
TIMMY. The waffles?
NETTIE. I can't remember the last time they stuck.
TIMMY. What's that to cry about?
NETTIE. I've looked forward to this morning for three years and nothing's right.
TIMMY. Why do you say that?
NETTIE. Not one thing.
TIMMY. What isn't right?
NETTIE. Not one single thing.
TIMMY. Will you please stop?
NETTIE. The things you've been saying—your attitude.
TIMMY. What things? What attitude?
NETTIE. You haven't even asked about Willis.
TIMMY. . . . How is he?
NETTIE. Every time I look at you, you avoid me.
TIMMY (*turning away*). That's ridiculous.
NETTIE. You're doing it now.
TIMMY. I am not!
NETTIE. How could you forget waffles were your favorite?
TIMMY. I just forgot.

NETTIE. Then you must have forgotten a lot of things.
TIMMY. *I'll tell you one thing I didn't forget.* (*She looks at him.*) The dance. (*No reaction from her.*) The one we were going to have the first morning I was home.
NETTIE. What made you think of that?
TIMMY. It's been on my mind all along.
NETTIE. I'll bet.
TIMMY. I was about to turn the radio on when you started crying.
NETTIE. I'll bet.
TIMMY. If you're through, I'll do it now. Are you through?
NETTIE. I haven't danced in so long I've probably forgotten how.

(*He goes to the living room, snaps on the radio, dials to a band playing a slow fox trot, returns to the kitchen.*)

TIMMY. Shall we have a go at it?
NETTIE. I can't remember the last time I danced.
TIMMY. Come on.
NETTIE. You really want to?
TIMMY. Yes.
NETTIE (*rising*). You asked for it.
TIMMY. That-a-girl. (*He puts his arms about her.*) Here we go. (*They move smoothly, gracefully.*) Forgot how to dance—who you kidding?
NETTIE. I guess it's one of those things you never forget.
TIMMY. Remember this? (*He goes into a maneuver that she follows perfectly.*) You've been taking lessons.
NETTIE. Of course.

(*They dance from the kitchen into the living room.*)

TIMMY. Come here off-ten?
NETTIE. Foist time.
TIMMY. Me likewise... By yuhself?
NETTIE. Widda goil friend.

(*The song ends.*)

ANNOUNCER'S VOICE. That's all the time we have on Dance Parade this morning. I hope—

(TIMMY *goes to the radio, dials, picks up a polka band going full blast.*)

TIMMY. What do you say?
NETTIE. The spirit's willing.
TIMMY. Let's go! (*They take off.*) Not bad... not bad.
NETTIE. What will the neighbors think?
TIMMY. The worst. (*The rhythm begins to accelerate.*) We're coming into the home stretch. Hang on.

(*They move faster and faster.*)

NETTIE. I'm getting dizzy.

(*As they whirl about the room they begin to laugh.*)

TIMMY. Hang on.

NETTIE. I can't do any more.

(*The laughter grows.*)

TIMMY. Hang on!
NETTIE. I can't!

(*The laughter becomes hysterical.*)

TIMMY. Hang on! Hang on!
NETTIE. I can't! I...

(*They trip, collapse to the floor.*)

TIMMY. You all right?
NETTIE. I think so.

(*Both breathe laboredly. The laughter subsides. He snaps the radio off, then sits on the floor facing her.*)

TIMMY. I'm dead... absolutely dead.
NETTIE. So am I.
TIMMY. I can't remember the last time I laughed like that.
NETTIE. I can... We were driving to the lake and stopped at that dinky carnival.
TIMMY. The time I got you to go on that ride.
NETTIE. Your father thought we'd lost our minds. He kept begging the man to stop the engine.

TIMMY. Which made us laugh all the harder.
NETTIE. Know something?
TIMMY. What?
NETTIE. I really believe you're here now.
TIMMY. So do I.
NETTIE. What are you going to do today?
TIMMY. I don't know.
NETTIE. Why don't you come to Mama's with me?
TIMMY. We're going there for dinner tomorrow.
NETTIE. Willis would love to see you.
TIMMY. I'll see him tomorrow.
NETTIE. When we told him you were coming home he began to sing. It's the first time he's done that in months.
TIMMY. All right, I'll go.
NETTIE. We won't stay long.
TIMMY. All right.

(*The door opens and* JOHN *enters, sees them on the floor.*)

JOHN. Well, hello (TIMMY *rises.*) Don't get up on my account.
TIMMY. We were dancing and fell down.
NETTIE (*to* JOHN). What did you forget?
JOHN. Nothing.
NETTIE (*rising*). Why did you come back?
JOHN. I changed my mind. (*To* TIMMY.) If you still want to go to the ball game, it's a date.
NETTIE. What about Ruskin?
JOHN. The hell with him. (*To* TIMMY.) Still want to go?
TIMMY. Yes.
NETTIE. What about Willis?
JOHN. What *about* Willis?

NETTIE. Timmy was going to see him this afternoon.
TIMMY. I'll see him tomorrow.
NETTIE. I told him you'd be over today.
TIMMY. Before you even asked me?
NETTIE. I thought sure you'd want to.
TIMMY. You had no right to do that.
NETTIE. What will I tell him?
TIMMY. Tell him I'll be there tomorrow.
NETTIE. He'll be disappointed.
TIMMY. That's not my fault.
JOHN. The game starts at twelve.
TIMMY. Just have to get my tie.
NETTIE. You haven't eaten.
TIMMY. We'll grab something on the way. (*He exits.*)
JOHN. I came out of Saint Francis and started for the subway. Was halfway there when I thought of Mr. Freeman: What wouldn't *he* give to be able to spend a day with his son? . . . It made me turn around and come back. (*She just looks at him.*) You're mad. (*No reply.*) You told me to take him to the game.
NETTIE. And you always do what I tell you.
JOHN. Bless us and save us.

(TIMMY, *knotting his tie, reappears, puts on his jacket, snaps to attention.*)

TIMMY. Corporal Cleary reporting for duty.
JOHN. Kiss your mother good-bye.
TIMMY. That's not a duty. (*He kisses* NETTIE *on the cheek. She receives the kiss impassively.*) So long, Mom.
JOHN. We won't be late.

(*He and* TIMMY *exit. She stands as she is.*)

*Curtain*

# Act I SCENE 2

TIME: *Late afternoon—the same day.*
AT RISE: JOHN *and* TIMMY *enter the apartment.* TIMMY *carries a bouquet of red roses.* JOHN *has just concluded a joke and they are both laughing.*

JOHN. I haven't told that one in years.
TIMMY. I was considered a very funny fellow. Thanks to you.
JOHN. Hello? . . . Anybody home? (*No answer.*) Still at her mother's.
TIMMY (*indicating the roses*). I better put these in water.

(*They move into the kitchen.*)

JOHN. Stand another beer?
TIMMY. Sure.

(*While* TIMMY *puts the roses in a vase,* JOHN *gets two cans of beer from the refrigerator.*)

JOHN (*opening the beers*). How did you remember all those jokes of mine?
TIMMY. Just came to me.

JOHN. I don't remember most of them myself . . . (*Hands* TIMMY *a beer.*) Here you go.
TIMMY. Thanks.
JOHN. What'll we drink to?
TIMMY. The Chicago Cubs.
JOHN. Think it'll help them?
TIMMY. Can it hurt?
JOHN (*raising the can*). To the Cubs
TIMMY. To the Cubs.

(*They both drink.*)

JOHN. Sixteen to three.
TIMMY. I'm still glad we went.
JOHN. So am I. (*Drinks.*) That was a beautiful catch Ott made.
TIMMY. Yes.
JOHN. For a moment I thought he lost it in the sun.
(TIMMY *says nothing.* JOHN *drinks.*) So they really went for the old man's jokes?
TIMMY. Especially the ones about Uncle Mike.
JOHN. Such as?
TIMMY. The Pennsylvania Hotel gag.
JOHN. Columbus told that one to the Indians.
TIMMY. Uncle Mike was a famous man in our outfit.
JOHN. Joking aside, he was quite a guy. Stood six three. Weighed close to two fifty.
TIMMY. I remember his picture.
JOHN. He was in the Spanish American War.
TIMMY. I know.
JOHN. Got hit by a bullet once that knocked him out. When he came to, he was lying in a field full of wounded men. The ones that were sure goners were marked with yellow

tags so no one would waste time on them. The others had blue tags. Mike found a yellow tag around his wrist. The fellow next to him who was unconscious had a blue one. Quick as a wink Mike switched the tags and . . . How about that? I'm telling *you* war stories. Go on—you do the talking.

TIMMY. About what?

JOHN. You must have seen some pretty bad things.

TIMMY. Not as much as a lot of others.

JOHN. Maybe you'd rather not talk about it.

TIMMY. I don't mind.

JOHN. I'd like to hear what you have to say.

TIMMY. I don't know how to begin.

JOHN. Anything that comes to mind.

TIMMY. Want to hear the bravest thing I ever did?

JOHN. Yes.

TIMMY. The first night we were in combat I slept with my boots off.

JOHN. Go on.

TIMMY. That's it.

JOHN. You slept with your boots off?

TIMMY. Doesn't sound like much, does it?

JOHN. Not offhand.

TIMMY. The fellows who eventually cracked up were all guys who couldn't sleep. If I hadn't decided to take my boots off I'd have ended up being one of them.

JOHN. I see.

TIMMY. Want to know the smartest thing I did?

JOHN. Sure.

TIMMY. I never volunteered. One day the lieutenant bawled me out for it. I said, "Sir, if there's anything you want me to do, you tell me and I'll do it. But if you wait for me to volunteer you'll wait forever."

JOHN. What did he say to that?

TIMMY. Nothing printable. The fact is I wasn't a very good soldier, Pop.

JOHN. You did everything they asked you.
TIMMY. The good ones do more. You'd have been a good one.
JOHN. What makes you say that?
TIMMY. I can tell.
JOHN. Well, thanks.
TIMMY. You're welcome.
JOHN. It's one of the big regrets of my life that I was never in the service.
TIMMY. I know.
JOHN. The day World War One was declared I went to the recruiting office. When they learned I was the sole support of the family, they turned me down.
TIMMY. I know.
JOHN. A lot of people made cracks. Especially guys like Clayton and Harper who waited to be drafted and then wangled safe jobs at Governors Island and the Navy Yard . . . I fixed their wagons one night—sent the army flying one way and the navy the other. That was the last about slacking I heard from *them* . . . Still it bothers me—missing out on the whole thing . . . I keep wondering what difference it might have made in my life . . . And then I wonder how I'd have made out . . . I wouldn't have settled for a desk job. I'd have gotten to the front.
TIMMY. I'm sure of that.
JOHN. But once there, how would I have done?
TIMMY. Fine.
JOHN. How do you know?
TIMMY. You're a born fighter.
JOHN. They say a lot of fellows who were terrors as civilians turned to jelly when they heard those bullets.
TIMMY. Not you.
JOHN. It doesn't seem so. But you can't be sure . . . That's always bothered me. (*Drinks the last of his beer.*) How about another?

TIMMY. Fine.
JOHN. Maybe we shouldn't.
TIMMY. Why?
JOHN. Your mother blames me for your getting sick last night; says I encouraged you to drink too much.
TIMMY. It wasn't what I drank. It was the excitement.
JOHN. That's what I told her.
TIMMY. *I'll* open two more.
JOHN. All right. (*While* TIMMY *gets the beers,* JOHN *regards the roses.*) Her father used to send her roses every birthday . . . A dozen red ones . . . Never missed . . . Even at the end.
TIMMY. Tell her they were your idea.
JOHN. What?
TIMMY. Tell her the roses were your idea.
JOHN. Why?
TIMMY. She'll get a kick out of it . . . All right?
JOHN. If you like.
TIMMY (*handing him a beer*). Here you go.
JOHN. Thanks.
TIMMY. You call it this time.
JOHN (*raising his beer*). To the two nicest fellows in the house.
TIMMY. I'll buy that. (*They drink.* TIMMY *regards the can.*) Funny how you acquire a taste for things.
JOHN. Yes.
TIMMY. When I was a kid I couldn't even stand the smell of beer.
JOHN. Believe it or not I was the same.
TIMMY. We seem to have gotten over it.
JOHN. Yes . . . Can I say something to you?
TIMMY. Sure.
JOHN. You won't take it the wrong way?
TIMMY. No.
JOHN. I owe you an apology.

TIMMY. For what?
JOHN. You were always sick; always home from school with one thing or another. I never thought you'd last in the army.
TIMMY. Neither did I.
JOHN. Really?
TIMMY. Really.
JOHN. When Dr. Goldman heard they took you he said it was ridiculous. When they put you in the infantry he said it was inhuman.
TIMMY. And when I survived?
JOHN. He said it was a miracle. (*They both laugh.*) I don't think it was a miracle. I think we just underestimated you . . . Especially me . . . That's what I wanted to apologize for.
TIMMY. Remember that corny thing you used to recite—about how a boy thinks his father is the greatest guy in the world until he's fifteen. Then the doubts start. By the time he's eighteen he's convinced his father is the worst guy in the world. At twenty-five the doubts start again. At thirty it occurs to him that the old man wasn't so bad after all. At forty—
JOHN. What about it?
TIMMY. There's some truth to it.
JOHN. I think you've had too much to drink.
TIMMY. I'm not saying you're a saint.
JOHN. That's a relief.
TIMMY. But taking into account where you started from, and the obstacles you had to overcome, what you've done is something to be proud of.
JOHN. Well, thank you.
TIMMY. How many guys that you grew up with even turned out legitimate?
JOHN. Not many.
TIMMY. And most of *them* are still scraping along where they started.

JOHN. That's true.
TIMMY. How many years of school did you have?
JOHN. I had to quit after the fourth grade.
TIMMY. I've met college graduates who don't know nearly as much as you about the things that really count.
JOHN. Must have been Yale men.
TIMMY. I'm serious.
JOHN. Speaking of college . . . If you get into one of those big ones and it's more than the G.I. Bill pays for, I'll help you out.
TIMMY. Thanks.
JOHN. That's just between you and me.
TIMMY. Why?
JOHN. I don't want people getting wrong notions.
TIMMY. About what?
JOHN. That I'm loaded.
TIMMY. *Are* you loaded?
JOHN. Don't be ridiculous.
TIMMY. That doesn't answer my question.
JOHN. The question's ridiculous.
TIMMY. That's still no answer.
JOHN. No, I'm not loaded.
TIMMY. How much do you have?
JOHN. What?
TIMMY. How much money do you have?
JOHN. Is this your idea of a joke?
TIMMY. No.
JOHN. Then why are you doing it?
TIMMY. I don't want to take money from you if you can't afford it.
JOHN. I can afford it.
TIMMY. Some of the places I applied at are pretty expensive.
JOHN. I can afford it!
TIMMY. Then you must be loaded.
JOHN. *I am not loaded!*

TIMMY. We have a summer place, a car. Now you tell me you can afford any school in the country. You must be fairly loaded.
JOHN. *If I hear that word once more, I'm marching right out the door!*

(TIMMY *is unable to suppress his laughter any longer.*)

TIMMY. You haven't changed a bit. (JOHN *regards him uncertainly.*) You look as though I'd asked you to betray your country.

(JOHN, *against his will, smiles.*)

JOHN. You son of a gun.
TIMMY. I really had you going.
JOHN. Some joke.
TIMMY. Oh, say, Pop.
JOHN. What?
TIMMY. How much *do* you have?
JOHN. *Enough's enough!* (TIMMY *laughs anew.*) I think we better change the subject.
TIMMY. How did you meet Mother? (JOHN *regards him.*) You said change the subject.
JOHN. You know all about that.
TIMMY. Just that you picked her up on the subway.
JOHN. It wasn't like that at all.
TIMMY. Then I don't know all about it.
JOHN. "Picked her up" makes it sound cheap.
TIMMY. Sorry.
JOHN. The first time I spoke to her was on the subway but there's more to it.

TIMMY. Tell me.
JOHN. Why?
TIMMY. I might become a writer and want to do a story about it someday.
JOHN. A writer?
TIMMY. Maybe.
JOHN. Well, that's the first I heard about that.
TIMMY. Me, too. Must be the beer... What year was it you met her?
JOHN. Nineteen twenty-one... A writer?
TIMMY. A writer... Where were you working then?
JOHN. At Emerson's...
TIMMY. And?
JOHN. One morning I saw her walk by. That afternoon she passed again. Same the next day. Turned out she worked around the corner. I... You sure you want to hear this?
TIMMY. Uh-huh.
JOHN. One evening I happened to be leaving at the same time she did. Turned out we took the same subway. She got off at Seventy-second Street... To make a long story short, I got a seat next to her one day and we started talking.
TIMMY. That's it?
JOHN. Yes.
TIMMY. Sounds like an ordinary pickup to me.
JOHN. *Well, it wasn't*... I left some things out.
TIMMY. Such as?
JOHN. I don't remember... It was twenty-five years ago.
TIMMY. The way I heard it, you followed her for a month before you finally got the nerve to speak.
JOHN. I thought you didn't know the story.
TIMMY. To convince her your intentions were honorable, you asked if you might call at her home. True or false? ...Well?
JOHN. True. (*Chuckles.*) You wouldn't believe how nervous I was. And she didn't make it any easier... Pretended

the whole thing was a complete surprise. Bernhardt couldn't have done it nicer . . . Or looked nicer . . . All in blue . . . Blue dress, blue hat, blue shoes . . . Everything blue . . . Light blue . . . And dignified . . . One look at her, you knew she was a lady . . . My family *called* her The Lady. To their minds it was an insult. (*Regards* TIMMY.) How did we get on this?

TIMMY. You were—

(*He is interrupted by the opening of the outside door.* NETTIE *enters.*)

JOHN. Join the party.

(*She enters the kitchen.*)

TIMMY. We're having a little hair of the dog.
NETTIE. How was the game?
JOHN. One-sided.
TIMMY. Pop was just telling me how you and he met.

(NETTIE *turns to* JOHN *questioningly.*)

JOHN. He asked me.
TIMMY (*to his mother, indicating his father*). His version is a little different from yours.
NETTIE. What do you mean?
TIMMY. He says *you* chased *him*.
NETTIE. That'll be the day.

TIMMY. Says you did everything but stand on your head to attract his attention. (NETTIE *is not sure now whether he's kidding or not.*) That's what he said.

(NETTIE *looks uncertainly from* TIMMY *to* JOHN. *They break up simultaneously.*)

NETTIE. You two.
JOHN. How about a beer?
NETTIE. No thanks.
JOHN. Come on—
TIMMY. Be a sport.
NETTIE. All right.
JOHN. That-a-girl.
NETTIE. Just a glass. (*To* TIMMY, *while* JOHN *gets the beer.*) What *did* he tell you?
TIMMY. He said you were dressed in blue and nobody ever looked nicer.
NETTIE. I'll bet.
TIMMY (*to* JOHN). Didn't you say that?
JOHN. I'm a stranger here.
NETTIE. Did he tell you how he used his friend Eddie Barnes?
JOHN. Bless us and save us.
NETTIE. Every night they'd get on the subway, stand right in front of me, and have a loud conversation about how well they were doing in business.
JOHN. It wasn't every night.
NETTIE. Poor Eddie had to go an hour out of his way.
TIMMY. That's what I call a friend.
JOHN. The best I ever had. (*Extends a glass of beer to* NETTIE.) Here you go. (*She stares past him.*) Here's your beer.

(*She continues looking off. He follows her gaze to the roses.*)

NETTIE. Where did they come from?
TIMMY. Pop got them . . . for you.
NETTIE (*to* JOHN). You did?
JOHN. Yes.

(*She goes to the roses.*)

NETTIE. They're beautiful . . . Thank you.
JOHN. You're welcome.
NETTIE. What made you do it?
JOHN. We happened to pass a place and I know you like them.
NETTIE. I haven't had red roses since Papa died. (*To* TIMMY.) He used to send me a dozen on my birthday. Never missed.
TIMMY. I remember.
NETTIE (*to* JOHN). Thank you.
JOHN. You're welcome.
NETTIE. I'm going to cry.

(*She does.*)

JOHN. You don't bring flowers—they cry. You do—they cry.
NETTIE. I'm sorry.
TIMMY. What's to be sorry?
NETTIE. He was the kindest, gentlest man that ever lived.
TIMMY. I know.
NETTIE. I'm all right now.

JOHN (*handing her the glass of beer*). Here's what you need.
NETTIE. Maybe so.
TIMMY (*raising his beer*). To happy days.
JOHN and NETTIE. To happy days.

(*They all drink.*)

NETTIE (*regarding the roses*). They're just beautiful.
JOHN (*anxious to change the subject*). Talking of Eddie Barnes before, God rest his soul, reminds me of the time old Emerson put up a second-hand car for the man who sold the most coffee over a three-month period. I won it, but couldn't drive. Eddie said he'd teach me. We didn't get two blocks from the office when he ran broadside into an ice truck.
NETTIE. How about that ride to Connecticut? He practically killed us all.
JOHN. What was the name of the place we stayed at?
NETTIE. The Rainbow Grove.
JOHN. That's right. Big fat red-haired dame ran it.
NETTIE. Mrs. Hanlon.
JOHN (*mimicking Mrs. Hanlon à la Mae West*). "My friends all call me Daisy." (*He and* NETTIE *laugh.*) I dubbed her the Will Rogers of Connecticut—she never met a man she didn't like.

(*They all laugh.*)

NETTIE. Remember the night you, Eddie, and a couple of others picked her up, bed and all, and left her sleeping in the middle of the baseball field.

JOHN. In the morning when we went out to play, she was still there.
TIMMY. What did you do?
JOHN. We ruled that any ball hitting her on the fly was a ground rule double. (*They all laugh.*) We had a lot of fun at that place.
NETTIE. Yes.
JOHN. I wonder if it's still there.
NETTIE. I wonder.
JOHN. Let's take a ride someday and see.
NETTIE. All right.

(*She starts to rise.*)

JOHN. Where you going?
NETTIE. Have to start supper.
JOHN. Forget it—we're eating out!
NETTIE. I bought a steak.
JOHN. It'll keep. (*To* TIMMY.) Where would you like to go, Champ?
NETTIE. Maybe he has a date.
JOHN. Bring her along.
TIMMY. I don't have a date.
NETTIE. I thought you'd be seeing that Davis girl?
TIMMY. That's finished.
NETTIE. She was a nice girl.
JOHN. She was a dunce.
NETTIE. John!
TIMMY. Pop's right.
NETTIE. You men are terrible.
TIMMY. You're too kind.
JOHN. Well, where are we going?
TIMMY. You two settle it while I see a man about a dog.

(*He exits.*)

JOHN. How about the Concourse Plaza?
NETTIE. All right.
JOHN. I had a nice day today.
NETTIE. I'm glad.
JOHN. He's quite a boy.
NETTIE. That's what I've been telling you for years.
JOHN. We talked about things. Really talked. The way Eddie and I used to . . . The hell with the Concourse Plaza! Let's go downtown! Let's go to the New Yorker!
NETTIE. You *are* in a good mood.
JOHN. Because I want to go downtown?
NETTIE. That and the roses.
JOHN. Are you going to talk about those roses all night?
NETTIE. I just wanted to thank you for them.
JOHN. You already have.
NETTIE. You sound as though you're sorry you got them.
JOHN. Don't be ridiculous.
NETTIE. Then what are you angry about?
JOHN. I'm just tired of hearing about them. A guy gets some roses—big deal.
NETTIE. You're embarrassed.
JOHN. I am not.
NETTIE. You did something nice and you're embarrassed.
JOHN. You don't know what you're talking about.
NETTIE. Don't worry, I won't tell anyone.
JOHN. *Nettie, please.*
NETTIE. All right, but I want to let you know how much I appreciate it.
JOHN. Good. I'm glad.
NETTIE. I do . . . I really do. (*On an impulse she touches his shoulder. The contact is mutually startling. Flustered, she turns away.*) We haven't been to the New

Yorker in years . . . I wonder if they still have the ice show? . . . Do you suppose we'll have any trouble getting in on a Saturday night?

(TIMMY *enters.*)

TIMMY. What did you decide?
JOHN. We're going to the Hotel New Yorker.
TIMMY. Well, digga digga doo.
JOHN. After that we're going to the Diamond Horseshoe. And then the Sawdust Trail.
TIMMY. Sounds like our night to howl.
JOHN. That's what it is.

(*He howls.*)

TIMMY. You call that a howl?

(*He howls louder. Now* JOHN *howls. Now* TIMMY. *Now* JOHN. *Now* TIMMY. *Each howl is louder than the last.*)

*Curtain*

# Act I SCENE 3

TIME: *Two A.M. Sunday morning.*
AT RISE: *The apartment is in darkness. From the hallway outside the apartment, we hear* TIMMY *and* JOHN *in loud but dubious harmony.*

TIMMY and JOHN (*offstage*). "Farewell, Piccadilly . . . Hello, Leicester Square . . . It's a long, long way to Tipperary . . . But my heart's right there."
NETTIE (*offstage*). You'll wake the Feldmans.
JOHN (*offstage*). Nothing could wake the Feldmans.

(TIMMY *and* JOHN *laugh.*)

NETTIE (*offstage*). Open the door.
JOHN (*offstage*). Can't find my keys.
TIMMY (*offstage—giggling*). I can't find the door.
NETTIE (*offstage*). Honestly.
JOHN (*offstage*). Where would you be if you were my keys?
NETTIE (*offstage*). Here—I'll do it.
JOHN (*offstage*). Did you ever see such pretty hair?
NETTIE (*offstage*). Stop.
TIMMY (*offstage*). Beautiful hair.

NETTIE (*offstage*). Will you please let me open this door?

(*A key turns. The door opens.* NETTIE, *followed by* JOHN *and* TIMMY, *enters. She turns on the lights.*)

JOHN.  Home to wife and mother.
NETTIE (*to* JOHN). Someday we'll break our necks because you refuse to leave a light.
TIMMY (*sings*). "By the light . . . (JOHN *joins in.*) Of the silvery moon—"
NETTIE.  That's just enough.
JOHN.  Whatever you say, Antoinette.
NETTIE.  I say to bed.
JOHN.  Shank of the evening. (*He grabs her around the waist and manages a squeeze before she breaks away. Ignoring the look of censure she directs at him, he turns to* TIMMY.) No sir, you can't beat a law degree. Springboard for anything.
TIMMY.  So they say.
NETTIE (*to* JOHN). Anyone can be a lawyer. How many people become writers?
JOHN.  That's my point.
NETTIE.  You should be proud to have a son who wants to try something different.
JOHN.  Did I say I wasn't proud of him?
TIMMY.  Abra ka dabra ka deedra slatter-in. (*They regard him.*) The fellow in the red jacket who leads the horses to the post at Jamaica always says that when they reach the starting gate. Abra ka dabra ka deedra slatter-in. And here are your horses for the fifth race . . . Long as you can say it, you're not drunk . . . *Abra ka dabra ka deedra slatter-in.*
JOHN.  Abra ka dabra . . .
TIMMY.  Ka deedra slatter-in.

NETTIE. Honestly.
JOHN. Ka zebra—
TIMMY. Not zebra. Deedra . . . Ka deedra slatter-in . . . Abra ka dabra ka deedra slatter-in.
JOHN. Abra . . . ka dabra . . . ka deedra . . . slatter-in.
TIMMY. Faster.
JOHN. Abra, ka dabra, ka deedra, slatter-in.
TIMMY. Faster.
JOHN. Abra ka dabra ka deedra slatter-in.
NETTIE. Have you both lost your minds?
JOHN. Nothing wrong with us that a little nightcap wouldn't cure.

(*He enters the kitchen.*)

NETTIE (*following him*). I'll nightcap you.
TIMMY. I can't bear to hear married people fight.
JOHN (*to* NETTIE). We ought to go dancing more.
NETTIE. Now I know you're drunk.
TIMMY (*calling from the living room*). Who was it that used to call us The Four Mortons?
JOHN (*calling back*). Harold Bowen.
TIMMY (*staring at the audience*). I wish we were.
JOHN (*to* NETTIE). Remember the first dance I took you to?
NETTIE. Of course.
JOHN. I'll bet you don't.
NETTIE. Of course I do.
TIMMY (*lost in contemplation of the audience*). I have this magical feeling about vaudeville.
JOHN (*to* NETTIE). Where was it, then?
NETTIE. The Crystal Terrace.
JOHN. And what was the first song?
NETTIE. It's too late for quiz games.

TIMMY. It doesn't matter how cheap and tinny the show is . . . Soon as the house lights go down and the band starts up, I could cry.
JOHN (*to* NETTIE). The first song we ever danced to was "Pretty Baby." A blond guy crooned it.
NETTIE. Through a gold megaphone.
JOHN. You *do* remember.
NETTIE. Of course.

(JOHN *moves to touch* NETTIE. *To elude him, she re-enters the living room. He follows.*)

TIMMY (*to the audience—à la Smith and Dale*[1]). "I've got snew in my blood" . . . "What's snew?" . . . "Nothing. What's snew with you?"
NETTIE (*to* JOHN—*indicating* TIMMY). What's he doing?
JOHN. Playing the Palace.
TIMMY (*to the audience*). "Take off the coat, my boy . . . Take . . . off . . . the . . . coat . . . Tay-ake . . . o-f-f-f . . . the coat-t-t-t-t."
JOHN and TIMMY. "The coat is off."
NETTIE (*to* TIMMY). Will you please go to bed?
TIMMY (*to the audience*). In closing I would like to do a dance made famous by the inimitable Pat Rooney.
(*Nods to* JOHN.) Maestro, if you please.

(JOHN *begins to hum "The Daughter of Rosie O'Grady" as both he and* TIMMY *dance in the manner of Pat Rooney.*)

---

[1] *Smith and Dale*: an old vaudeville team, famous for a routine featuring many puns.

NETTIE.  John! Timmy! (*They stop dancing.*) Mama expects us at twelve.
TIMMY (*to the audience*).  We're running a bit long, folks: No dance tonight. My mother thanks you. My father thanks you. My sister thanks you. And the Feldmans thank you. (*He goes into Jimmy Durante's closing song.*) "Good night . . . Good night . . . Good night—"
NETTIE.  *Good night.*
TIMMY (*kisses* NETTIE).  Good night, Mrs. Cleary—whoever you are.
NETTIE.  Good night, dear.
TIMMY (*to* JOHN—*indicating the audience*).  Tough house, but I warmed them up for you.
JOHN.  Thanks.
TIMMY.  Don't look now, but your leg's broken.
JOHN.  The show must go on.
TIMMY (*to* NETTIE—*indicating* JOHN).  Plucky lad. (*Extends his hand to* JOHN.) Honor to share the bill with you.
JOHN (*shaking with him*).  Likewise.
TIMMY.  Sleep well, chaps.
JOHN.  Night, Champ.
NETTIE.  Sure you don't want an Alka Seltzer?
TIMMY.  Abra ka dabra ka deedra slatter-in . . . see you in the morning.
JOHN.  With the help of God.
TIMMY (*moving toward his room*).  Abra ka dabra ka deedra slatter-in . . . Abra ka dabra ka deedra slatter-in . . . And here are your horses for . . .

(*He enters his room, closes the door.*)

NETTIE.  Home two days and both nights to bed like that.
JOHN.  He's entitled. You should hear some of the things

he's been through. They overran one of those concentration camps—
NETTIE. I don't want to hear about it now.
JOHN. You're right. It's no way to end a happy evening.
NETTIE. I think we have some aspirin in the kitchen.

(*She moves into the kitchen. He follows, watches her take a bottle of aspirin from a cabinet.*)

JOHN. You didn't say anything before about a headache.
NETTIE. I don't have a headache.
JOHN. Then what—
NETTIE. I read that if you put an aspirin in cut flowers they keep longer. (*She drops an aspirin in the vase, regards the roses.*) I wonder what made you get them?
JOHN. I don't know.
NETTIE. There must have been some reason.
JOHN. I just thought it would be nice to do.

(*She turns to him.*)

NETTIE. It was.

(*They regard each other a moment.*)

JOHN. I like your dress.
NETTIE. You've seen it before.
JOHN. It looks different . . . Everything about you looks different.
NETTIE. What Mass are you going to?

JOHN. Ten o'clock.
NETTIE (*picking up the vase of roses and starting toward the living room*). I better set the alarm.
JOHN. Nettie? (*She turns to him.*) I had a good time tonight.
NETTIE. So did I.

(NETTIE *enters the living room and places the roses on a table.*)

JOHN (*following her into the living room*). Did you really? Or were you putting it on for his sake?
NETTIE. I really did.
JOHN. So did I.
NETTIE. I'll set the alarm for nine-fifteen.

(*She starts away again.*)

JOHN. Now that he's back we'll have lots of good times.

(*She stops.*)

NETTIE. What's wrong between you and I has nothing to do with him.
JOHN. I didn't say it did.
NETTIE. We have to solve our own problems.
JOHN (*coming up behind her*). Of course.
NETTIE. They can't be solved in one night.
JOHN (*touching her*). I know.
NETTIE. One nice evening doesn't make everything different.
JOHN. Did I say it did?

(*His lips brush the nape of her neck.*)

NETTIE. I guess you don't understand.
JOHN. I forgot how nice you smelled.
NETTIE. You'll spoil everything.
JOHN. I want things right between us.
NETTIE. You think this is going to make them right?
JOHN (*his hand moving to her breasts*). We have to start some place.
NETTIE (*breaking away*). Start?
JOHN. Bless us and save us.
NETTIE. *That's not my idea of a start.*
JOHN. Nettie, I want you . . . I want you like I never wanted anything in my life.
NETTIE (*covering her ears*). Stop.
JOHN. *Please?*
NETTIE. You're drunk.
JOHN. *Do you think I could ask again if I wasn't?*
NETTIE. I'm not one of your hotel lobby whores.
JOHN. If you were I wouldn't have to ask.
NETTIE. A couple of drinks, a couple of jokes, and let's jump in bed.
JOHN. Maybe that's my mistake.
NETTIE. How do you suppose Ruskin managed without you today?
JOHN. Maybe you don't want to be asked!

(*He seizes her.*)

NETTIE. Let me alone.
JOHN (*as they struggle*). *You've had the drinks! You've had the jokes!*

NETTIE.   *Stop!*

(*She breaks free of him; regards him for a moment, then picks up the vase of roses and hurls them against the floor. The impact is shattering. They both freeze. For a moment there is silence. Now* TIMMY's *door opens.*)

TIMMY (*entering*).   What happened?
NETTIE.   The roses . . . I knocked them over.
TIMMY.   Sounded like a bomb.
NETTIE.   I'm sorry I woke you. (TIMMY *bends to pick up a piece of the vase.*) Don't . . . I'll clean up. You go back to bed. (*He hesitates.*) Please.
TIMMY.   All right . . . Good night.
NETTIE.   Good night.
TIMMY.   Good night, Pop.

(JOHN, *his back to* TIMMY, *remains silent.* TIMMY *hesitates a moment, then goes off to his room and closes his door.*)

NETTIE (*to* JOHN).   You moved me this afternoon . . . When you brought the roses, I felt something stir I thought was dead forever. (*Regards the roses on the floor.*) And now this . . . I don't understand.
JOHN (*without turning*).   I had nothing to do with the roses . . . They were *his* idea.

(*She bends and starts to pick up the roses.*)

*Curtain*

## Act II SCENE 1

Time: *Nine-fifteen a.m. Sunday morning.*
At Rise: JOHN *and* NETTIE *are at the breakfast table.*

JOHN.  Coffee's weak.
NETTIE.  Add water.
JOHN.  I said *weak* . . . Waste of time bringing good coffee into this house . . . (*He looks for a reaction. She offers none.*) I'm thinking about renting the lake house this summer . . . (*Still no reaction from her.*) Business is off . . . (*Still no reaction.*) Well, what do you say?
NETTIE.  About what?
JOHN.  Renting the lake house.
NETTIE.  Timmy will be disappointed.
JOHN.  How about you?
NETTIE.  I'm in favor of it.
JOHN.  Of course you are.
NETTIE.  I wonder why.

(TIMMY *enters.*)

TIMMY.  Morning.

NETTIE. Good morning.

(TIMMY *kisses her.*)

TIMMY (*to* JOHN). Morning.
JOHN. Nice of you to join us.
TIMMY. My pleasure.
JOHN. This isn't a hotel. We have our meals at certain times.

(TIMMY *now senses his father's irritation.*)

TIMMY. You should have woke me.
NETTIE (*to* TIMMY). It's all right.
JOHN. Of course it is.
NETTIE (*to* TIMMY, *who regards his father puzzledly*). Sit down. (TIMMY *sits.*) What do you want?
TIMMY. Coffee.
NETTIE. Just coffee?
TIMMY. Stomach's a bit shaky.
NETTIE. You should have taken that Alka Seltzer.
TIMMY. I'll be all right.
JOHN. Two days—two hangovers. Is that what they taught you in the army?
TIMMY (*to* JOHN). Cream, please? (JOHN *passes the cream.*) Thank you.
JOHN. I'm thinking of renting the lake house.
TIMMY. How come?
JOHN. I can use the money.
TIMMY. Oh . . .
JOHN. That all you're going to say?

TIMMY. What do you expect me to say?
JOHN. I thought that house meant something to you.
TIMMY. It does. But if you need the money—
JOHN. A bunch of strangers sleeping in our beds, using our things—doesn't bother you at all?
TIMMY. If it has to be it has to be.
JOHN. Of course! I forgot! What's a little summer cottage, after the earth-shattering things you've been through?
TIMMY (*to* NETTIE—*holding up the cream pitcher*). Do you have more cream?
NETTIE (*taking the pitcher*). Yes.
JOHN. What do you want more cream for?
TIMMY. Coffee's strong.
JOHN. It's weak.
TIMMY. It's too strong for me. (NETTIE *returns the refilled pitcher to him.*) Thanks.

(*He adds cream to his coffee.*)

JOHN. A few months in the army and they're experts on everything. Even coffee.
TIMMY. Who said that?
JOHN. By the time I was your age I was in the coffee business nine years . . . Nine years . . . When I was seventeen they sent me to Brazil for three months.
TIMMY. I know.
JOHN. I'd never even been out of New York before but I went down there on my own and did my job.
TIMMY. For Emerson, wasn't it?
JOHN. No uniform. No buddies. No Uncle Sam to lean on. Just myself . . . All alone in that strange place.
TIMMY. That's the time you grew the mustache to look older.

JOHN. Who's telling the story?
TIMMY. Sorry.
JOHN. Thirty-five years in the business and *he's* going to tell me about coffee.
TIMMY. I wasn't telling you anything about anything. I just said that for me, the coffee was too strong.
JOHN. It isn't strong!
TIMMY (*to* NETTIE). What time's dinner?
NETTIE. Mama expects us at twelve.
JOHN. I suppose you'll wear your uniform.
TIMMY. It's the only thing I have that fits.
JOHN. Are you sure? I mean maybe you haven't grown as much as you think.

(TIMMY, *studiously trying to avoid a fight, turns to* NETTIE.)

TIMMY. Ravioli?
NETTIE. And meat balls.
JOHN. G.I. Bill, home loans, discharge bonus, unemployment insurance—you boys did pretty well for yourselves.
NETTIE. They did pretty well for us, too.
JOHN (*sings*). "Oh, say can you see."
TIMMY. What's your point, Pop?
JOHN. The war's over.
TIMMY. I'll buy that.
JOHN. The world doesn't owe anyone a living—including veterans.
TIMMY. I'll buy that too.
JOHN. Let the Jews support you.
TIMMY. Come again?
JOHN. Wasn't for them we wouldn't have gotten in it in the first place.

TIMMY. I thought you broke that record.
JOHN. Lousy kikes.
NETTIE. John!
TIMMY (*to* NETTIE). I changed my mind—I'll have some toast.
JOHN (*to* TIMMY). Don't tell me you've lost your great love for the Jews?
NETTIE. *Stop it!*
TIMMY (*to* NETTIE). It's all right.
JOHN. How nice of you to let me talk in my own house. And me not even a veteran.
TIMMY. Would you mind telling me what you're mad about?
JOHN. Who's mad?
NETTIE (*to* TIMMY). Anything on the toast?
TIMMY. Honey, if you've got it.
JOHN. A man states a few facts and right away he's mad.
NETTIE (*at the cupboard*). How about strawberry jam?
TIMMY. No.
JOHN. If I get a halfway decent offer I might sell the lake house.
NETTIE. Peach?
TIMMY. All right.
JOHN. Hurry up with your breakfast.
TIMMY. What for?
JOHN. Mass starts in twenty minutes and you're not even dressed.
TIMMY. Mass?
JOHN. Mass.
TIMMY. I haven't been to Mass in over two years. You know that.
JOHN. Lots of bad habits you boys picked up that you'll have to get over.
TIMMY. Not going to Mass isn't a habit I picked up. It's a decision I came to after a lot of thought.

JOHN. What way is that for a Catholic to talk?
TIMMY. I haven't considered myself a Catholic for quite a while.
JOHN. Must be something wrong with my ears.
NETTIE (*to* JOHN). You knew this was coming. Why pretend it's such a shock?
JOHN. Now there's a familiar alliance. (*To* TIMMY.) So you've outgrown the Faith?
TIMMY. It doesn't answer my needs.
JOHN. Outgrown your old clothes and outgrown the Faith.
TIMMY. Pop, will you listen to me—
JOHN. Billions of people have believed in it since the beginning of time but it's not good enough for you.
TIMMY. It's not a question of good enough.
JOHN. What do you say when people ask what religion you are?
TIMMY. Nothing.
JOHN. You say you're nothing?
TIMMY. Yes.
JOHN. The Clearys have been Catholics since . . . since the beginning of time. And now you, a Cleary, are going to tell people that you're nothing?
TIMMY. Yes.
JOHN. *You're an atheist!*
NETTIE. John!
JOHN. When you come to the blank after religion on those college applications, put down atheist. Make a big hit in those Ivy League places, from what I hear.
TIMMY. I'm not an atheist.
JOHN. Then what are you?
TIMMY. I don't know . . . But I'd like a chance to find out.
JOHN. You don't know what you believe in?
TIMMY. Do *you?*
JOHN. Yes.
TIMMY. Tell me . . . Well, go on!

JOHN. I believe in the Father, the Son and the Holy Ghost . . . I believe that God created man in his own image . . . I—

TIMMY. Pop, look . . . if your faith works for you, I'm glad. I'm very glad. I wish it worked for me . . . But it doesn't.

JOHN. Do you believe in God—yes or no?

TIMMY. I don't believe in Heaven, or Hell, or Purgatory, or—

JOHN. *Yes or no?*

TIMMY. I believe there's something bigger than myself. What you call it or what it is I don't know.

JOHN. Well, this is a fine how-do-you-do.

NETTIE (*to* JOHN). Yesterday you said he was a man. A man has a right to decide such things for himself.

JOHN. "Good morning, Father Riley." "Good morning, Mr. Cleary. I understand your boy's out of service." "Yes, Father." "Where is he this fine Sunday morning, Mr. Cleary?" "Home, Father." "Is he sick, Mr. Cleary?" "No, Father." "Then why isn't he here in church, Mr. Cleary?" "He's become an atheist, Father."

TIMMY. I'm not an atheist!

JOHN. Whatever you are, I won't have it! I'm the boss of this house. If you want to go on living here you'll do as I say. And I say you're going to church with me this morning.

NETTIE (*to* JOHN). *Do you know what you're doing?*

JOHN (*to* NETTIE). Keep out! (*To* TIMMY.) Well?

NETTIE (*to* TIMMY). Don't pay any attention to him.

TIMMY (*to* NETTIE). It's all right. (*To* JOHN.) I'll go to church with you. (*Rises.*) Be out in a minute.

(*He starts from the room.*)

JOHN. Forget it!

TIMMY. What?

JOHN. I said forget it. The Lord doesn't want anybody in His house who has to be dragged there. (*To* NETTIE *as he puts on his jacket.*) Score another one for your side.

TIMMY. It has nothing to do with her.

JOHN (*to* TIMMY). Wait till you're down on all fours someday—you'll be glad to see a priest then.

(*He starts out.*)

NETTIE. We'll meet you at Mama's.

JOHN. I won't be there.

NETTIE. She expects us.

JOHN. We all have our disappointments.

TIMMY. I said I'd go with you.

(JOHN *exits, slamming the door.*)

NETTIE. Now what was that all about?

TIMMY (*furious with himself*). I should have gone with him.

NETTIE. I'll never understand that man.

TIMMY. Why didn't I just go? Why did I have to make an issue?

NETTIE. It wasn't your fault.

TIMMY. It never *is*.

NETTIE. When he's in one of those moods there's nothing anyone can do.

TIMMY. The alliance, he called us.

NETTIE. Everyone's entitled to their own beliefs.

TIMMY. That's what we must seem like to him—an alliance. Always two against one. Always us against him . . . Why?

NETTIE. If you're through eating, I'll clear the table.
TIMMY. Didn't you hear me?
NETTIE. Evidently your father's not the only one who got up on the wrong side of the bed this morning.
TIMMY. *I'm not talking about this morning.*
NETTIE. There's no need to shout.
TIMMY. You, and him, and me, and what's been going on here for twenty years . . . It's got to stop.
NETTIE. What's got to stop?
TIMMY. We've got to stop ganging up on him.
NETTIE. Is that what we've been doing?
TIMMY. You said you've never understood him.
NETTIE. And never will.
TIMMY. Have you ever really tried? . . .
NETTIE. Go on.
TIMMY. Have you ever tried to see things from his point of view?
NETTIE. What things?
TIMMY. The lake house, for instance.
NETTIE. The lake house?
TIMMY. It's the pride and joy of his life and you're always knocking it.
NETTIE. Do you know why?
TIMMY. Because he bought it without consulting you.
NETTIE. Drove me out to this Godforsaken lake. Pointed to a bungalow with no heat or hot water and said, "That's where we'll be spending our summers from now on."
TIMMY. An hour's ride from New York City isn't exactly Godforsaken.
NETTIE. It wasn't an hour's ride twenty years ago.
TIMMY. The point is, would he have gotten it any other way? If he had come to you and said he wanted to buy a cottage on a lake in New Jersey, would you have said yes?
NETTIE. I might have.

TIMMY. No. Not if it had been a palace with fifty servants.
NETTIE. I don't like the country.
TIMMY. We'd have spent every summer right here.
NETTIE. My idea of a vacation is to travel—see something new.
TIMMY. You had a chance to see Brazil.
NETTIE. That was different.
TIMMY. The fellow who took that job is a millionaire today.
NETTIE. And still living in Brazil.
TIMMY. Which is not to be compared with the Bronx.
NETTIE. So it's my fault we're not millionaires.
TIMMY. Who knows—your mother might have loved Brazil! (*This causes her to turn from him.*) You violently objected to moving from Yorkville to the Bronx . . . Why?
NETTIE (*clearing the table in an effort to avoid him.*) I hate the Bronx.
TIMMY (*pursuing her*). But you insisted that your mother move up here.
NETTIE. They tore down her building. She had to move somewhere.
TIMMY. Except for summers at the lake, have you ever gone two days without seeing her?
NETTIE. Only because of Willis. (*He starts from the room.*) Where are you going?
TIMMY. To get dressed. Then I'm going to church and apologize to him for acting like a fool.
NETTIE. You'll be at Mama's for dinner?
TIMMY. Only if he'll come with me.
NETTIE. You disappointed Willis yesterday. You can't do it again.
TIMMY. Oh yes I can!
NETTIE. How cruel.
TIMMY. Not as cruel as your dragging me over there every day when I was little. And when I was bigger, and

couldn't go every day, concentrating on Sunday. "Is it too much to give your crippled cousin one day a week?" And when I didn't go there on Sunday, I felt so guilty that I couldn't enjoy myself anyway . . . I hate Sunday, and I don't think I'll ever get over it. But I'm going to try.

NETTIE. How fortunate for the cripples in this world that everyone isn't as selfish as you.

TIMMY. Why do you keep calling him a cripple? That's not the worst thing wrong with Willis. It's his mind. He's like a four-year-old.

NETTIE. Can a four-year-old read a book?

TIMMY (*pressing his attack relentlessly*). Yes, he reads. After you drilling him every day for twenty years. But does he have any idea what he's reading about? . . . If you and the rest of them over there want to throw your lives away on him, you go ahead and do it! But don't try and sacrifice me to the cause! (NETTIE, *stunned by* TIMMY's *assault, exits from the kitchen, disappears into the bedroom. Immediately regretful at having vented his feelings so strongly,* TIMMY *moves into the living room; is pondering the best way to apologize, when* NETTIE, *carrying a pocketbook, appears, takes a coat from the hall closet, puts it on.*) Where are you going? (*No answer.*) Your mother doesn't expect us till twelve. (*No answer.*) Give me a minute to dress and I'll go with you. (*No answer.*) Now look—(*As* NETTIE *reaches for her pocketbook,* TIMMY *also reaches for it in an effort to prevent her departure. He wrests it from her. As he does so, his face registers surprise.*) This is like lead. (*He opens the bag, regards the contents, looks at her puzzledly.*) You've got all your coins in here . . . You're taking your coins . . . What for? (*She extends her hand for the bag. He surrenders it. She moves toward the door.*) Will you please say something?

NETTIE. Thank you for the roses.

(*She exits.*)

*Curtain*

# Act II SCENE 2

TIME: *Ten P.M. Sunday.*
AT RISE: TIMMY, *highball glass in hand, whiskey bottle on the coffee table before him, sits on the sofa in the living room. It is plain that he has been drinking for some time.* JOHN, *cold sober, moves about the room nervously.*

TIMMY. I remember sitting here like this the night she went to have John.
JOHN. Why would she just walk out and not tell anyone where she was going?

TIMMY.  I was six.

JOHN.  Without any reason.

TIMMY.  Dr. Goldman came at midnight and took her to the hospital.

JOHN.  It doesn't make sense.

TIMMY.  After they left, I started to cry. You did too.

JOHN.  It's not like her.

TIMMY.  I asked you if you loved her. You nodded. I asked you to say it. You hesitated. I got hysterical. To quiet me you finally said, "I love her."

JOHN.  Maybe she's at Sophie's.

TIMMY.  No. (JOHN *regards him questioningly*.) I called Sophie.

JOHN (*looking at a pocket watch*).  It's after ten.

TIMMY.  I called everybody.

JOHN.  She's been gone twelve hours.

TIMMY.  They all said they'd call back if they heard from her.

JOHN.  If she's not here by eleven o'clock I'm calling the police.

TIMMY.  I wonder what difference it would have made if John lived.

JOHN.  I wonder what department you call.

TIMMY.  I remember you and I going to visit her at the hospital on a Sunday afternoon. I had to wait downstairs. First time I ever heard the word incubator . . . Incubator.

JOHN.  I guess you call Missing Persons.

TIMMY.  As we left the hospital and started down the Concourse, we ran into an exotic Spanish-looking woman whom you'd met on one of your trips to Brazil. She was a dancer. Very beautiful. You and she spoke awhile and then you and I went to a movie. Fred Astaire and Ginger Rogers in *Flying Down to Rio*.

JOHN.  What are you talking about?

TIMMY.  I always thought that was a coincidence—meeting a South American woman and then seeing a picture about Rio . . . *Was* it a coincidence?
JOHN.  What?
TIMMY (*sings*).  "Hey Rio, Rio by the sea-o. Got to get to Rio and I've got to make time."
JOHN.  You're drunk.
TIMMY.  Abra ka dabra ka deedra slatter-in.
JOHN.  Fine time you picked for it.
TIMMY.  A bunch of chorus girls stood on the wings of a silver plane singing that song—"Hey Rio. Flying down to Rio—"
JOHN.  You're the last one who saw her. The police will want to question you.
TIMMY.  She left the house at ten A.M., your Honor. Didn't say boo but I assumed she was going to her mother's. Brown coat. Brown hat. When I got to her mother's, she wasn't there. They hadn't seen her—hadn't heard from her. I had two helpings of ravioli and meat balls. Came back here to wait. When she didn't call by three o'clock I started to worry—
JOHN.  And drink.
TIMMY.  *When she didn't call by three o'clock I started to worry* . . . I tried to get in touch with my father. Called all the bars I could think of—"Is Mr. Cleary there?" . . . "If he comes in would you please tell him to call his house?" . . . It was like old times.
JOHN.  I told you—I had dinner and went to a movie.
TIMMY.  "*Is* Mr. Cleary there?"—Shows how long I've been away. You never say, "*Is* Mr. Cleary there?" You say, "Let me speak to Mr. Cleary." As though you *knew* he was there.
JOHN.  I was at a movie.
TIMMY.  Did it have a happy ending?
JOHN.  *Gilda*, with Rita Hayworth and Glenn Ford.
TIMMY.  I didn't ask you what it was.

JOHN. At the Loew's Paradise.
TIMMY. *I didn't ask you what it was!*
JOHN. What's the matter with you?
TIMMY (*about to pour another drink*). Join me?
JOHN. No, and I think you've had enough.
TIMMY. First time I ever saw you refuse a drink.
JOHN. I want you to stop.
TIMMY. But you're powerless to stop me. It's a lousy position to be in, *I* know.
JOHN. That's your last one.

(*He starts to remove the bottle.*)

TIMMY. Take it and I leave!

(JOHN *hesitates, puts the bottle down.*)

JOHN. Joy, joy, said Mrs. Malloy.
TIMMY. Louder louder, said Mrs. . . . What rhymes with louder?
JOHN. You were sick Friday night. Sick last night.

(*The phone rings. By the time* TIMMY *gets to his feet* JOHN *is picking up the receiver.*)

JOHN (*on the phone*). Hello? . . . Oh . . . (*The abrupt disinterest in his voice causes* TIMMY *to sit down.*) Nothing . . . I said we haven't heard anything . . . I know how long she's been gone . . . Of course I'm concerned

... *I don't care how I sound—I'm concerned* ... *If she's not here by eleven, that's what I'm going to do* ... *That's a comforting bit of information.* (*He hangs up, returns to the living room.*) Her mother again. Wanted to let me know how many muggings there's been lately.

TIMMY. I've got it! Earl Browder.

JOHN. What?

TIMMY. Louder, louder, and Mrs. Earl Browder.

JOHN. I'm glad you can take the whole thing so calmly.

TIMMY. To quote a famous authority: "I don't care how I sound—I'm concerned."

JOHN (*regards his watch*). Ten after ten.

TIMMY. Trouble with you is you haven't had enough experience in these matters.

JOHN. Where the devil can she be?

TIMMY. I'm an old hand.

JOHN. Never done anything like this before in her life.

TIMMY. All those nights I lay in bed waiting for your key to turn in the door. Part of me praying you'd come home safe, part of me dreading the sound of that key because I knew there'd be a fight.

JOHN. I'll give her a few minutes more.

TIMMY. All those mornings I woke up sick. Had to miss school. The boy's delicate, everyone said, has a weak constitution.

JOHN. I'll give her till half-past.

TIMMY. From the day I left this house I was never sick. Not once. Took me a long time to see the connection.

JOHN. Where can she go? She has no money.

TIMMY. Wrong.

JOHN. What?

TIMMY. Nothing.

JOHN. You said wrong.

TIMMY (*sings*). "Hey Rio. Rio by the—"

JOHN. I want to know what you meant.
TIMMY. She took her coins. (JOHN *goes into the bedroom*.)
TIMMY (*quietly*). "Hey Rio. Rio by the sea-o."

(JOHN *reappears*.)

JOHN. Why didn't you mention it before?
TIMMY. Slipped my mind.
JOHN. Over fifty dollars in dimes and quarters, and she took them all.
TIMMY. Person could go quite a ways with fifty dollars.
JOHN. You saw her take them?
TIMMY. Yes.
JOHN. Didn't it strike you as peculiar?
TIMMY. Everything strikes me as peculiar.
JOHN. There's something you're not telling me.
TIMMY. We all have our little secrets.
JOHN. There *is* something!
TIMMY. Take you and your money for instance.
JOHN. I want to know what it is.
TIMMY. For all I know, we're millionaires.
JOHN. I want to know why she walked out.
TIMMY. Just between us chickens, how much do you have?

(TIMMY *reaches for the bottle to pour another drink, but* JOHN *snatches it out of his reach*.)

JOHN. Answer me.
TIMMY. If you don't put that bottle down, I'm leaving.
JOHN. I want an answer!
TIMMY (*rising*). See you around the pool hall.

JOHN (*shoving him down hard on the sofa*). *I want an answer!*
TIMMY. Hell of a way to treat a veteran.
JOHN. I've taken all the crap from you I'm going to.
TIMMY. You want an answer. I want a drink. It's a deal.

(*He reaches for the bottle but* JOHN *keeps it from him.*)

JOHN. First the answer.
TIMMY. I forget the question.
JOHN. Why did your mother leave this house? . . . Well?
TIMMY. We had an argument.
JOHN. About what?
TIMMY. I don't remember.
JOHN. Probably something to do with your drinking.
TIMMY. Yes, that's what it was. She said I drank too much
JOHN. She's right.
TIMMY. Yes.
JOHN. I never thought I'd see the day when you and she would argue.
TIMMY. Neither did I.
JOHN. She didn't say where she was going? Just took the coins and left?
TIMMY. That's right.
JOHN. Beats me.

(*He starts toward the kitchen.*)

TIMMY. Where you going?
JOHN. To get something to eat.
TIMMY. *Eat?*
JOHN. I didn't have any supper.

TIMMY. A minute ago you were so worried you couldn't even sit down.
JOHN. I'm just going to have a sandwich.
TIMMY. Have a banquet!
JOHN. What are you getting mad at *me* for? You're the one who argued with her.
TIMMY. Which absolves you completely! She might jump off a bridge but *your* conscience is clear!
JOHN. A person doesn't take a bunch of change along if they're planning to do something like that.
TIMMY. *She thanked me for the roses!* (JOHN *just looks at him.*) Don't you have any consideration for other people's feelings?
JOHN. Consideration?
TIMMY. Don't you know how much it pleased her to think they were from you?
JOHN. *You* talk about consideration?
TIMMY. How could you do it?
JOHN. Do you have any idea how I looked forward to this morning? To Mass, and dropping in at Rafferty's afterwards with you in your uniform?
TIMMY. Always the injured party.
JOHN. You'll be the injured party in about two minutes.
TIMMY. I already am.
JOHN. Real rough you had it. Good food. Good clothes. Always a roof over your head.
TIMMY. Heigh-ho, everybody, it's count-your-blessings time.
JOHN. I'll tell you what rough is—being so hungry you begged. Being thrown out in the street with your few sticks of furniture for all the neighbors to enjoy. Never sleeping in a bed with less than two other people. Always hiding from collectors. Having to leave school at the age of ten because your father was crippled for life and it was your job to support the house . . . You had it rough, all right.

TIMMY. The subject was roses.
JOHN. Where I couldn't have gone with your advantages . . . What I couldn't have been.
TIMMY. I still want to know why you told her about the roses.
JOHN. We were having words and it slipped out.
TIMMY. Words about what? . . . Well?
JOHN. Stop pushing or I'll tell you.
TIMMY. Go on! Go on!
JOHN. *The humping I'm getting is not worth the humping I'm getting.*
TIMMY (*rising*). You pig.
JOHN. I'm warning you!
TIMMY. *You pig.* (JOHN's *right hand shoots out, catches* TIMMY *hard across the side of his face.* NETTIE *enters.*) Bon soir. (NETTIE *regards them with an air of detached curiosity.*) Had one too many . . . Lost my ka deedra slatter-in.

(NETTIE *removes her hat and coat.*)

JOHN. Where have you been? (NETTIE *lays her hat, coat and pocketbook on a chair in the foyer.*) I was about to call the police. (NETTIE *gives no indication that she even hears him.*) I want to know where you've been. (NETTIE *moves through the living room, stops in front of* TIMMY, *who has just poured himself another drink.*) Are you going to tell me where you've been?
NETTIE. You wouldn't believe me.
JOHN. Of course I'd believe you.
NETTIE (*to* TIMMY). You don't look well.
TIMMY. Appearances are deceiving—I feel terrible.
JOHN. Why wouldn't I believe you?

NETTIE. You just wouldn't.
JOHN. Tell me and see.
NETTIE. I went to the movies.
JOHN. Go on.
NETTIE. That's it.
JOHN. You just went to the movies?
NETTIE. That's right.
JOHN. You've been gone over twelve hours.
NETTIE. I stayed for several shows.
JOHN. Are you trying to tell me you were at a movie for twelve hours?
NETTIE. I knew you wouldn't believe me.
TIMMY. *I* believe you.
NETTIE. Thank you.
TIMMY. What did you see?
NETTIE. That means you *don't* believe me.
TIMMY. No, I guess not.
JOHN. I demand to know where you were.
NETTIE. I went to the Hotel Astor, picked up a man, had a few drinks, a few jokes, went to his room and—
JOHN. Stop it!
NETTIE. I was just getting to the best part.
JOHN. You're making a fool of yourself.
NETTIE. Is there anything I could say that you *would* believe?
TIMMY. Say you took a bus downtown, walked around, visited a museum, had dinner, went to Radio City, and came home.
NETTIE. I took a bus downtown, walked around, visited a museum, had dinner . . .
TIMMY. Went to Radio City and came home.
NETTIE. Went to Radio City and came home.
TIMMY. I'll buy that. (*To* JOHN.) If you had any sense you'd buy it, too.

JOHN. I don't have any sense. I'm just a poor, ignorant slob whose wife's been missing twelve hours—and I want to know where she was.

TIMMY. What difference does it make?

JOHN. Stay out of this!

TIMMY. How?

JOHN (*to* NETTIE). What are you going to tell your mother?

NETTIE. Nothing.

JOHN. The poor woman's almost out of her mind.

TIMMY. There's a joke there some place.

JOHN. At least call her and say you're home.

NETTIE. She'll want an explanation. When I tell her, she won't believe me any more than you did.

JOHN. I'll believe you when you tell the truth.

TIMMY. What *is* truth? (JOHN *shoots him a furious glance.*) Sorry.

NETTIE. I'll tell you this . . . In all my life, the past twelve hours are the only real freedom I've ever known.

TIMMY. Did you enjoy it?

NETTIE. Every moment.

TIMMY. Why did you come back?

NETTIE. I'm a coward.

JOHN. *Will somebody tell me what's going on?*

TIMMY (*to the audience*). You heard the question. (*He peers out into the theatre, points.*) Up there in the balcony. The bearded gentleman with the . . . (*He stops abruptly, rubs his stomach, regards the audience wanly.*) Sorry, folks, but I'm about to be ill.

(*He hastens offstage.* NETTIE *follows him.* JOHN *takes advantage of her absence to examine her pocketbook, is going through it when she returns.*)

NETTIE. He wouldn't let me hold his head, ordered me out of the bathroom, locked the door.

JOHN. What happened to your coins?
NETTIE. I spent them.
JOHN. How?
NETTIE. I took a bus downtown, walked around, visited a museum—

(JOHN *interrupts her by slamming the pocketbook to the table.*)

JOHN. Wasn't for his drinking, none of this would have happened.
NETTIE. Why do you say that?
JOHN. If he didn't drink, you and he wouldn't have argued. (*She regards him uncomprehendingly.*) Isn't that why you left? Because you had an argument about his drinking?
NETTIE. We had an argument, but it wasn't about drinking.
JOHN. What was it about?
NETTIE. You, mostly.
JOHN. Go on.
NETTIE. He thinks I don't give you enough credit . . . Feels you're quite a guy . . . Said we had to stop ganging up on you.

(JOHN *turns away.*)

*Curtain*

## Act II SCENE 3

Time: *Two A.M. Monday.*
At Rise: *The apartment is in darkness. Now a crack of light appears beneath the door to* TIMMY's *room. The door opens.* TIMMY, *in pajamas, emerges, goes to the living room, turns on a lamp which reveals* NETTIE, *in nightgown and robe, sitting on the sofa.*

NETTIE. I couldn't sleep.
TIMMY. Neither could I. Came out to get a magazine.
NETTIE. You feel all right?
TIMMY. Yes.

(*He looks through a pile of magazines, selects one.*)

NETTIE. What time is it?
TIMMY. Almost two . . . Are *you* all right?
NETTIE. Yes.

TIMMY. Well, I guess I'll turn in. (*She offers no comment.*) Good night.

(*Again, no response. He starts away.*)

NETTIE. Isn't there something you want to tell me?
TIMMY. As a matter of fact there is . . . but it'll keep till morning.
NETTIE. You've decided to leave.
TIMMY. Yes.
NETTIE. When?
TIMMY. It's not a sudden decision.
NETTIE. When are you leaving?
TIMMY. In the morning. (*He looks for a comment from her, but she remains silent.*) This fellow I went to high school with has a flat on Twenty-second Street. His roommate just got married and he's looking for a replacement. I figured . . . (*He becomes aware that she isn't listening.*) Hey . . . (*Still no reaction.*) Hey. (*She regards him absently.*) Give you a penny for them.
NETTIE. An apple core.
TIMMY. What?
NETTIE. An apple core . . . I was due to start working for a law firm. Passed all the interviews and had been notified to report for work the following Monday . . . On Sunday, my sister and I were walking in the park when a blond boy who had a crush on me but was too bashful to speak, demonstrated his affection by throwing an apple core which struck me here. (*She indicates the area beneath her left eye.*) When I woke up Monday morning, I had the most beautiful black eye you ever saw. Too embarrassed to start a new job looking like that, I called in sick. They called back to say the

position had been filled by someone else . . . The next job I found was the one that brought your father and I together . . . I often think of that apple core and wonder what my life would be like if it had never been thrown.

TIMMY. Everyone wonders about things like that.

NETTIE. I was going in early to type up some dictation I'd taken the night before . . . Front Street was deserted . . . As I walked, I had the sensation of being watched . . . I glanced up at the office I was passing and saw this young man, your father, staring down . . . He regarded me intensely, almost angrily, for a moment, then suddenly realized I was looking back at him and turned away . . . In that moment, I knew that that young man and I were not suited to each other . . . And at the same time I knew we would become involved . . . that it was inevitable.

TIMMY. Why? You had others to choose from.

NETTIE. Oh yes . . . All gentle, considerate men. All very much like my father . . . One of them was the baker from Paterson, New Jersey, that we always joke about.

TIMMY. The fellow who brought a hatbox full of pastries whenever he called on you.

NETTIE. Yes . . . What a sweet man . . . How he begged me to marry.

TIMMY. What was it that drew you to Pop?

NETTIE. I think it was his energy . . . a certain wildness. He was not like my father at all . . . I was attracted . . . and I was afraid. I've always been a little afraid of him . . . And then he was clearly a young man who was going places. Twenty-four when I met him and making well over a hundred a week. Great money in those days and his prospects were unlimited . . . Money was never plentiful in our house. We weren't poor like his people, you understand. Never without rent, or food, or tickets to the opera, or nice clothes. But still we weren't well-to-do . . . My father brought home stories from the hotel about the various bigwigs who came in and what they wore and how they talked and acted. And we went to the opera. And we had friends who were cultured. Musical Sunday afternoons. Those were Papa's happiest moments . . . Yes, I liked good things. Things that the baker from Paterson and the others could never give me . . . But your father surely would. The way he was going he would be a millionaire . . . That was his dream, you know—to be a millionaire by the time he was forty . . . Nineteen twenty-nine took care of that. He was never quite the same afterwards . . . But when I met him he was cock of the walk. Good-looking, witty young Irishman. Everyone liked him and those who didn't at least feared him because he was a fierce fellow. Everyone wanted to go into business with him. Everyone wanted to be social with him . . . He was immediately at home on a ship, a train . . . in any bar. Strangers thought he was magnificent. And he *was* . . . as long as the situation was impersonal . . . At his best in an impersonal situation . . . But that doesn't include the home, the family . . . The baker from Paterson was all tongue-tied outside, but in the home he would have been beautiful . . . Go to bed now.

(*He kisses her on the forehead.*)

TIMMY. Want the light off?
NETTIE. Please.

(*He moves to the lamp, is about to turn it off, hesitates.*)

TIMMY. When I left this house three years ago, I blamed *him* for everything that was wrong here . . . When I came home, I blamed *you* . . . Now I suspect that no one's to blame . . . Not even me. (*He turns the light off.*) Good night.
NETTIE. Good night.

(TIMMY *exits into his room, closes the door. For a moment there is silence. Then* . . .)

NETTIE. "Who loves you, Nettie?" . . . "You do, Papa." . . . "Why, Nettie?" "Because I'm a nice girl, Papa."

*Curtain*

## Act II SCENE 4

Time: *Nine A.M. Monday.*
At Rise: JOHN *and* NETTIE *are in the kitchen.*

JOHN. One word from you . . . That's all it would take.
NETTIE. I'm not so sure.
JOHN. Try.
NETTIE. No.
JOHN. Do you want him to go?
NETTIE. No.
JOHN. Then say something before it's too late.
NETTIE. What do you want for breakfast?
JOHN. Who cares about breakfast?
NETTIE. Timmy's having scrambled eggs.
JOHN. *Am I the only one who's upset by what's going on here?*
NETTIE. No.
JOHN. Then how can you just stand there?
NETTIE. Would you feel better if I wept?
JOHN. You'll weep when he's gone.

NETTIE. But not now.
JOHN. All I want you to do is tell him how you feel.
NETTIE. He knows that.
JOHN. You won't speak to him.
NETTIE. I can't.
JOHN. You're the one who'll miss him most . . . With me it's different. I've got my business.
NETTIE. I envy you.
JOHN. Just ask him to wait a couple of days and think it over.
NETTIE. After a couple of days, we'd be used to having him around. It would be that much harder to see him leave.
JOHN. He might change his mind. Might not want to leave.
NETTIE. He has to leave sometime.
JOHN. But not now. Not like this.
NETTIE. Twenty-second Street isn't the end of the world.
JOHN. If he leaves this house today I don't want to see him ever again!
NETTIE. If you say that to him, make it clear that you're speaking for yourself.
JOHN. Who's this fellow he's moving in with?
NETTIE. A boy he knew at high school.
JOHN. Everything he wants right here—food, clothing, a room of his own. And he has to move into a dirty cold-water flat.
NETTIE. I think I understand his feeling.
JOHN. Home two days and gone again. The neighbors will have a field day.
NETTIE. I'm going in to call him now.
JOHN. I want to see him alone.
NETTIE. If you're wise you won't start a row.
JOHN. *I want to see him alone.*
NETTIE. All right.

(*She goes inside, knocks at* TIMMY's *door.*)

TIMMY'S VOICE.  Come in.

(*She enters the room, closes the door after her.*)

JOHN (*addresses* TIMMY's *place at the table*).  I understand you've decided to leave us . . . (*Not satisfied with this opening, he tries another.*) What's this nonsense about your leaving? . . . (*And another.*) Your mother tells me you're moving out. I would like to know why. (*The first part of this opening pleases him, the last part doesn't. He tries variations on it.*) I *demand* to know why . . . Would you be so good as to tell me why? . . . Why, God-damn it?

(*He is puzzling over these various approaches when* TIMMY *enters the kitchen.*)

TIMMY.  Good morning.
JOHN.  Morning.
TIMMY.  Mother said you wanted to see me.
JOHN.  Sleep well?
TIMMY.  Yes.
JOHN.  Good . . .
TIMMY.  You wanted to see me?
JOHN.  Mother says you're leaving.
TIMMY.  Yes.
JOHN.  Rather sudden, isn't it?
TIMMY.  Not really.
JOHN.  Mind telling me why?
TIMMY.  I just think it's best.
JOHN.  For who?
TIMMY.  Everyone.

JOHN. Crap! (TIMMY *starts from the room.*) Wait. (*The note of entreaty in his voice causes* TIMMY *to halt.*) I didn't mean that . . . The fact is I don't blame you for wanting to leave. I had no business hitting you.
TIMMY. That's not why I'm going.
JOHN. If there was any way I could undo last night, I would.
TIMMY. It's not a question of last night.
JOHN. If I had to do it over again I'd cut my arm off.
TIMMY. Pop, listen—
JOHN. I don't know what gets into me sometimes.
TIMMY. Pop! (JOHN *looks at him.*) I'm not leaving because of anything that happened last night . . . I always intended to leave.
JOHN. You never mentioned it.
TIMMY. I planned to stay a couple of weeks and then go.
JOHN. A couple of days isn't a couple of weeks.
TIMMY. It's not like I'm going to China.
JOHN. Why two days instead of two weeks?
TIMMY. Because I know that if I stay two weeks I'll *never* leave.
JOHN. If it's what I said yesterday, about me being the boss and you'd have to do what I said—forget it.
TIMMY. It's not that.
JOHN. I was just letting off steam.
TIMMY. *It's not that.*
JOHN. As far as I'm concerned you're a man—you can come and go as you please, do as you please. That goes for religion, drinking, anything.
TIMMY. How can I make you understand?
JOHN. Even girls. I know how it is to be your age. Give me a little advance notice and I'll see that you have the house to yourself whenever you want.
TIMMY. Pop, for Chrisake.

JOHN (*flares momentarily*). *What kind of language is that?* (*Then hastily.*) I'm sorry. I didn't mean that. Talk any way you want.
TIMMY. I don't know what to say to you.
JOHN. What I said yesterday about the Jews, I was just trying to get a rise out of you.
TIMMY. I know.
JOHN. The time those bums from Saint Matthew's jumped the I-cash-clothes man. I was the one who saved him.
TIMMY. I know.
JOHN. Whole crowd of people watching but I was the only one who did anything.
TIMMY. Do you think I could forget that?
JOHN. Stay another week. Just a week.
TIMMY. I can't.
JOHN. Stay till Wednesday.
TIMMY. No.
JOHN. Do you have any idea how your mother looked forward to your coming home?
TIMMY. Yes.
JOHN. Then how can you do it?
TIMMY. We're just going around in circles.
JOHN. What happens to the lake house?
TIMMY. What do you mean?
JOHN. Without you, what's the good of it?
TIMMY. I'll be spending time there.
JOHN. I thought we'd have a real summer together like before the war.
TIMMY. You're making this a lot tougher than it has to be.
JOHN. *Did you expect me to say nothing? Like her?* . . .
TIMMY. Are you through?
JOHN (*trying a new tack*). I know what the trouble is. You know what the trouble is? You're like me . . . Stubborn . . . All the Clearys are stubborn . . . Would rather die than admit a mistake . . . Is that a fact? Yes or no?

TIMMY. I don't know.

JOHN (*points to himself*). Well, here's one donkey who's seen the light. I've been wrong in my dealings with you and I admit it.

TIMMY. Pop—

JOHN. Not just wrong last night, but all along. Well, those days are gone forever, and I'll prove it . . . You know how much money I have?

TIMMY. I don't want to know.

JOHN. Fourteen thousand three hundred and fifty-seven dollars.

TIMMY. Pop!

JOHN. Plus a bit more in stocks . . . Now *you* admit that *you* made a mistake—admit you don't really want to leave and we'll forget the whole thing.

TIMMY. I *don't* want to leave.

JOHN. See—

TIMMY. But I'm leaving.

JOHN (*turning away*). *Then go and good riddance!*

TIMMY. Listen to me.

JOHN. The sooner the better.

TIMMY. *Listen to me!* (*Pauses—then goes on quietly, intensely.*) There was a dream I used to have about you and I . . . It was always the same . . . I'd be told that you were dead and I'd run crying into the street . . . Someone would stop me and ask why I was crying and I'd say, "My father's dead and he never said he loved me."

JOHN (*trying unsuccessfully to shut out* TIMMY's *words*). I only tried to make you stay for her sake.

TIMMY. I had that dream again last night . . . Was thinking about it this morning when something occurred to me that I'd never thought of before.

JOHN. She's the one who'll miss you.

TIMMY. It's true you've never said you love me. But it's also true that I've never said those words to you.

JOHN. I don't know what you're talking about.
TIMMY. I say them now—
JOHN. *I don't know what you're talking about.*
TIMMY. I love you, Pop. (JOHN's *eyes squeeze shut, his entire body stiffens, as he fights to repress what he feels.*) *I love you.* (*For another moment,* JOHN *continues his losing battle, then, overwhelmed, turns, extends his arms.* TIMMY *goes to him. Both in tears, they embrace.* NETTIE *emerges from* TIMMY's *room, closes the door with emphasis to alert them to her approach.* TIMMY *and* JOHN *separate hastily.*)
JOHN. What I said about the money—that's strictly between us.
TIMMY. I understand.

(NETTIE *enters the kitchen. If she is aware of anything unusual in their appearance or manner, she doesn't show it.*)

NETTIE. Ready for breakfast? (*They nod.*) Sit down.

(*They sit. She pours the coffee.*)

NETTIE (*to* TIMMY). Your bag is packed and ready to go.
TIMMY. I've changed my mind.
NETTIE. What?
TIMMY. I've changed my mind. I'm going to stay a few more days.
JOHN. I'm afraid that's out of the question. (TIMMY *and* NETTIE *regard him incredulously.*) When you said you were going, I called the painters. They're coming in to do your room tomorrow... You know how hard it is to get the painters. If we don't take them now, it'll be months before they're free again.
TIMMY. Then I guess I better leave as scheduled.
JOHN. I think so. (*To* NETTIE.) Don't you?

NETTIE. ... Yes.

(JOHN *tastes the coffee—scowls.*)

JOHN. I don't know why I bother to bring good coffee into this house. If it isn't too weak, it's too strong. If it isn't too strong, it's too hot. If it isn't ...

*Curtain*

FOR DISCUSSION

## Act I  SCENE 1

1. The opening speeches betray a strong ambivalence—mixture of conflicting emotions—on the part of John and Nettie Cleary, toward each other and toward their son. How would you characterize these emotions? Point to the speeches that establish this mood.
2. The scene indicates that Timmy Cleary had left home to join the army at the age of eighteen. What do you learn of his relations with his parents before this time? What does this suggest about possible future problems?
3. John Cleary interpolates bits of doggerel into the conversation. ("Bless us and save us, said Mrs. Davis.") Why does the playwright have him do this? What effect do you think it has on his wife? Do you get the feeling that he may have been indulging this mannerism throughout their more than two decades of married life?
4. Why does Timmy "alert" his parents before entering the kitchen? How do they react? What does this tell you about the family group?
5. Why do you think Mrs. Cleary reacts so strongly when Timmy repeats his father's doggerel verses about "Mrs. Davis" and "Mrs. Malloy"?
6. Mrs. Cleary indicates in several ways that she is emotionally overwrought and uncertain about her relationship with her son. Point out several of these "giveaways." Why is each of these incidents appropriate and dramatically effective?

7. Note the references to Willis, whom Timmy is supposed to see. Why doesn't the playwright tell us immediately just who Willis is?
8. The dancing incident in this scene is the kind of "business" that actors relish. Why? What do you gather from the way mother and son "kid" each other during the dance?
9. Why does John return unexpectedly? How do you think his wife feels about this?

## Act I  SCENE 2

1. Timmy tells his father that he is sure that he (the father) would have made a good soldier. The father takes it as a compliment, but is it intended entirely as a compliment? Explain.
2. Whose idea was it to present Mrs. Cleary with a bouquet of roses? Why do the father and son agree that they will tell Mrs. Cleary that the idea originated with her husband? How does this symbolize and clarify the basic emotional tensions among these three people?
3. What effect is gained by having John and Nettie reminisce about some of the incidents of their courtship and the early days of their married life?
4. Note that toward the close of this scene, after a good deal of intervening talk, the playwright returns to the theme of the roses. Why does he do this?

## Act I  SCENE 3

1. How does this scene develop the idea that there is a deep rift between the husband and the wife?
2. What does Nettie mean when she says, "What's wrong between you and I has nothing to do with him"?
3. Incidentally, why does the playwright have Nettie use the self-consciously "genteel" (and grammatically incorrect) form "between you and I"?
4. How does Nettie's action in breaking the vase with the roses foreshadow the late developments in the play? Is this an effective "first act curtain"? Explain.

## Act II  SCENE 1

1. This scene shows a sharp shift in John Cleary's mood toward his son. How would you characterize the change? Do you think it is psychologically sound?
2. What is the dramatic purpose of John's crudely anti-Semitic remarks? How do his wife and son react?
3. How does the argument between John and Timmy about going to church, with the sudden changes of position on both sides, reveal the growing emotional tensions?
4. In this connection, what does John mean when he says to his wife, "Score another one for your side"?
5. How do the details about the lake house point up what has been happening to this marriage for many years?
6. Toward the end of this scene, we finally learn who Willis is. How does this contribute to the overall psychological atmosphere and the dramatic effect?
7. Imagine that you were the director of this play. How would you want Nettie to deliver the closing line of this scene?

## Act II  SCENE 2

1. At the beginning of this scene, Timmy is talking about his brother who died in infancy, while John is talking about getting in touch with the police to find his wife. What effect is gained by this apparently aimless and non-responsive conversation?
2. This scene develops our knowledge of the reason for the strained, unhappy relations between father and son. Show how the playwright conveys this information.
3. In this scene, Timmy is given the line, "The subject was roses." What is he trying to emphasize to his father by saying this? What does it reveal about his own frame of mind?
4. When Nettie returns after her unexplained 12-hour absence, each of the three members of the family reacts in a characteristic way. Describe the reaction, and indicate in each case whether you think it is psychologically sound, based on what you have learned of the character.

## Act II  SCENE 3

1. In her long reminiscence, Nettie contrasts John with her other suitor—"the baker from Paterson." Why did she choose John? She feels now she might have been happier choosing the baker. Do you agree?
2. Note the closing speech of this scene by Nettie. Whom is she talking to? What event of her early life is she recovering? What does it tell you about her? How does it help to intensify the mood that has been established?

## Act II  SCENE 4

1. At the outset of this scene, John is outspokenly upset about Timmy's impending departure, while Nettie is calm and restrained. Yet, both feel deeply about this. Explain their contrasting reactions in terms of their personalities and of their relations with Timmy and with each other.
2. How does John convey his intense eagerness to have Timmy stay? Is there something pathetic in his efforts to "bribe" his son to stay?
3. Why does Timmy feel that he has to get out quickly—or not at all?
4. Why does John raise again, quite gratuitously, the matter of his anti-Semitic remarks of the previous day?
5. Does it seem strange to you that precisely at this moment when the family group is breaking up, Timmy finally tells his father he loves him, and the two embrace? Or is it psychologically sound?
6. At the very close, there is a sudden change of mind by Timmy about leaving, but John refuses to accept this. Yet, just the moment before, John has been imploring him to stay. How do you interpret John's attitude?

### ABOUT THE PLAY AS A WHOLE

1. *The Subject Was Roses* might be characterized as a representative of the "realistic." What characteristics of the play place it in this general category? How does it differ from other "realistic" plays that you are familiar with?

2. In the introduction, we suggested that the general situation at the outset of *The Subject Was Roses* is not unlike that of a soap opera or even a TV situation comedy. Yet the play is most assuredly not a soap opera, of the kind that you can see any day on your TV screen. Can you explain the characteristics, resources, and values that make this drama of American family life so different from the typical soap opera?

3. Frank Gilroy has been much praised for the quality of the dialogue in *The Subject Was Roses*. One critic has said, "His characters reveal themselves in the authentic accents of the New York Irish middle class. The speech is ethnic without being caricatured, realistic without being flat, emotion-ridden without being incoherent or overwrought." Do you agree? Point to specific speeches that illustrate these characteristics or other characteristics that you have in mind.

4. In telling the history of this play, Mr. Gilroy indicates that one of the great difficulties in putting on the original production (in 1964) was in casting the play's three roles. Actor after actor read for the play, and either turned it down or was turned down. Can you suggest why it was so difficult to find actors capable of filling these roles satisfactorily? Which role do you think would be most difficult to interpret effectively? Do you think that once the right actors have been found, they would be likely to find the roles exceptionally satisfying?

5. In Act Two, Scene Three, Timmy says to his mother, "When I left this house three years ago, I blamed *him* for everything that was wrong here . . . When I came home, I blamed *you* . . . Now I suspect that no one's to blame . . . Not even me." Do you feel that this is a sound observation on what has "gone wrong" with the Cleary family? If "no one is to blame," does this make the situation more or less poignant?

6. Each of the three characters in this play is weighed down with a deep sense of failure, disappointment, lack of personal fulfillment. Which of the characters do you find the most pathetic and worthy of your sympathy? Why?

7. Do you see any hope for the three Clearys? Do you think they can come to terms with their lives and continue to live with a reasonable degree of happiness and dignity? What kinds of adjustments or changes in attitude must they make for this purpose? Apply these questions to each of the three characters.

8. Do you think that this play is well titled? Can you think of another title that might be more suitable than *The Subject was Roses*?
9. Suppose that you were asked to tell in a very few words what *The Subject Was Roses* is all about. What would you say? (Try to pin down the basic theme, without wandering off into details.)

FOR COMPOSITION

1. The relations between Timmy Cleary and parents are, in a sense, an example of that contemporary cliché, the "generation gap." Write an essay on "The Generation Gap As I Know It." If your own experience has been very different from that of the Clearys, see if you can pin down the factors that account for the difference.
2. Do you find the ending of *The Subject Was Roses* dramatically and psychologically satisfying? Discuss in written form some other way (or ways) in which the play might have been resolved.
3. In a play such as this, the characters take on the dimensions of reality. They seem to be actual people, who have not only a past and present but also a future. Write a theme in which you describe the situation of the Clearys a year (or, if you prefer, several years) after the close of the play. Try to base your predictions on what you have learned of the personalities and needs of the three family members.
4. The entire action of this play takes place in a rather ordinary middle-class apartment. The film version, of course, showed many other locales (the streets, a night club, etc.) and also brought in characters who were only mentioned in the dialogue of the play. Do you feel that because of these greater physical resources the film is necessarily more effective than the play? Or less effective? In a composition, discuss the problems—the opportunities, as well as the pitfalls—of converting stage plays into films. For "documentation," you may use not only *The Subject Was Roses* but any other play you know in its original form and which you have seen in a screen version.

# Tennessee Williams

Often the playwrights of twentieth century America have clashed with their middle-class, respectable audiences. From one point of view, the century seems a series of skirmishes in which the writer attacks what he sees as the self-satisfied assumptions of "typical America." Not too surprisingly, the public reacts in outrage or anger, lashing out at the writer, denouncing him as sick, immoral, or decadent. Of all the writers who have incurred the wrath of the public, none has been attacked more ferociously or more often than Tennessee Williams. For many, Williams' name is synonymous with the disturbing subject matter and themes produced by the most alienated of modern artists.

It is surprising, then, to realize that Williams, almost from the beginning of his career, has been among the most popular of American playwrights. *The Glass Menagerie,* his first successful play, long ago took its undisputed place among the classics of the American stage. When the play opened on Broadway in 1945, its acclaim was instant and virtually unanimous. Its popular appeal has been so great and lasting that it has been revived several times both on Broadway and on a major television network.

Williams' detractors, unable to resist the charm of *The Glass Menagerie*, habitually assert that this play is not typical of his work. In actuality, however, there are more similarities than differences between this and other of Williams' plays. Williams has always exhibited a deep sympathy for the outcasts or misfits in modern society. Like Laura Wingfield, his characters often cannot meet and fulfill the demands of the world in which they live; they are too frail, too sensitive, too unique to fit in.

Another character frequently seen in Williams' plays is the impoverished gentlewoman, the lady who, like Laura's mother Amanda, looks to the imagined grandeur of the past to find values she can affirm or an image of herself in which she can take pride. Tom, her son, is an example of the frustrated artist—another type Williams often employs to explore the conflict between the creative person and a materialistic society which he cannot abide.

Finally, the Wingfields' situation—the futile but valiant fight for survival—is a situation repeated in some of Williams' most famous plays, such as *A Streetcar Named Desire* and *Cat on a Hot Tin Roof*. Of his own work, Williams has said, "Every artist has a basic premise pervading his whole life, and that premise can provide the impulse to everything he creates. For me, the dominating premise has been the need for understanding and tenderness and fortitude among individuals trapped by circumstances."[1]

*The Glass Menagerie* is now recognized as one of the most lyrical and moving of American dramas. Williams reveals dramatically how love and hate, closeness and remoteness, are present among members of a family. He has explored this theme so imaginatively that long after you have finished the play, you will remember Amanda, Laura, Tom, and the Gentleman Caller. But Williams' play is true enough to extend beyond the specific characters, the specific family, and the specific situation to say something universal about people.

[1] Lincoln Barnett, "Tennessee Williams," *Life* XXIV (February 18, 1948), p. 113.

# The Glass Menagerie

> "Nobody,
> not even the rain,
> has such small hands"
> —E. E. Cummings

**CHARACTERS**

AMANDA WINGFIELD (*the mother*)
A little woman of great but confused vitality clinging frantically to another time and place. Her characterization must be carefully created, not copied from type. She is not paranoiac, but her life is paranoia.[1] There is much to admire in AMANDA, and as much to love and pity as there is to laugh at. Certainly she has endurance and a kind of heroism, and though her foolishness makes her unwittingly cruel at times, there is tenderness in her slight person.

LAURA WINGFIELD (*her daughter*)
AMANDA, *having failed to establish contact with reality, continues to live vitally in her illusions, but* LAURA'S

---

[1] *paranoiac . . . paranoia:* Paranoia is a mental disorder characterized by delusions of persecution. Williams suggests that Amanda must cope with many setbacks which might make some persons feel persecuted.

*situation is even graver. A childhood illness has left her crippled, one leg slightly shorter than the other, and held in a brace. This defect need not be more than suggested on the stage. Stemming from this,* LAURA'S *separation increases till she is like a piece of her own glass collection, too exquisitely fragile to move from the shelf.*

TOM WINGFIELD (*her son*)
*And the narrator of the play. A poet with a job in a warehouse. His nature is not remorseless, but to escape from a trap he has to act without pity.*

JIM O'CONNOR (*the gentleman caller*)
*A nice, ordinary, young man.*

SCENE: An alley in St. Louis.

TIME: Now and in the Past.

# Production Notes

Being a "memory play," *The Glass Menagerie* can be presented with unusual freedom of convention. Because of its considerably delicate or tenuous material, atmospheric touches and subtleties of direction play a particularly important part. Expressionism and all other unconventional techniques in drama have only one valid aim, and that is a closer approach to truth. When a play employs unconventional techniques, it is not, or certainly shouldn't be, trying to escape its responsibility of dealing with reality, or interpreting experience, but is actually or should be attempting to find a closer approach, a more penetrating and vivid expression of things as they are. The straight realistic play with its genuine frigidaire and authentic ice cubes, its characters that speak exactly as its audience speaks, corresponds to the academic landscape and has the same virtue of a photographic likeness. Everyone should know nowadays the unimportance of the photographic in art: that truth, life, or reality is an organic thing which the poetic imagination can represent or suggest, in essence, only through transformation, through changing into other forms than those which were merely present in appearance.

These remarks are not meant as a preface only to this particular play. They have to do with a conception of a new, plastic theatre which must take the place of the exhausted theatre of realistic conventions if the theatre is to resume vitality as a part of our culture.

## THE SCREEN DEVICE

There is *only one important difference between the original and acting version of the play* and that is the *omission* in the latter of the device which I tentatively included in my *original* script. This device was the use of a screen on which were projected magic-lantern slides bearing images or titles. I do not regret the omission of this device from the present Broadway production. The extraordinary power of Miss Taylor's performance[2] made it suitable to have the utmost simplicity in the physical production. But I think it may be interesting to some readers to see how this device was conceived. So I am putting it into the published manuscript. These images and legends, projected from behind, were cast on a section of wall between the front-room and dining-room areas, which should be indistinguishable from the rest when not in use.

The purpose of this will probably be apparent. It is to give accent to certain values in each scene. Each scene contains a particular point (or several) which is structurally the most important. In an episodic play, such as this, the basic structure or narrative line may be obscured from the audience; the effect may seem fragmentary rather than architectural. This may not be the fault of the play so much as a lack of attention in the audience. The legend or image upon the screen will strengthen the effect of what is merely allusion in the writing and allow the primary point to be made more simply and lightly than if the entire responsibility were on the spoken lines. Aside from this structural value, I think the screen will have a definite emotional appeal, less definable but just as important. An imaginative producer or director may invent many other uses for this device than those indicated in the present script. In fact the possibilities of the device seem much larger to me than the instance of this play can possibly utilize.

## THE MUSIC

Another extra-literary accent in this play is provided by the use of music. A single recurring tune, "The Glass Menagerie," is used to

[2] *Miss Taylor's performance:* Laurette Taylor (1884-1946), famous American actress who portrayed Amanda in the first production of the play on Broadway.

give emotional emphasis to suitable passages. This tune is like circus music, not when you are on the grounds or in the immediate vicinity of the parade, but when you are at some distance and very likely thinking of something else. It seems under those circumstances to continue almost interminably and it weaves in and out of your preoccupied consciousness; then it is the lightest, most delicate music in the world and perhaps the saddest. It expresses the surface vivacity of life with the underlying strain of immutable and inexpressible sorrow. When you look at a piece of delicately spun glass you think of two things: how beautiful it is and how easily it can be broken. Both of those ideas should be woven into the recurring tune, which dips in and out of the play as if it were carried on a wind that changes. It serves as a thread of connection and allusion between the narrator with his separate point in time and space and the subject of his story. Between each episode it returns as reference to the emotion, nostalgia, which is the first condition of the play. It is primarily LAURA'S music and therefore comes out most clearly when the play focuses upon her and the lovely fragility of glass which is her image.

## THE LIGHTING

The lighting in the play is not realistic. In keeping with the atmosphere of memory, the stage is dim. Shafts of light are focused on selected areas or actors, sometimes in contradistinction to what is the apparent center. For instance, in the quarrel scene between TOM and AMANDA, in which LAURA has no active part, the clearest pool of light is on her figure. This is also true of the supper scene, when her silent figure on the sofa should remain the visual center. The light upon LAURA should be distinct from the others, having a peculiar pristine clarity such as light used in early religious portraits of female saints or madonnas. A certain correspondence to light in religious paintings, such as El Greco's,[3] where the figures are radiant in atmosphere that is relatively dusky, could be effectively used throughout the play. (It will also permit a more effective use of the screen.) A free, imaginative use of light can be of enormous value in giving a mobile, plastic quality to plays of a more or less static nature.

T.W.

---

[3] *El Greco:* Sixteenth-century Greek artist who painted many of his important canvases in the Spanish town of Toledo, where the townsfolk called him "the Greek." He is known for his elongated figures and his dramatic effects gained with lighting.

# Part I.
# Preparation for a Gentleman Caller

## Scene 1

The Wingfield apartment is in the rear of the building, one of those vast hive-like conglomerations of cellular living-units that flower as warty growths in overcrowded urban centers of lower middle-class population and are symptomatic of the impulse of this largest and fundamentally enslaved section of American society to avoid fluidity and differentiation and to exist and function as one interfused mass of automatism.

The apartment faces an alley and is entered by a fire escape, a structure whose name is a touch of accidental poetic truth, for all of these huge buildings are always burning with the slow and implacable fires of human desperation. The fire escape is included in the set—that is, the landing of it and steps descending from it.

The scene is memory and is therefore non-realistic. Memory takes a lot of poetic license. It omits some details; others are exaggerated, according to the emotional value of the articles it touches, for memory is seated predominantly in the heart. The interior is therefore rather dim and poetic.

At the rise of the curtain, the audience is faced with the dark, grim rear wall of the Wingfield tenement. This building, which runs parallel to the footlights, is flanked on both sides by dark, narrow alleys which run into murky canyons of tangled clotheslines, garbage cans and the sinister latticework of neighboring fire escapes. It is up and down these side alleys that exterior entrances and exits are made, during the play. At the end of TOM'S opening commentary, the dark tenement wall slowly reveals *(by means of a transparency) the interior of the ground floor Wingfield apartment.*

*Downstage is the living room, which also serves as a sleeping room for* LAURA, *the sofa unfolding to make her bed. Upstage, center, and divided by a wide arch or second proscenium with transparent faded portieres (or second curtain), is the dining room. In an old-fashioned what-not in the living room are seen scores of transparent glass animals. A blown-up photograph of the father hangs on the wall of the living room, facing the audience, to the left of the archway. It is the face of a very handsome young man in a doughboy's First World War cap. He is gallantly smiling, ineluctably smiling, as if to say, "I will be smiling forever."*

*The audience hears and sees the opening scene in the dining room through both the transparent fourth wall of the building and the transparent gauze portieres of the dining room arch. It is during this revealing scene that the fourth wall slowly ascends, out of sight. This transparent exterior wall is not brought down again until the very end of the play, during* TOM'S *final speech.*

*The narrator is an undisguised convention of the play. He takes whatever license with dramatic convention as is convenient to his purposes.*

TOM *enters dressed as a merchant sailor from alley, stage left, and strolls across the front of the stage to the fire escape. There he stops and lights a cigarette. He addresses the audience.*

TOM. Yes, I have tricks in my pocket, I have things up my sleeve. But I am the opposite of a stage magician. He gives you illusion that has the appearance of truth. I give you truth in the pleasant disguise of illusion.

To begin with, I turn back time. I reverse it to that quaint period, the thirties, when the huge middle class of America was matriculating in a school for the blind. Their eyes had failed them, or they had failed their eyes, and so they were having their fingers pressed forcibly down on the fiery Braille alphabet of a dissolving economy.

In Spain there was revolution. Here there was only shouting and confusion.

In Spain there was Guernica.[4] Here there were disturbances of labor, sometimes pretty violent, in otherwise peaceful cities such as Chicago, Cleveland, Saint Louis...

This is the social background of the play.

(MUSIC.)

The play is memory.

Being a memory play, it is dimly lighted, it is sentimental, it is not realistic.

In memory everything seems to happen to music. That explains the fiddle in the wings.

I am the narrator of the play, and also a character in it.

The other characters are my mother, Amanda, my sister, Laura, and a gentleman caller who appears in the final scenes.

He is the most realistic character in the play, being an emissary from a world of reality that we were somehow set apart from.

But since I have a poet's weakness for symbols, I am using this character also as a symbol; he is the long delayed but always expected something that we live for.

There is a fifth character in the play who doesn't appear except in this larger-than-life-size photograph over the mantel.

This is our father who left us a long time ago.

He was a telephone man who fell in love with long distances; he gave up his job with the telephone company and skipped the light fantastic out of town...

The last we heard of him was a picture postcard from Mazatlan, on the Pacific coast of Mexico, containing a message of two words—"Hello—Good-bye!" and no address.

I think the rest of the play will explain itself...

---

[4]*Guernica:* a town bombed during the Spanish Civil War which came to symbolize Fascist cruelty and Republican valor

(AMANDA'S *voice becomes audible through the portieres.*)
(LEGEND ON SCREEN: *"Où Sont les Neiges."*[5])
(*He divides the portieres and enters the upstage area.*)
(AMANDA *and* LAURA *are seated at a drop-leaf table. Eating is indicated by gestures without food or utensils.* AMANDA *faces the audience.* TOM *and* LAURA *are seated in profile.*)
(*The interior has lit up softly and through the scrim we see* AMANDA *and* LAURA *seated at the table in the upstage area.*)

AMANDA (*calling*). Tom?

TOM. Yes, Mother.

AMANDA. We can't say grace until you come to the table!

TOM. Coming, Mother. (*He bows slightly and withdraws, reappearing for a few moments later in his place at the table.*)

AMANDA (*to her son*). Honey, don't *push* with your *fingers*. If you have to push with something, the thing to push with is a crust of bread. And chew — chew! Animals have sections in their stomachs which enable them to digest food without mastication, but human beings are supposed to chew their food before they swallow it down. Eat food leisurely, son, and really enjoy it. A well-cooked meal has lots of delicate flavors that have to be held in the mouth for appreciation. So chew your food and give your salivary glands a chance to function!

(TOM *deliberately lays his imaginary fork down and pushes his chair back from the table.*)

TOM. I haven't enjoyed one bite of this dinner because of your constant directions on how to eat it. It's you that make me rush through meals with your hawk-like attention to every bite I take. Sickening — spoils my appetite

---

[5]*Où Sont les Neiges:* part of a famous poetic line by François Villon which means, "Where are the snows of yesteryear?"

—all this discussion of—animal's secretion—salivary glands—mastication!

AMANDA (*lightly*). Temperament like a Metropolitan star! (*He rises and crosses downstage*.) You're not excused from the table.

TOM. I'm getting a cigarette.

AMANDA. You smoke too much.

(LAURA *rises*.)

LAURA. I'll bring in the blancmange.

(*He remains standing with his cigarette by the portieres during the following*.)

AMANDA (*rising*). No, sister, no, sister—you be the lady this time and I'll be the servant.

LAURA. I'm already up.

AMANDA. Resume your seat, little sister—I want you to stay fresh and pretty—for gentlemen callers!

LAURA. I'm not expecting any gentlemen callers.

AMANDA (*crossing out to kitchenette. Airily*). Sometimes they come when they are least expected! Why, I remember one Sunday afternoon in Blue Mountain—(*Enters kitchenette*.)

TOM. I know what's coming!

LAURA. Yes. But let her tell it.

TOM. Again?

LAURA. She loves to tell it.

(AMANDA *returns with bowl of dessert*.)

AMANDA. One Sunday afternoon in Blue Mountain—your mother received—*seventeen!*—gentlemen callers! Why, sometimes there weren't chairs enough to accommodate them all. We had to send the servant over to bring in folding chairs from the parish house.

TOM (*remaining at portieres*). How did you entertain those gentlemen callers?

AMANDA. I understood the art of conversation!

TOM. I bet you could talk.
AMANDA. Girls in those days *knew* how to talk, I can tell you.
TOM. Yes?

(IMAGE: AMANDA *as a girl on a porch, greeting callers.*)

AMANDA. They knew how to entertain their gentlemen callers. It wasn't enough for a girl to be possessed of a pretty face and a graceful figure — although I wasn't slighted in either respect. She also needed to have a nimble wit and a tongue to meet all occasions.
TOM. What did you talk about?
AMANDA. Things of importance going on in the world! Never anything coarse or common or vulgar. (*She addresses* TOM *as though he were seated in the vacant chair at the table though he remains by portieres. He plays this scene as though he held the book.*) My callers were gentlemen — all! Among my callers were some of the most prominent young planters of the Mississippi Delta — planters and sons of planters!

(TOM *motions for music and a spot of light on* AMANDA.) (*Her eyes lift, her face glows, her voice becomes rich and elegiac.*)
(SCREEN LEGEND: "*Où Sont les Neiges.*")

There was young Champ Laughlin who later became vice-president of the Delta Planters Bank.
Hadley Stevenson who was drowned in Moon Lake and left his widow one hundred and fifty thousand in Government bonds.
There were the Cutrere brothers, Wesley and Bates. Bates was one of my bright particular beaux! He got in a quarrel with that wild Wainwright boy. They shot it out on the floor of Moon Lake Casino. Bates was shot through the stomach. Died in the ambulance on his way to Memphis. His widow was also well-provided for, came into eight or ten thousand acres, that's all. She married him on the rebound — never loved her — carried my picture on him the night he died!

And there was that boy that every girl in the Delta had set her cap for! That beautiful, brilliant young Fitzhugh boy from Greene County!

TOM. What did he leave his widow?

AMANDA. He never married! Gracious, you talk as though all of my old admirers had turned up their toes to the daisies!

TOM. Isn't this the first you've mentioned that still survives?

AMANDA. That Fitzhugh boy went North and made a fortune—came to be known as the Wolf of Wall Street! He had the Midas touch, whatever he touched turned to gold!

And I could have been Mrs. Duncan J. Fitzhugh, mind you! But—I picked your *father!*

LAURA (*rising*). Mother, let me clear the table.

AMANDA. No, dear, you go in front and study your typewriter chart. Or practice your shorthand a little. Stay fresh and pretty!—It's almost time for our gentlemen callers to start arriving. (*She flounces girlishly toward the kitchenette.*) How many do you suppose we're going to entertain this afternoon?

(TOM *throws down the paper and jumps up with a groan.*)

LAURA (*alone in the dining room*). I don't believe we're going to receive any, Mother.

AMANDA (*reappearing, airily*). What? No one—not one? You must be joking! (LAURA *nervously echoes her laugh. She slips in a fugitive manner through the half-open portieres and draws them gently behind her. A shaft of very clear light is thrown on her face against the faded tapestry of the curtains.* MUSIC: *"The Glass Menagerie" under faintly. Lightly.*) Not one gentleman caller? It can't be true! There must be a flood, there must have been a tornado!

LAURA. It isn't a flood, it's not a tornado, Mother. I'm just not popular like you were in Blue Mountain. . . . (TOM *utters another groan.* LAURA *glances at him with a faint, apologetic smile. Her voice catching a little.*) Mother's afraid I'm going to be an old maid.

**The Scene Dims Out with "Glass Menagerie" Music**

# Scene 2

"Laura, Haven't You Ever Liked Some Boy?"

On the dark stage the screen is lighted with the image of blue roses.

Gradually LAURA'S figure becomes apparent and the screen goes out.

The music subsides.

LAURA is seated in the delicate ivory chair at the small claw-foot table.

She wears a dress of soft violet material for a kimono — her hair tied back from her forehead with a ribbon.

She is washing and polishing her collection of glass.

AMANDA appears on the fire escape steps. At the sound of her ascent, LAURA catches her breath, thrusts the bowl of ornaments away and seats herself stiffly before the diagram of the typewriter keyboard as though it held her spellbound.

Something has happened to AMANDA. It is written in her face as she climbs to the landing: a look that is grim and hopeless and a little absurd.

She has on one of those cheap or imitation velvety-looking cloth coats with imitation fur collar. Her hat is five or six years old, one of those dreadful cloche hats that were worn in the late twenties and she is clasping an enormous black patent-leather pocketbook with nickel clasps and initials. This is her full-dress outfit, the one she usually wears to the D.A.R.[1]

Before entering she looks through the door.

She purses her lips, opens her eyes very wide, rolls them upward and shakes her head.

Then she slowly lets herself in the door. Seeing her mother's expression LAURA touches her lips with a nervous gesture.

---

[1] *D.A.R.:* Daughters of the American Revolution. Amanda's membership in this organization suggests that she belongs to a very old family and that the past is a source of much pride for her.

LAURA. Hello, Mother, I was— (*She makes a nervous gesture toward the chart on the wall.* AMANDA *leans against the shut door and stares at* LAURA *with a martyred look.*)

AMANDA. Deception? Deception? (*She slowly removes her hat and gloves, continuing the sweet suffering stare. She lets the hat and gloves fall on the floor—a bit of acting.*)

LAURA (*shakily*). How was the D.A.R. meeting? (AMANDA *slowly opens her purse and removes a dainty white handkerchief which she shakes out delicately and delicately touches to her lips and nostrils.*) Didn't you go to the D.A.R. meeting, Mother?

AMANDA (*faintly, almost inaudibly*). —No. —No. (*Then more forcibly.*) I did not have the strength—to go to the D.A.R. In fact, I did not have the courage! I wanted to find a hole in the ground and hide myself in it forever! (*She crosses slowly to the wall and removes the diagram of the typewriter keyboard. She holds it in front of her for a second, staring at it sweetly and sorrowfully—then bites her lips and tears it in two pieces.*)

LAURA (*faintly*). Why did you do that, Mother? (AMANDA *repeats the same procedure with the chart of the Gregg Alphabet.*) Why are you—

AMANDA. Why? Why? How old are you, Laura?

LAURA. Mother, you know my age.

AMANDA. I thought that you were an adult; it seems that I was mistaken. (*She crosses slowly to the sofa and sinks down and stares at* LAURA.)

LAURA. Please don't stare at me, Mother.

(AMANDA *closes her eyes and lowers her head. Count ten.*)

AMANDA. What are we going to do, what is going to become of us, what is the future?

(*Count ten.*)

LAURA. Has something happened, Mother? (AMANDA *draws a long breath and takes out the handkerchief again. Dabbing process.*) Mother, has—something happened?

AMANDA. I'll be all right in a minute, I'm just bewildered— (*Count five.*)—by life....

LAURA. Mother, I wish that you would tell me what's happened!

AMANDA. As you know, I was supposed to be inducted into my office at the D.A.R. this afternoon. (IMAGE: *A swarm of typewriters.*) But I stopped off at Rubicam's Business College to speak to your teachers about your having a cold and ask them what progress they thought you were making down there.

LAURA. Oh....

AMANDA. I went to the typing instructor and introduced myself as your mother. She didn't know who you were. Wingfield, she said. We don't have any such student enrolled at the school!

I assured her she did, that you had been going to classes since early in January.

"I wonder," she said, "if you could be talking about that terribly shy little girl who dropped out of school after only a few days' attendance?"

"No," I said, "Laura, my daughter, has been going to school every day for the past six weeks!"

"Excuse me," she said. She took the attendance book out and there was your name, unmistakably printed, and all the dates you were absent until they decided that you had dropped out of school.

I still said, "No, there must have been some mistake! There must have been some mix-up in the records!"

And she said, "No—I remember her perfectly now. Her hands shook so that she couldn't hit the right keys! The first time we gave a speed-test, she broke down completely—was sick at the stomach and almost had to be carried into the wash-room! After that morning she never showed up any more. We phoned the house but never got any answer" —while I was working at Famous and Barr, I suppose, demonstrating those— Oh!

I felt so weak I could barely keep on my feet!

I had to sit down while they got me a glass of water!

Fifty dollars' tuition, all of our plans—my hopes and

ambitions for you—just gone up the spout, just gone up the spout like that.

(LAURA *draws a long breath and gets awkwardly to her feet. She crosses to the victrola and winds it up.*)

What are you doing?
LAURA. Oh! (*She releases the handle and returns to her seat.*)
AMANDA. Laura, where have you been going when you've gone out pretending that you were going to business college?
LAURA. I've just been going out walking.
AMANDA. That's not true.
LAURA. It is. I just went walking.
AMANDA. Walking? Walking? In winter? Deliberately courting pneumonia in that light coat? Where did you walk to, Laura?
LAURA. All sorts of places—mostly in the park.
AMANDA. Even after you'd started catching that cold?
LAURA. It was the lesser of two evils, Mother. (IMAGE *Winter scene in park.*) I couldn't go back up. I—threw up—on the floor!
AMANDA. From half past seven till after five every day you mean to tell me you walked around in the park, because you wanted to make me think that you were still going to Rubicam's Business College?
LAURA. It wasn't as bad as it sounds. I went inside places to get warmed up.
AMANDA. Inside where?
LAURA. I went in the art museum and the bird-houses at the Zoo. I visited the penguins every day! Sometimes I did without lunch and went to the movies. Lately I've been spending most of my afternoons in the Jewel-box, that big glass house[2] where they raise the tropical flowers.
AMANDA. You did all this to deceive me, just for deception? (LAURA *looks down.*) Why?

[2] *big glass house:* part of the St. Louis zoo in which fragile or exotic flowers can be viewed

LAURA. Mother, when you're disappointed, you get that awful suffering look on your face, like the picture of Jesus' mother in the museum!
AMANDA. Hush!
LAURA. I couldn't face it.

(*Pause. A whisper of strings.*)
(LEGEND: *"The Crust of Humility."*)

AMANDA (*hopelessly fingering the huge pocketbook*). So what are we going to do the rest of our lives? Stay home and watch the parades go by? Amuse ourselves with the glass menagerie, darling? Eternally play those wornout phonograph records your father left as a painful reminder of him?

We won't have a business career—we've given that up because it gave us nervous indigestion! (*Laughs wearily.*) What is there left but dependency all our lives? I know so well what becomes of unmarried women who aren't prepared to occupy a position. I've seen such pitiful cases in the South—barely tolerated spinsters living upon the grudging patronage of sister's husband or brother's wife!—stuck away in some little mouse-trap of a room—encouraged by one in-law to visit another—little birdlike women without any nest—eating the crust of humility all their life!

Is that the future that we've mapped out for ourselves?
I swear it's the only alternative I can think of!
It isn't a very pleasant alternative, is it?
Of course—some girls *do marry*.

(LAURA *twists her hands nervously.*)

Haven't you ever liked some boy?
LAURA. Yes. I liked one once. (*Rises.*) I came across his picture a while ago.
AMANDA. (*with some interest*). He gave you his picture?
LAURA. No, it's in the yearbook.
AMANDA. (*disappointed*). Oh—a high-school boy.

(SCREEN IMAGE: *Jim as high-school hero bearing a silver cup.*)

LAURA. Yes. His name was Jim. (LAURA *lifts the heavy annual from the claw-foot table.*) Here he is in *The Pirates of Penzance*.[3]

AMANDA (*absently*). The what?

LAURA. The operetta the senior class put on. He had a wonderful voice and we sat across the aisle from each other Mondays, Wednesdays and Fridays in the Aud. Here he is with the silver cup for debating! See his grin?

AMANDA (*absently*). He must have had a jolly disposition.

LAURA. He used to call me—Blue Roses.

(IMAGE: *Blue roses.*)

AMANDA. Why did he call you such a name as that?

LAURA. When I had that attack of pleurosis—he asked me what was the matter when I came back. I said pleurosis—he thought that I said Blue Roses! So that's what he always called me after that. Whenever he saw me, he'd holler, "Hello, Blue Roses!" I didn't care for the girl that he went out with. Emily Meisenbach. Emily was the best-dressed girl at Soldan. She never struck me, though, as being sincere . . . It says in the Personal Section—they're engaged. That's—six years ago! They must be married by now.

AMANDA. Girls that aren't cut out for business careers usually wind up married to some nice man. (*Gets up with a spark of revival.*) Sister, that's what you'll do!

(LAURA *utters a startled, doubtful laugh. She reaches quickly for a piece of glass.*)

LAURA. But, Mother—

AMANDA. Yes? (*Crossing to photograph.*)

---

[3] *The Pirates of Penzance:* a light-hearted operetta by Gilbert and Sullivan

LAURA (*in a tone of frightened apology*). I'm—crippled!

(IMAGE: *Screen.*)

AMANDA. Nonsense! Laura, I've told you never, never to use that word. Why, you're not crippled, you just have a little defect—hardly noticeable, even! When people have some slight disadvantage like that, they cultivate other things to make up for it—develop charm—and vivacity—and—*charm!* That's all you have to do! (*She turns again to the photograph.*) One thing your father had *plenty of*—was *charm!*

(TOM *motions to the fiddle in the wings.*)

*The Scene Fades Out with Music*

# Scene 3

LEGEND ON SCREEN: *"After the fiasco—"*

TOM *speaks from the fire escape landing.*

TOM. After the fiasco at Rubicam's Business College, the idea of getting a gentleman caller for Laura began to play a more and more important part in Mother's calculations.

It became an obsession. Like some archetype of the universal unconscious,[1] the image of the gentleman caller haunted our small apartment. . . .

(IMAGE: *Young man at door with flowers.*)

---

[1] *archetype of the universal unconscious:* a concept of Carl Jung (1875-1961), a psychologist who believed that humans inherit certain images from the history of their race and model elements of their lives on these images

An evening at home rarely passed without some allusion to this image, this spectre, this hope. . . .

Even when he wasn't mentioned, his presence hung in Mother's preoccupied look and in my sister's frightened, apologetic manner—hung like a sentence passed upon the Wingfields!

Mother was a woman of action as well as words. She began to take logical steps in the planned direction.

Late that winter and in the early spring—realizing that extra money would be needed to properly feather the nest and plume the bird—she conducted a vigorous campaign on the telephone, roping in subscribers to one of those magazines for matrons called *The Home-maker's Companion,* the type of journal that features the serialized sublimations of ladies of letters who think in terms of slim, tapering waists, eyes like wood-smoke in autumn, fingers that soothe and caress like strains of music, bodies as powerful as Etruscan sculpture.

(SCREEN IMAGE: *Glamor magazine cover.*)

(AMANDA *enters with phone on long extension cord. She is spotted in the dim stage.*)

AMANDA. Ida Scott? This is Amanda Wingfield!
We *missed* you at the D.A.R. last Monday!
I said to myself: She's probably suffering with that sinus condition! How is that sinus condition?
Horrors! Heaven have mercy!—You're a Christian martyr, yes, that's what you are, a Christian martyr!
Well, I just now happened to notice that your subscription to the *Companion's* about to expire! Yes, it expires with the next issue, honey!—just when that wonderful new serial by Bessie Mae Hopper is getting off to such an exciting start. Oh, honey, it's something that you can't miss! You remember how *Gone With the Wind* took everybody by storm? You simply couldn't go out if you hadn't read it. All everybody *talked* was Scarlett O'Hara. Well,

this is a book that critics already compare to *Gone With the Wind*. It's the *Gone With the Wind* of the post-World War generation! — What? — Burning? — Oh, honey, don't let them burn, go take a look in the oven and I'll hold the wire! Heavens — I think she's hung up!

DIM OUT
(LEGEND ON SCREEN: *"You think I'm in love with continental shoemakers?"*)
(*Before the stage is lighted, the violent voices of* TOM *and* AMANDA *are heard.*)
(*They are quarreling behind the portieres. In front of them stands* LAURA *with clenched hands and panicky expression.*)
(*A clear pool of light on her figure throughout this scene.*)

TOM. What in God's name am I —
AMANDA (*shrilly*). Don't you use that —
TOM. Supposed to do!
AMANDA. Expression! Not in my —
TOM. Ohhh!
AMANDA. Presence! Have you gone out of your senses?
TOM. I have, that's true, *driven* out!
AMANDA. What is the matter with you, you — big — big — IDIOT!
TOM. Look! — I've got *no thing*, no single thing —
AMANDA. Lower your voice!
TOM. In my life here that I can call my OWN! Everything is —
AMANDA. Stop that shouting!
TOM. Yesterday you confiscated my books! You had the nerve to —
AMANDA. I took that horrible novel back to the library — yes! That hideous book by that insane Mr. Lawrence.[2] (TOM *laughs wildly.*) I cannot control the output of diseased

---

[2] *Mr. Lawrence:* D. H. Lawrence (1885-1930), a highly acclaimed English writer whose work initially outraged some because of its advocacy of bodily pleasures

minds or people who cater to them— (TOM *laughs still more wildly.*) BUT I WON'T ALLOW SUCH FILTH BROUGHT INTO MY HOUSE! No, no, no, no, no!

TOM.   House, house! Who pays rent on it, who makes a slave of himself to—

AMANDA (*fairly screeching*).   Don't you DARE to—

TOM.   No, no, *I* mustn't say things! *I've* got to just—

AMANDA.   Let me tell you—

TOM.   I don't want to hear any more! (*He tears the portieres open. The upstage area is lit with a turgid smoky red glow.*)

(AMANDA'S *hair is in metal curlers and she wears a very old bathrobe, much too large for her slight figure, a relic of the faithless Mr. Wingfield.*)
(*An upright typewriter and a wild disarray of manuscripts is on the drop-leaf table. The quarrel was probably precipitated by* AMANDA'S *interruption of his creative labor. A chair lying overthrown on the floor.*)
(*Their gesticulating shadows are cast on the ceiling by the fiery glow.*)

AMANDA.   You *will* hear more, you—

TOM.   No, I won't hear more, I'm going out!

AMANDA.   You come right back in—

TOM.   Out, out, out! Because I'm—

AMANDA.   Come back here, Tom Wingfield! I'm not through talking to you!

TOM.   Oh, go—

LAURA (*desperately*).   —Tom!

AMANDA.   You're going to listen, and no more insolence from you! I'm at the end of my patience!

(*He comes back toward her.*)

TOM.   What do you think I'm at? Aren't I supposed to have any patience to reach the end of, Mother? I know, I know. It seems unimportant to you, what I'm *doing*—what I *want* to do—having a little *difference* between them! You don't think that—

AMANDA. I think you've been doing things that you're ashamed of. That's why you act like this. I don't believe that you go every night to the movies. Nobody goes to the movies night after night. Nobody in their right minds goes to the movies as often as you pretend to. People don't go to the movies at nearly midnight, and movies don't let out at two A.M. Come in stumbling. Muttering to yourself like a maniac! You get three hours' sleep and then go to work. Oh, I can picture the way you're doing down there. Moping, doping, because you're in no condition.

TOM (*wildly*). No, I'm in no condition!

AMANDA. What right have you got to jeopardize your job? Jeopardize the security of us all? How do you think we'd manage if you were—

TOM. Listen! You think I'm crazy *about* the *warehouse?* (*He bends fiercely toward her slight figure.*) You think I'm in love with the Continental Shoemakers? You think I want to spend fifty-five *years* down there in that—*celotex interior!* with—*fluorescent*—*tubes!* Look! I'd rather somebody picked up a crowbar and battered out my brains—than go back mornings! I *go!* Every time you come in yelling that damn *"Rise and Shine!" "Rise and Shine!"* I say to myself, "How *lucky dead* people are!" But I get up. I *go!* For sixty-five dollars a month I give up all that I dream of doing and being *ever!* And you say self—*self's* all I ever think of. Why, listen, if self is what I thought of, Mother, I'd be where he is—GONE! (*Pointing to father's picture.*) As far as the system of transportation reaches! (*He starts past her. She grabs his arm.*) Don't grab at me, Mother!

AMANDA. Where are you going?

TOM. I'm going to the *movies!*

AMANDA. I don't believe that lie!

TOM (*crouching toward her, overtowering her tiny figure. She backs away, gasping*). I'm going to opium dens! Yes, opium dens, dens of vice and criminals' hang-outs,

Mother. I've joined the Hogan gang, I'm a hired assassin, I carry a tommy-gun in a violin case! They call me Killer, Killer Wingfield, I'm leading a double-life, a simple, honest warehouse worker by day, by night a dynamic *czar* of the *underworld, Mother.* I go to gambling casinos, I spin away fortunes on the roulette table! I wear a patch over one eye and a false mustache, sometimes I put on green whiskers. On those occasions they call me—*El Diablo!*[3] Oh, I could tell you things to make you sleepless! My enemies plan to dynamite this place. They're going to blow us all sky-high some night! I'll be glad, very happy, and so will you! You'll go up, up on a broomstick, over Blue Mountain with seventeen gentlemen callers! You ugly—babbling old—*witch*. . . . (*He goes through a series of violent, clumsy movements, seizing his overcoat, lunging to the door, pulling it fiercely open. The women watch him, aghast. His arm catches in the sleeve of the coat as he struggles to pull it on. For a moment he is pinioned by the bulky garment. With an outraged groan he tears the coat off again, splitting the shoulder of it, and hurls it across the room. It strikes against the shelf of* LAURA'S *glass collection, there is a tinkle of shattering glass.* LAURA *cries out as if wounded.*)

(MUSIC. LEGEND: *"The Glass Menagerie."*)

LAURA (*shrilly*). My glass!—menagerie. . . . (*She covers her face and turns away.*)

(*But* AMANDA *is still stunned and stupefied by the "ugly witch" so that she barely notices this occurrence. Now she recovers her speech.*)

AMANDA (*in an awful voice*). I won't speak to you—until you apologize! (*She crosses through portieres and draws*

---

[3] *El Diablo:* Spanish term for the Devil

*them together behind her.* TOM *is left with* LAURA. LAURA *clings weakly to the mantel with her face averted.* TOM *stares at her stupidly for a moment. Then he crosses to shelf. Drops awkwardly on his knees to collect the fallen glass, glancing at* LAURA *as if he would speak but couldn't.)*

"The Glass Menagerie" steals in as The Scene Dims Out

# Scene 4

*The interior is dark. Faint light in the alley.*
*A deep-voiced bell in a church is tolling the hour of five as the scene commences.*

TOM *appears at the top of the alley. After each solemn boom of the bell in the tower, he shakes a little noise-maker or rattle as if to express the tiny spasm of man in contrast to the sustained power and dignity of the Almighty. This and the unsteadiness of his advance make it evident that he has been drinking.*

*As he climbs the few steps to the fire escape landing light steals up inside.* LAURA *appears in night-dress, observing* TOM'S *empty bed in the front room.*

TOM *fishes in his pockets for door-key, removing a motley assortment of articles in the search, including a perfect shower of movie-ticket stubs and an empty bottle. At last he finds the key, but just as he is about to insert it, it slips from his fingers. He strikes a match and crouches below the door.*

TOM (*bitterly*).   One crack—and it falls through!

(LAURA *opens the door.*)

LAURA. Tom! Tom, what are you doing?
TOM. Looking for a door-key.
LAURA. Where have you been all this time?
TOM. I have been to the movies.
LAURA. All this time at the movies?
TOM. There was a very long program. There was a Garbo picture and a Mickey Mouse and a travelogue and a newsreel and a preview of coming attractions. And there was an organ solo and a collection for the milk-fund —simultaneously—which ended up in a terrible fight between a fat lady and an usher!
LAURA (*innocently*). Did you have to stay through everything?
TOM. Of course! And, oh, I forgot! There was a big stage show! The headliner on this stage show was Malvolio the Magician. He performed wonderful tricks, many of them, such as pouring water back and forth between pitchers. First it turned to wine and then it turned to beer and then it turned to whiskey. I know it was whiskey it finally turned into because he needed somebody to come up out of the audience to help him, and I came up—both shows! It was Kentucky Straight Bourbon. A very generous fellow, he gave souvenirs. (*He pulls from his back pocket a shimmering rainbow-colored scarf.*) He gave me this. This is his magic scarf. You can have it, Laura. You wave it over a canary cage and you get a bowl of gold-fish. You wave it over the gold-fish bowl and they fly away canaries. . . . But the wonderfullest trick of all was the coffin trick. We nailed him into a coffin and he got out of the coffin without removing one nail. (*He has come inside.*) There is a trick that would come in handy for me—get me out of this 2 by 4 situation! (*Flops onto bed and starts removing shoes.*)
LAURA. Tom—Shhh!
TOM. What're you shushing me for?
LAURA. You'll wake up Mother.
TOM. Goody, goody! Pay 'er back for all those "Rise an' Shines." (*Lies down, groaning.*) You know it don't take much intelligence to get yourself into a nailed-up coffin,

Laura. But who in hell ever got himself out of one without removing one nail?

(*As if in answer, the father's grinning photograph lights up.*)

SCENE DIMS OUT

(*Immediately following: The church bell is heard striking six. At the sixth stroke the alarm clock goes off in* AMANDA'S *room, and after a few moments we hear her calling: "Rise and Shine! Rise and Shine! Laura, go tell your brother to rise and shine!"*)

TOM (*sitting up slowly*).   I'll rise — but I won't shine.

(*The light increases.*)

AMANDA.   Laura, tell your brother his coffee is ready.

(LAURA *slips into front room.*)

LAURA.   Tom! — It's nearly seven. Don't make Mother nervous. (*He stares at her stupidly. Beseechingly.*) Tom, speak to Mother this morning. Make up with her, apologize, speak to her!
TOM.   She won't to me. It's her that started not speaking.
LAURA.   If you just say you're sorry she'll start speaking.
TOM.   Her not speaking — is that such a tragedy?
LAURA.   Please — please!
AMANDA (*calling from kitchenette*).   Laura, are you going to do what I asked you to do, or do I have to get dressed and go out myself?
LAURA.   Going, going — soon as I get on my coat! (*She pulls on a shapeless felt hat with nervous, jerky movement, pleadingly glancing at* TOM. *Rushes awkwardly for coat. The coat is one of* AMANDA'S, *inaccurately made-over, the sleeves too short for* LAURA.) Butter and what else?
AMANDA (*entering upstage*).   Just butter. Tell them to charge it.

LAURA.  Mother, they make such faces when I do that.
AMANDA.  Sticks and stones can break our bones, but the expression on Mr. Garfinkel's face won't harm us! Tell your brother his coffee is getting cold.
LAURA (*at door*).  Do what I asked you, will you, will you, Tom?

(*He looks sullenly away.*)

AMANDA.  Laura, go now or just don't go at all!
LAURA (*rushing out*).  Going—going! (*A second later she cries out.* TOM *springs up and crosses to door.* AMANDA *rushes anxiously in.* TOM *opens the door.*)
TOM.  Laura?
LAURA.  I'm all right. I slipped, but I'm all right.
AMANDA (*peering anxiously after her*).  If anyone breaks a leg on those fire escape steps, the landlord ought to be sued for every cent he possesses! (*She shuts door. Remembers she isn't speaking and returns to other room.*) (*As* TOM *enters listlessly for his coffee, she turns her back to him and stands rigidly facing the window on the gloomy gray vault of the areaway. Its light on her face with its aged but childish features is cruelly sharp, satirical as a Daumier print.*[1])
(MUSIC UNDER: "*Ave Maria.*")
(TOM *glances sheepishly but sullenly at her averted figure and slumps at the table. The coffee is scalding hot; he sips it and gasps and spits it back in the cup. At his gasp,* AMANDA *catches her breath and half turns. Then catches herself and turns back to window.*)
(TOM *blows on his coffee, glancing sidewise at his mother. She clears her throat.* TOM *clears his. He starts to rise. Sinks back down again, scratches his head, clears his throat again.* AMANDA *coughs.* TOM *raises his cup in both hands to blow on it, his eyes staring over the rim of it at his mother for several moments. Then he slowly sets the cup down and awkwardly and hesitantly rises from the chair.*)

[1] *Daumier:* Honoré Daumier, a nineteenth-century French artist known for his bitingly satiric lithographs

TOM (*hoarsely*). Mother. I—I apologize, Mother. (AMANDA *draws a quick, shuddering breath. Her face works grotesquely. She breaks into childlike tears.*) I'm sorry for what I said, for everything that I said, I didn't mean it.
AMANDA (*sobbingly*). My devotion has made me a witch and so I make myself hateful to my children!
TOM. *No*, you *don't*.
AMANDA. I worry so much, don't sleep, it makes me nervous!
TOM (*gently*). I understand that.
AMANDA. I've had to put up a solitary battle all these years. But you're my right-hand bower! Don't fall down, don't fail!
TOM (*gently*). I try, Mother.
AMANDA (*with great enthusiasm*). Try and you will SUCCEED! (*The notion makes her breathless.*) Why, you— you're just *full* of natural endowments! Both of my children—they're *unusual* children! Don't you think I know it? I'm so—*proud!* Happy and—feel I've—so much to be thankful for but— Promise me one thing, Son!
TOM. What, Mother?
AMANDA. Promise, son, you'll—never be a drunkard!
TOM (*turns to her grinning*). I will never be a drunkard, Mother.
AMANDA. That's what frightened me so, that you'd be drinking! Eat a bowl of Purina!
TOM. Just coffee, Mother.
AMANDA. Shredded wheat biscuit?
TOM. No. No, Mother, just coffee.
AMANDA. You can't put in a day's work on an empty stomach. You've got ten minutes—don't gulp! Drinking too-hot liquids makes cancer of the stomach. . . . Put cream in.
TOM. No, thank you.
AMANDA. To cool it.
TOM. No! No, thank you, I want it black.
AMANDA. I know, but it's not good for you. We have to do all that we can to build ourselves up. In these trying times we live in, all that we have to cling to is—each other. . . . That's why it's so important to— Tom, I— I sent out your sister so I could discuss something with you. If you hadn't spoken I would have spoken to you. (*Sits down.*)

TOM (*gently*). What is it, Mother, that you want to discuss?
AMANDA. Laura!

> (TOM *puts his cup down slowly.*)
> (LEGEND ON SCREEN: *"Laura."*)
> (MUSIC: *"The Glass Menagerie."*)

TOM. —Oh.—Laura . . .
AMANDA (*touching his sleeve*). You know how Laura is. So quiet but—still water runs deep! She notices things and I think she—broods about them. (TOM *looks up.*) A few days ago I came in and she was crying.
TOM. What about?
AMANDA. You.
TOM. Me?
AMANDA. She has an idea that you're not happy here.
TOM. What gave her that idea?
AMANDA. What gives her any idea? However, you do act strangely. I—I'm not criticizing, understand *that!* I know your ambitions do not lie in the warehouse, that like everybody in the whole wide world—you've had to—make sacrifices, but—Tom—Tom—life's not easy, it calls for—Spartan endurance! There's so many things in my heart that I cannot describe to you! I've never told you but I—*loved* your father. . . .
TOM (*gently*). I know that, Mother.
AMANDA. And you—when I see you taking after his ways! Staying out late—and—well, you *had* been drinking the night you were in that—terrifying condition! Laura says that you hate the apartment and that you go out nights to get away from it! Is that true, Tom?
TOM. No. You say there's so much in your heart that you can't describe to me. That's true of me, too. There's so much in my heart that I can't describe to *you*! So let's respect each other's—
AMANDA. But, why—*why*, Tom—are you always so *restless*? Where do you *go* to, nights?
TOM. I—go to the movies.
AMANDA. Why do you go to the movies so much, Tom?
TOM. I go to the movies because—I like adventure. Adven-

ture is something I don't have much of at work, so I go to the movies.

AMANDA. But, Tom, you go to the movies *entirely too much!*

TOM. I like a lot of adventure.

(AMANDA *looks baffled, then hurt. As the familiar inquisition resumes he becomes hard and impatient again.* AMANDA *slips back into her querulous attitude toward him.*)
(IMAGE ON SCREEN: *Sailing vessel with Jolly Roger.*)

AMANDA. Most young men find adventure in their careers.

TOM. Then most young men are not employed in a warehouse.

AMANDA. The world is full of young men employed in warehouses and offices and factories.

TOM. Do all of them find adventure in their careers?

AMANDA. They do or they do without it! Not everybody has a craze for adventure.

TOM. Man is by instinct a lover, a hunter, a fighter, and none of those instincts are given much play at the warehouse!

AMANDA. Man is by instinct! Don't quote instinct to me! Instinct is something that people have got away from! It belongs to animals! Christian adults don't want it!

TOM. What do Christian adults want, then, Mother?

AMANDA. Superior things! Things of the mind and the spirit! Only animals have to satisfy instincts! Surely your aims are somewhat higher than theirs! Than monkeys — pigs —

TOM. I reckon they're not.

AMANDA. You're joking. However, that isn't what I wanted to discuss.

TOM (*rising*). I haven't much time.

AMANDA (*pushing his shoulders*). Sit down.

TOM. You want me to punch in red at the warehouse, Mother?

AMANDA. You have five minutes. I want to talk about Laura.

(LEGEND: *"Plans and Provisions."*)

TOM. All right! What about Laura?

AMANDA. We have to be making some plans and provisions for her. She's older than you, two years, and nothing has happened. She just drifts along doing nothing. It frightens me terribly how she just drifts along.

TOM. I guess she's the type that people call home girls.

AMANDA. There's no such type, and if there is, it's a pity! That is unless the home is hers, with a husband!

TOM. What?

AMANDA. Oh, I can see the handwriting on the wall as plain as I see the nose in front of my face! It's terrifying!

More and more you remind me of your father! He was out all hours without explanation! — then *left! Good-bye!*

And me with the bag to hold. I saw that letter you got from the Merchant Marine. I know what you're dreaming of. I'm not standing here blindfolded.

Very well, then. Then *do* it!

But not till there's somebody to take your place.

TOM. What do you mean?

AMANDA. I mean that as soon as Laura has got somebody to care of her, married, a home of her own, independent — why, then you'll be free to go wherever you please, on land, on sea, whichever way the wind blows you!

But until that time you've got to look out for your sister. I don't say me because I'm old and don't matter! I say for your sister because she's young and dependent.

I put her in business college — a dismal failure! Frightened her so it made her sick at the stomach.

I took her over to the Young People's League at the church. Another fiasco. She spoke to nobody, nobody spoke to her. Now all she does is fool with those pieces of glass and play those worn-out records. What kind of a life is that for a girl to lead?

TOM. What can I do about it?

AMANDA. Overcome selfishness!

Self, self, self is all that you ever think of!

(TOM *springs up and crosses to get his coat. It is ugly and bulky. He pulls on a cap with earmuffs.*)

Where is your muffler? Put your wool muffler on!

(*He snatches it angrily from the closet and tosses it around his neck and pulls both ends tight.*)

Tom! I haven't said what I had in mind to ask you.
TOM.  I'm too late to—
AMANDA (*catching his arm—very importunately. Then shyly*). Down at the warehouse, aren't there some—nice young men?
TOM.  No!
AMANDA.  There *must* be—*some* . . .
TOM.  Mother—(*Gesture.*)
AMANDA.  Find out one that's clean-living—doesn't drink and—ask him out for sister!
TOM.  What?
AMANDA.  For *sister!* To *meet!* Get *acquainted!*
TOM (*stamping to door*).  Oh, my go-osh!
AMANDA.  Will you? (*He opens door. Imploringly.*) Will you? (*He starts down.*) Will you? *Will* you, dear?
TOM (*calling back*).  Yes!

(AMANDA *closes the door hesitantly and with a troubled but faintly hopeful expression.*)
(SCREEN IMAGE: *Glamor magazine cover.*)
(*Spot* AMANDA *at phone.*)

AMANDA.  Ella Cartwright? This is Amanda Wingfield!
How are you, honey?
How is that kidney condition? (*Count five.*)
Horrors! (*Count five.*)
You're a Christian martyr, yes, honey, that's what you are, a Christian martyr!
Well, I just now happened to notice in my little red book that your subscription to the *Companion* has just run out! I knew that you wouldn't want to miss out on the wonderful serial starting in this new issue. It's by Bessie Mae Hopper, the first thing she's written since *Honeymoon for Three.*
Wasn't that a strange and interesting story? Well, this one is even lovelier, I believe. It has a sophisticated,

society background. It's all about the horsey set on Long Island!

*Fade Out*

# Scene 5

LEGEND ON SCREEN: *"Annunciation." Fade with music.*

*It is early dusk of a spring evening. Supper has just been finished in the Wingfield apartment.* AMANDA *and* LAURA *in light-colored dresses are removing dishes from the table, in the upstage area, which is shadowy, their movements formalized almost as a dance or ritual, their moving forms as pale and silent as moths.*

TOM, *in white shirt and trousers, rises from the table and crosses toward the fire escape.*

AMANDA (*as he passes her*). Son, will you do me a favor?

TOM. What?

AMANDA. Comb your hair! You look so pretty when your hair is combed! (TOM *slouches on sofa with evening paper. Enormous caption "Franco Triumphs."*[1]) There is only one respect in which I would like you to emulate your father.

TOM. What respect is that?

AMANDA. The care he always took of his appearance. He never allowed himself to look untidy. (*He throws down the paper and crosses to fire escape.*) Where are you going?

TOM. I'm going out to smoke.

AMANDA. You smoke too much. A pack a day at fifteen cents a pack. How much would that amount to in a month? Thirty times fifteen is how much, Tom? Figure it out and you will be astounded at what you could save. Enough to give you a night-school course in accounting at Wash-

---

[1] *Franco Triumphs:* reference to the outcome of the Spanish Civil War, after which the Fascist general Franco became head of the Spanish government

ington U! Just think what a wonderful thing that would be for you, Son!

(TOM *is unmoved by the thought.*)

TOM. I'd rather smoke. (*He steps out on landing, letting the screen door slam.*)
AMANDA (*sharply*). I know! That's the tragedy of it. . . . (*Alone, she turns to look at her husband's picture.*)

(DANCE MUSIC: *"All the World is Waiting for the Sunrise!"*)

TOM (*to the audience*). Across the alley from us was the Paradise Dance Hall. On evenings in spring the windows and doors were open and the music came outdoors. Sometimes the lights were turned out except for a large glass sphere that hung from the ceiling. It would turn slowly about and filter the dusk with delicate rainbow colors. Then the orchestra played a waltz or a tango, something that had a slow and sensuous rhythm. Couples would come outside, to the relative privacy of the alley. You could see them kissing behind ash-pits and telephone poles.

This was the compensation for lives that passed like mine, without any change or adventure.

Adventure and change were imminent in this year. They were waiting around the corner for all these kids.

Suspended in the mist over Berchtesgaden,[2] caught in the folds of Chamberlain's umbrella—

In Spain there was Guernica!

But here there was only hot swing music and liquor, dance halls, bars, and movies, and sex that hung in the gloom like a chandelier and flooded the world with brief, deceptive rainbows. . . .

All the world was waiting for bombardments!

[2] *Berchtesgaden:* the mountain retreat of Adolf Hitler which Great Britain's Prime Minister Neville Chamberlain visited in 1938. Chamberlain agreed to Hitler's annexation of part of Czechoslovakia as reward for Hitler's promise to commit no further aggression.

(AMANDA *turns from the picture and comes outside.*)

AMANDA (*sighing*). A fire escape landing's a poor excuse for a porch. (*She spreads a newspaper on a step and sits down, gracefully and demurely as if she were settling into a swing on a Mississippi veranda.*) What are you looking at?
TOM. The moon.
AMANDA. Is there a moon this evening?
TOM. It's rising over Garfinkel's Delicatessen.
AMANDA. So it is! A little silver slipper of a moon. Have you made a wish on it yet?
TOM. Um-hum.
AMANDA. What did you wish for?
TOM. That's a secret.
AMANDA. A secret, huh? Well, I won't tell mine either. I will be just as mysterious as you.
TOM. I bet I can guess what yours is.
AMANDA. Is my head so transparent?
TOM. You're not a sphinx.
AMANDA. No, I don't have secrets. I'll tell you what I wished for on the moon. Success and happiness for my precious children! I wish for that whenever there's a moon, and when there isn't a moon, I wish for it, too.
TOM. I thought perhaps you wished for a gentleman caller.
AMANDA. Why do you say that?
TOM. Don't you remember asking me to fetch one?
AMANDA. I remember suggesting that it would be nice for your sister if you brought home some nice young man from the warehouse. I think that I've made that suggestion more than once.
TOM. Yes, you have made it repeatedly.
AMANDA. Well?
TOM. We are going to have one.
AMANDA. What?
TOM. A gentleman caller!

(*The Annunciation is celebrated with music.*)
(AMANDA *rises.*)
(IMAGE ON SCREEN: *Caller with bouquet.*)

AMANDA. You mean you have asked some nice young man to come over?
TOM. Yep. I've asked him to dinner.
AMANDA. You really did?
TOM. I did!
AMANDA. You did, and did he — *accept?*
TOM. He did!
AMANDA. Well, well — well, well! That's — lovely!
TOM. I thought that you would be pleased.
AMANDA. It's definite, then?
TOM. Very definite.
AMANDA. Soon?
TOM. Very soon.
AMANDA. For heaven's sake, stop putting on and tell me some things, will you?
TOM. What things do you want me to tell you?
AMANDA. *Naturally* I would like to know when he's *coming!*
TOM. He's coming tomorrow.
AMANDA. *Tomorrow?*
TOM. Yep. Tomorrow.
AMANDA. But, Tom!
TOM. Yes, Mother?
AMANDA. Tomorrow gives me no time!
TOM Time for what?
AMANDA. Preparations! Why didn't you phone me at once, as soon as you asked him, the minute that he accepted? Then, don't you see, I could have been getting ready!
TOM. You don't have to make any fuss.
AMANDA. Oh, Tom, Tom, Tom, of course I have to make a fuss! I want things nice, not sloppy! Not thrown together. I'll certainly have to do some fast thinking, won't I?
TOM. I don't see why you have to think at all.
AMANDA. You just don't know. We can't have a gentleman caller in a pig-sty! All my wedding silver has to be polished, the monogrammed table linen ought to be laundered! The windows have to be washed and fresh curtains put up. And how about clothes? We have to *wear* something, don't we?
TOM. Mother, this boy is no one to make a fuss over!

AMANDA. Do you realize he's the first young man we've introduced to your sister?
  It's terrible, dreadful, disgraceful that poor little sister has never received a single gentleman caller! Tom, come inside! (*She opens the screen door.*)
TOM. What for?
AMANDA. I want to ask you some things.
TOM. If you're going to make such a fuss, I'll call it off, I'll tell him not to come!
AMANDA. You certainly won't do anything of the kind. Nothing offends people worse than broken engagements. It simply means I'll have to work like a Turk! We won't be brilliant, but we will pass inspection. Come on inside. (TOM *follows, groaning.*) Sit down.
TOM. Any particular place you would like me to sit?
AMANDA. Thank heavens I've got that new sofa! I'm also making payments on a floor lamp I'll have sent out! And put the chintz covers on, they'll brighten things up! Of course I'd hoped to have these walls repapered. . . . What is the young man's name?
TOM His name is O'Connor.
AMANDA. That, of course, means fish—tomorrow is Friday! I'll have that salmon loaf—with Durkee's dressing! What does he do? He works at the warehouse?
TOM. Of course! How else would I—
AMANDA. Tom, he—doesn't drink?
TOM. Why do you ask me that?
AMANDA. Your father *did!*
TOM. Don't get started on that!
AMANDA. He *does* drink, then?
TOM. Not that I know of!
AMANDA. Make sure, be certain! The last thing I want for my daughter's a boy who drinks!
TOM. Aren't you being a little bit premature? Mr. O'Connor has not yet appeared on the scene!
AMANDA. But will tomorrow. To meet your sister, and what do I know about his character? Nothing! Old maids are better off than wives of drunkards!
TOM. Oh, my God!
AMANDA. Be still!

TOM (*leaning forward to whisper*). Lots of fellows meet girls whom they don't marry!
AMANDA. Oh, talk sensibly, Tom—and don't be sarcastic! (*She has gotten a hairbrush.*)
TOM. What are you doing?
AMANDA. I'm brushing that cowlick down!
What is this young man's position at the warehouse?
TOM (*submitting grimly to the brush and the interrogation*). This young man's position is that of a shipping clerk, Mother.
AMANDA. Sounds to me like a fairly responsible job, the sort of a job *you* would be in if you just had more *get-up*.
What is his salary? Have you any idea?
TOM. I would judge it to be approximately eighty-five dollars a month.
AMANDA. Well—not princely, but—
TOM. Twenty more than I make.
AMANDA. Yes, how well I know! But for a family man, eighty-five dollars a month is not much more than you can just get by on....
TOM. Yes, but Mr. O'Connor is not a family man.
AMANDA. He might be, mightn't he? Some time in the future?
TOM. I see. Plans and provisions.
AMANDA. You are the only young man that I know of who ignores the fact that the future becomes the present, the present the past, and the past turns into everlasting regret if you don't plan for it!
TOM. I will think that over and see what I can make of it.
AMANDA. Don't be supercilious with your mother! Tell me some more about this—what do you call him?
TOM. James D. O'Connor. The D. is for Delaney.
AMANDA. Irish on *both* sides! *Gracious!* And doesn't drink?
TOM. Shall I call him up and ask him right this minute?
AMANDA. The only way to find out about those things is to make discreet inquiries at the proper moment. When I was a girl in Blue Mountain and it was suspected that a young man drank, the girl whose attentions he had been receiving, if any girl *was*, would sometimes speak to the minister of his church, or rather her father would if her father was living, and sort of feel him out on the young

man's character. That is the way such things are discreetly handled to keep a young woman from making a tragic mistake!

TOM. Then how did you happen to make a tragic mistake?

AMANDA. That innocent look of your father's had everyone fooled!

He *smiled* — the world was *enchanted!*

No girl can do worse than put herself at the mercy of a handsome appearance!

I hope that Mr. O'Connor is not too good-looking.

TOM. No, he's not too good-looking. He's covered with freckles and hasn't too much of a nose.

AMANDA. He's not right-down homely, though?

TOM. Not right-down homely. Just medium homely, I'd say.

AMANDA. Character's what to look for in a man.

TOM. That's what I've always said, Mother.

AMANDA. You've never said anything of the kind and I suspect you would never give it a thought.

TOM. Don't be so suspicious of me.

AMANDA. At least I hope he's the type that's up and coming.

TOM. I think he really goes in for self-improvement.

AMANDA. What reason have you to think so?

TOM. He goes to night school.

AMANDA (*beaming*). Splendid! What does he do, I mean study?

TOM. Radio engineering and public speaking!

AMANDA. Then he has visions of being advanced in the world!

Any young man who studies public speaking is aiming to have an executive job some day!

And radio engineering? A thing for the future!

Both of these facts are very illuminating. Those are the sort of things that a mother should know concerning any young man who comes to call on her daughter. Seriously or — not.

TOM. One little warning. He doesn't know about Laura. I didn't let on that we had dark ulterior motives. I just said, why don't you come and have dinner with us? He said okay and that was the whole conversation.

AMANDA. I bet it was! You're eloquent as an oyster.
However, he'll know about Laura when he gets here. When he sees how lovely and sweet and pretty she is, he'll thank his lucky stars he was asked to dinner.

TOM. Mother, you mustn't expect too much of Laura.

AMANDA. What do you mean?

TOM. Laura seems all those things to you and me because she's ours and we love her. We don't even notice she's crippled any more.

AMANDA. Don't say crippled! You know that I never allow that word to be used!

TOM. But face facts, Mother. She is and — that's not all —

AMANDA. What do you mean "not all"?

TOM. Laura is very different from other girls.

AMANDA. I think the difference is all to her advantage.

TOM. Not quite all — in the eyes of others — strangers — she's terribly shy and lives in a world of her own and those things make her seem a little peculiar to people outside the house.

AMANDA. Don't say peculiar.

TOM. Face the facts. She is.

(*The dance-hall music changes to a tango that has a minor and somewhat ominous tone.*)

AMANDA. In what way is she peculiar — may I ask?

TOM (*gently*). She lives in a world of her own — a world of — little glass ornaments, Mother. . . . (*Gets up.* AMANDA *remains holding brush, looking at him, troubled.*) She plays old phonograph records and — that's about all — (*He glances at himself in the mirror and crosses to door.*)

AMANDA (*sharply*). Where are you going?

TOM. I'm going to the movies. (*Out screen door.*)

AMANDA. Not to the movies, every night to the movies! (*Follows quickly to screen door.*) I don't believe you always go to the movies! (*He is gone.* AMANDA *looks worriedly after him for a moment. Then vitality and optimism return and she turns from the door. Crossing to portieres.*) Laura! Laura! (LAURA *answers from kitchenette.*)

LAURA. Yes, Mother.
AMANDA. Let those dishes go and come in front! (LAURA *appears with dish towel. Gaily.*) Laura, come here and make a wish on the moon!

(SCREEN IMAGE: *Moon.*)

LAURA (*entering*). Moon—moon?
AMANDA. A little silver slipper of a moon. Look over your left shoulder, Laura, and make a wish!

(LAURA *looks faintly puzzled as if called out of sleep.* AMANDA *seizes her shoulders and turns her at an angle by the door.*)

Now!
Now, darling, *wish!*
LAURA. What shall I wish for, Mother?
AMANDA (*her voice trembling and her eyes suddenly filling with tears*). Happiness! Good fortune!

*The violin rises and the stage dims out.*

*Curtain*

## Part II. The Gentleman Calls

## Scene 6

IMAGE: *High school hero.*

TOM. And so the following evening I brought Jim home to dinner. I had known Jim slightly in high school. In high school Jim was a hero. He had tremendous Irish good nature and vitality with the scrubbed and polished look of white chinaware. He seemed to move in a continual spotlight. He was a star in basketball, captain of the debating club, president of the senior class and the glee club and he sang the male lead in the annual light operas.

He was always running or bounding, never just walking. He seemed always at the point of defeating the law of gravity. He was shooting with such velocity through his adolescence that you would logically expect him to arrive at nothing short of the White House by the time he was thirty. But Jim apparently ran into more interference after his graduation from Soldan. His speed had definitely slowed. Six years after he left high school he was holding a job that wasn't much better than mine.

(IMAGE: *Clerk*.)

He was the only one at the warehouse with whom I was on friendly terms. I was valuable to him as someone who could remember his former glory, who had seen him win basketball games and the silver cup in debating. He knew of my secret practice of retiring to a cabinet of the wash-room to work on poems when business was slack in the warehouse. He called me Shakespeare. And while the other boys in the warehouse regarded me with suspicious hostility, Jim took a humorous attitude toward me. Gradually his attitude affected the others, their hostility wore off and they also began to smile at me as people smile at an oddly fashioned dog who trots across their path at some distance.

I knew that Jim and Laura had known each other at Soldan, and I had heard Laura speak admiringly of his voice. I didn't know if Jim remembered her or not. In high school Laura had been as unobtrusive as Jim had been astonishing. If he did remember Laura, it was not as my sister, for when I asked him to dinner, he grinned and said, "You know, Shakespeare, I never thought of you as having folks!"

He was about to discover that I did. . . .

(*Light up stage*.)
(LEGEND ON SCREEN: "*The Accent of a Coming Foot*.")
(*Friday evening. It is about five o'clock of a late spring evening which comes "scattering poems in the sky*.")
(A *delicate lemony light is in the Wingfield apartment*.)

(AMANDA *has worked like a Turk in preparation for the gentleman caller. The results are astonishing. The new floor lamp with its rose-silk shade is in place, a colored paper lantern conceals the broken light fixture in the ceiling, new billowing white curtains are at the windows, chintz covers are on chairs and sofa, a pair of new sofa pillows make their initial appearance.*)
(*Open boxes and tissue paper are scattered on the floor.*)
LAURA *stands in the middle with lifted arms while* AMANDA *crouches before her, adjusting the hem of the new dress, devout and ritualistic. The dress is colored and designed by memory. The arrangement of* LAURA'S *hair is changed; it is softer and more becoming. A fragile, unearthly prettiness has come out in* LAURA: *she is like a piece of translucent glass touched by light, given a momentary radiance, not actual, not lasting.*)

AMANDA (*impatiently*). Why are you trembling?
LAURA. Mother, you've made me so nervous!
AMANDA. How have I made you nervous?
LAURA. By all this fuss! You make it seem so important!
AMANDA. I don't understand you, Laura. You couldn't be satisfied with just sitting home, and yet whenever I try to arrange something for you, you seem to resist it.

(*She gets up.*)

LAURA. You make it seem like we were setting a trap.
AMANDA. All pretty girls are a trap, a pretty trap, and men expect them to be.

(LEGEND: "*A Pretty Trap.*")

Now look at yourself, young lady. This is the prettiest you will ever be!
I've got to fix myself now! You're going to be surprised by your mother's appearance! (*She crosses through portieres, humming gaily.*)

(LAURA *moves slowly to the long mirror and stares solemnly at herself.*)
(*A wind blows the white curtains inward in a slow, graceful motion and with a faint, sorrowful sighing.*)

AMANDA (*off stage*). It isn't dark enough yet. (*She turns slowly before the mirror with a troubled look.*)

(LEGEND ON SCREEN: *"This Is My Sister: Celebrate Her with Strings!"* MUSIC.)

AMANDA (*laughing, off*). I'm going to show you something. I'm going to make a spectacular appearance!
LAURA. What is it, Mother?
AMANDA. Possess your soul in patience — you will see! Something I've resurrected from that old trunk! Styles haven't changed so terribly much after all. . . .

(*She parts the portieres.*)

Now just look at your mother!

(*She wears a girlish frock of yellowed voile with a blue silk sash. She carries a bunch of jonquils — the legend of her youth is nearly revived. Feverishly.*)

This is the dress in which I led the cotillion. Won the cakewalk twice at Sunset Hill, wore one spring to the Governor's ball in Jackson!
See how I sashayed around the ballroom, Laura?

(*She raises her skirt and does a mincing step around the room.*)

I wore it on Sundays for my gentlemen callers! I had it on the day I met your father —
I had malaria fever all that spring. The change of climate from East Tennessee to the Delta — weakened resistance — I had a little temperature all the time — not enough

to be serious—just enough to make me restless and giddy! —Invitations poured in—parties all over the Delta! "Stay in bed," said Mother, "you have fever!"—but I just wouldn't.—I took quinine but kept on going, going!— Evenings, dances!—Afternoons, long, long rides! Picnics —lovely!—So lovely, that country in May.—All lacy with dogwood, literally flooded with jonquils!—That was the spring I had the craze for jonquils. Jonquils became an absolute obsession. Mother said, "Honey, there's no more room for jonquils." And still I kept on bringing in more jonquils. Whenever, wherever I saw them, I'd say, "Stop! Stop! I see jonquils!" I made the young men help me gather the jonquils! It was a joke, Amanda and her jonquils! Finally there were no more vases to hold them, every available space was filled with jonquils. No vases to hold them? All right, I'll hold them myself! And then I—(*She stops in front of the picture.* MUSIC.) met your father!

Malaria fever and jonquils and then—this—boy....

(*She switches on the rose-colored lamp.*)

I hope they get here before it starts to rain.

(*She crosses upstage and places the jonquils in bowl on table.*)

I gave your brother a little extra change so he and Mr. O'Connor could take the service car home.

LAURA (*with altered look*). What did you say his name was?
AMANDA. O'Connor.
LAURA. What is his first name?
AMANDA. I don't remember. Oh, yes, I do. It was—Jim!

(LAURA *sways slightly and catches hold of a chair.*)
(LEGEND ON SCREEN: "*Not Jim!*")

LAURA (*faintly*). Not—Jim!
AMANDA. Yes, that was it, it was Jim! I've never known a Jim that wasn't nice!

(MUSIC: *Ominous*.)

LAURA.  Are you sure his name is Jim O'Connor?
AMANDA.  Yes. Why?
LAURA.  Is he the one that Tom used to know in high school?
AMANDA.  He didn't say so. I think he just got to know him at the warehouse.
LAURA.  There was a Jim O'Connor we both knew in high school — (*Then, with effort.*) If that is the one that Tom is bringing to dinner — you'll have to excuse me, I won't come to the table.
AMANDA.  What sort of nonsense is this?
LAURA.  You asked me once if I'd ever liked a boy. Don't you remember I showed you this boy's picture?
AMANDA.  You mean the boy you showed me in the yearbook?
LAURA.  Yes, that boy.
AMANDA.  Laura, Laura, were you in love with that boy?
LAURA.  I don't know, Mother. All I know is I couldn't sit at the table if it was him!
AMANDA.  It won't be him! It isn't the least bit likely. But whether it is or not, you will come to the table. You will not be excused.
LAURA.  I'll have to be, Mother.
AMANDA.  I don't intend to humor your silliness, Laura. I've had too much from you and your brother, both!
   So just sit down and compose yourself till they come. Tom has forgotten his key so you'll have to let them in, when they arrive.
LAURA (*panicky*).  Oh, Mother — *you* answer the door!
AMANDA (*lightly*).  I'll be in the kitchen — busy!
LAURA.  Oh, Mother, please answer the door, don't make me do it!
AMANDA (*crossing into kitchenette*).  I've got to fix the dressing for the salmon. Fuss, fuss — silliness! — over a gentleman caller!

(*Door swings shut.* LAURA *is left alone.*)
(LEGEND: *"Terror!"*)
(*She utters a low moan and turns off the lamp, sits stiffly on the edge of the sofa, knotting her fingers together.*)

(LEGEND ON SCREEN: *"The Opening of a Door!"*)
(TOM *and* JIM *appear on the fire escape steps and climb to landing. Hearing their approach,* LAURA *rises with a panicky gesture. She retreats to the portieres.*)
(*The doorbell.* LAURA *catches her breath and touches her throat. Low drums.*)

AMANDA (*calling*). Laura, sweetheart! The door!

(LAURA *stares at it without moving.*)

JIM. I think we just beat the rain.
TOM. Uh-huh. (*He rings again, nervously.*)

(JIM *whistles and fishes for a cigarette.*)

AMANDA (*very, very gaily*). Laura, that is your brother and Mr. O'Connor! Will you let them in, darling?

(LAURA *crosses toward kitchenette door.*)

LAURA (*breathlessly*). Mother—you go to the door!

(AMANDA *steps out of kitchenette and stares furiously at* LAURA. *She points imperiously at the door.*)

LAURA. Please, please!
AMANDA (*in a fierce whisper*). What is the matter with you, you silly thing?
LAURA (*desperately*). Please, you answer it, *please!*
AMANDA. I told you I wasn't going to humor you, Laura. Why have you chosen this moment to lose your mind?
LAURA. Please, please, please, you go!
AMANDA. You'll have to go to the door because I can't!
LAURA (*despairingly*). I can't either!
AMANDA. Why?
LAURA. I'm *sick!*
AMANDA. I'm sick, too—of your nonsense! Why can't you and your brother be normal people? Fantastic whims and behavior!

(TOM *gives a long ring.*)

Preposterous goings on! Can you give me one reason— (*Calls out lyrically.*) COMING! JUST ONE SECOND!—why you should be afraid to open a door? Now you answer it, Laura!

LAURA. Oh, oh, oh . . . (*She returns through the portieres. Darts to the victrola and winds it frantically and turns it on.*)
AMANDA. Laura Wingfield, you march right to that door!
LAURA. Yes—Yes, Mother!

(*A faraway, scratchy rendition of "Dardanella" softens the air and gives her strength to move through it. She slips to the door and draws it cautiously open.*)
(TOM *enters with the caller,* JIM O'CONNOR.)

TOM. Laura, this is Jim. Jim, this is my sister, Laura.
JIM (*stepping inside*). I didn't know that Shakespeare had a sister!
LAURA (*retreating stiff and trembling from the door*). How—how do you do?
JIM (*heartily extending his hand*). Okay!

(LAURA *touches it hesitantly with hers.*)

JIM. Your hand's *cold*, Laura!
LAURA. Yes, well—I've been playing the victrola. . . .
JIM. Must have been playing classical music on it! You ought to play a little hot swing music to warm you up!
LAURA. Excuse me—I haven't finished playing the victrola. . . . (*She turns awkwardly and hurries into the front room. She pauses a second by the victrola. Then catches her breath and darts through the portieres like a frightened deer.*)
JIM (*grinning*). What was the matter?
TOM. Oh—with Laura? Laura is—terribly shy.
JIM. Shy, huh? It's unusual to meet a shy girl nowadays. I don't believe you ever mentioned you had a sister.

TOM. Well, now you know. I have one. Here is the *Post Dispatch*. You want a piece of it?
JIM. Uh-huh.
TOM. What piece? The comics?
JIM. Sports! (*Glances at it.*) Ole Dizzy Dean[1] is on his bad behavior.
TOM (*disinterest*). Yeah? (*Lights cigarette and crosses back to fire escape door.*)
JIM. Where are *you* going?
TOM. I'm going out on the terrace.
JIM (*goes after him*). You know, Shakespeare—I'm going to sell you a bill of goods!
TOM. What goods?
JIM. A course I'm taking.
TOM. Huh?
JIM. In public speaking! You and me, we're not the warehouse type.
TOM. Thanks—that's good news.
   But what has public speaking got to do with it?
JIM. It fits you for—executive positions!
TOM. Awww.
JIM. I tell you it's done a helluva lot for me.

(IMAGE: *Executive at desk.*)

TOM. In what respect?
JIM. In every! Ask yourself what is the difference between you an' me and men in the office down front? Brains?—No!—Ability?—No! Then what? Just one little thing—
TOM. What is that one little thing?
JIM. Primarily it amounts to—social poise! Being able to square up to people and hold your own on any social level!
AMANDA (*off stage*). Tom?
TOM. Yes, Mother.
AMANDA. Well, you just make yourselves comfortable in there.
TOM. Yes, Mother.

[1] *Dizzy Dean*: colorful pitcher for the St. Louis Cardinals who later became a popular sports announcer

AMANDA. Ask Mr. O'Connor if he would like to wash his hands.
JIM. Aw, no—no—thank you—I took care of that at the warehouse. Tom—
TOM. Yes?
JIM. Mr. Mendoza was speaking to me about you.
TOM. Favorably?
JIM. What do you think?
TOM. Well—
JIM. You're going to be out of a job if you don't wake up.
TOM. I am waking up—
JIM. You show no signs.
TOM. The signs are interior.

> (IMAGE ON SCREEN: *The sailing vessel with Jolly Roger again.*)

TOM. I'm planning to change. (*He leans over the rail speaking with quiet exhilaration. The incandescent marquees and signs of the first-run movie houses light his face from across the alley. He looks like a voyager.*) I'm right at the point of committing myself to a future that doesn't include the warehouse and Mr. Mendoza or even a night-school course in public speaking.
JIM. What are you gassing about?
TOM. I'm tired of the movies.
JIM. Movies!
TOM. Yes, movies! Look at them—(*A wave toward the marvels of Grand Avenue.*) All of those glamorous people—having adventures—hogging it all, gobbling the whole thing up! You know what happens? People go to the *movies* instead of *moving!* Hollywood characters are supposed to have all the adventures for everybody in America, while everybody in America sits in a dark room and watches them have them! Yes, until there's a war. That's when adventure becomes available to the masses! *Everyone's* dish, not only Gable's! Then the people in the dark room come out of the dark room to have some adventures themselves—Goody, goody!—It's our turn now, to go to the South Sea Island—to make a safari—to be exotic, far-off!—But I'm not patient. I don't want to

wait till then. I'm tired of the *movies* and I am *about to move!*

JIM (*incredulously*). Move?

TOM. Yes.

JIM. When?

TOM. Soon!

JIM. Where? Where?

(*Theme three music seems to answer the question, while Tom thinks it over. He searches among his pockets.*)

TOM. I'm starting to boil inside. I know I seem dreamy, but inside—well, I'm boiling!—Whenever I pick up a shoe, I shudder a little thinking how short life is and what I am doing!—Whatever that means, I know it doesn't mean shoes—except as something to wear on a traveler's feet! (*Finds paper.*) Look—

JIM. What?

TOM. I'm a member.

JIM (*reading*). The Union of Merchant Seamen.

TOM. I paid my dues this month, instead of the light bill.

JIM. You will regret it when they turn the lights off.

TOM. I won't be here.

JIM. How about your mother?

TOM. I'm like my father. See how he grins? And he's been absent going on sixteen years!

JIM. You're just talking, you drip. How does your mother feel about it?

TOM. Shhh!—Here comes Mother! Mother is not acquainted with my plans!

AMANDA (*enters portieres*). Where are you all?

TOM. On the terrace, Mother.

(*They start inside. She advances to them.* TOM *is distinctly shocked at her appearance. Even* JIM *blinks a little. He is making his first contact with girlish Southern vivacity and in spite of the night-school course in public speaking is somewhat thrown off the beam by the unexpected outlay of social charm.*)

(*Certain responses are attempted by* JIM *but are swept aside by* AMANDA'S *gay laughter and chatter.* TOM *is embarrassed but after the first shock* JIM *reacts very warmly. Grins and chuckles, is altogether won over.*)
(IMAGE: *Amanda as a girl.*)

AMANDA (*coyly smiling, shaking her girlish ringlets*). Well, well, well, so this is Mr. O'Connor. Introductions entirely unnecessary. I've heard so much about you from my boy. I finally said to him, Tom—good gracious!—why don't you bring this paragon to supper? I'd like to meet this nice young man at the warehouse!—Instead of just hearing him sing your praises so much!

I don't know why my son is so stand-offish—that's not Southern behavior!

Let's sit down and—I think we could stand a little more air in here! Tom, leave the door open. I felt a nice fresh breeze a moment ago. Where has it gone to?

Mmm, so warm already! And not quite summer, even. We're going to burn up when summer really gets started.

However, we're having—we're having a very light supper. I think light things are better fo' this time of year. The same as light clothes are. Light clothes an' light food are what warm weather calls fo'. You know our blood gets so thick during th' winter—it takes a while fo' us to *adjust* ou'selves!—when the season changes. . . .

It's come so quick this year. I wasn't prepared. All of a sudden—heavens! Already summer!—I ran to the trunk an' pulled out this light dress—Terribly old! Historical almost! But feels so good—so good an' co-ol, y' know. . . .

TOM. Mother—
AMANDA. Yes, honey?
TOM. How about—supper?
AMANDA. Honey, you go ask Sister if supper is ready! You know that Sister is in full charge of supper!

Tell her you hungry boys are waiting for it.

(*To* JIM.)

Have you met Laura?

JIM. She —
AMANDA. Let you in? Oh, good, you've met already! It's rare for a girl as sweet an' pretty as Laura to be domestic! But Laura is, thank heavens, not only pretty but also very domestic. I'm not at all. I never was a bit. I never could make a thing but angel-food cake. Well, in the South we had so many servants. Gone, gone, gone. All vestige of gracious living! Gone completely! I wasn't prepared for what the future brought me. All of my gentlemen callers were sons of planters and so of course I assumed that I would be married to one and raise my family on a large piece of land with plenty of servants. But man proposes — and woman accepts the proposal! — To vary that old, old saying a little bit — I married no planter! I married a man who worked for the telephone company! — That gallantly smiling gentleman over there! (*Points to the picture.*) A telephone man who — fell in love with long-distance! — Now he travels and I don't even know where! — But what am I going on for about my — tribulations?

Tell me yours — I hope you don't have any! Tom?

TOM (*returning*). Yes, Mother?
AMANDA. Is supper nearly ready?
TOM. It looks to me like supper is on the table.
AMANDA. Let me look — (*She rises prettily and looks through portieres.*) Oh, lovely! — But where is Sister?
TOM. Laura is not feeling well and she says that she thinks she'd better not come to the table.
AMANDA. What? — Nonsense! — Laura? Oh, Laura!
LAURA (*off stage, faintly*). Yes, Mother.
AMANDA. You really must come to the table. We won't be seated until you come to the table!

Come in, Mr. O'Connor. You sit over there, and I'll — Laura? Laura Wingfield!

You're keeping us waiting, honey! We can't say grace until you come to the table!

(*The back door is pushed weakly open and* LAURA *comes in. She is obviously quite faint, her lips trembling, her eyes wide and staring. She moves unsteadily toward the table.*)

(LEGEND: *"Terror!"*)
(*Outside a summer storm is coming abruptly. The white curtains billow inward at the windows and there is a sorrowful murmur and deep blue dusk.*)
(LAURA *suddenly stumbles—she catches at a chair with a faint moan.*)

TOM. Laura!
AMANDA. Laura!

(*There is a clap of thunder.*)
(LEGEND: *"Ah!"*)
(*Despairingly.*)

Why, Laura, you *are* sick, darling! Tom, help your sister into the living room, dear!
Sit in the living room, Laura—rest on the sofa.
Well!

(*To the gentleman caller.*)

Standing over the hot stove made her ill!—I told her that it was just too warm this evening, but—

(TOM *comes back in.* LAURA *is on the sofa.*)

Is Laura all right now?
TOM. Yes.
AMANDA. What *is* that? Rain? A nice cool rain has come up!

(*She gives the gentleman caller a frightened look.*)

I think we may—have grace—now . . .

(TOM *looks at her stupidly.*)

Tom, honey—you say grace!
TOM. Oh . . .
"For these and all thy mercies—"

(*They bow their heads,* AMANDA *stealing a nervous glance at* JIM. *In the living room* LAURA, *stretched on the sofa,* clenches her hands to her lips, to hold back a shuddering sob.)

God's Holy Name be praised—

*The Scene Dims Out*

# Scene 7

A Souvenir.

*Half an hour later. Dinner is just being finished in the upstage area which is concealed by the drawn portieres.*

*As the curtain rises* LAURA *is still huddled upon the sofa, her feet drawn under her, her head resting on a pale blue pillow, her eyes wide and mysteriously watchful. The new floor lamp with its shade of rose-colored silk gives a soft, becoming light to her face, bringing out the fragile, unearthly prettiness which usually escapes attention. There is a steady murmur of rain, but it is slackening and stops soon after the scene begins; the air outside becomes pale and luminous as the moon breaks out.*

*A moment after the curtain rises, the lights in both rooms flicker and go out.*

JIM. Hey, there, Mr. Light Bulb!

(AMANDA *laughs nervously.*)
(LEGEND: *"Suspension of a Public Service."*)

AMANDA. Where was Moses when the lights went out? Ha-ha. Do you know the answer to that one, Mr. O'Connor?
JIM. No, Ma'am, what's the answer?
AMANDA. In the dark!

(JIM *laughs appreciatively.*)

Everybody sit still. I'll light the candles. Isn't it lucky we have them on the table? Where's a match? Which of you gentlemen can provide a match?

JIM. Here.

AMANDA. Thank you, sir.

JIM. Not at all, Ma'am!

AMANDA. I guess the fuse has burnt out. Mr. O'Connor, can you tell a burnt-out fuse? I know I can't and Tom is a total loss when it comes to mechanics.

(SOUND: *Getting up: Voices recede a little to kitchenette.*)

Oh, be careful you don't bump into something. We don't want our gentleman caller to break his neck. Now wouldn't that be a fine howdy-do?

JIM. Ha-Ha!
Where is the fuse-box?

AMANDA. Right here next to the stove. Can you see anything?

JIM. Just a minute.

AMANDA. Isn't electricity a mysterious thing?
Wasn't it Benjamin Franklin who tied a key to a kite?
We live in such a mysterious universe, don't we? Some people say that science clears up all the mysteries for us. In my opinion it only creates more!
Have you found it yet?

JIM. No, Ma'am. All these fuses look okay to me.

AMANDA. Tom!

TOM. Yes, Mother?

AMANDA. That light bill I gave you several days ago. The one I told you we got the notices about?

(LEGEND: *"Ha!"*)

TOM. Oh.—Yeah.

AMANDA. You didn't neglect to pay it by any chance?

TOM. Why, I—

AMANDA. Didn't! I might have known it!

JIM. Shakespeare probably wrote a poem on that light bill, Mrs. Wingfield.

AMANDA. I might have known better than to trust him with it! There's such a high price for negligence in this world!

JIM. Maybe the poem will win a ten-dollar prize.

AMANDA. We'll just have to spend the remainder of the evening in the nineteenth century, before Mr. Edison made the Mazda lamp!

JIM. Candlelight is my favorite kind of light.

AMANDA. That shows you're romantic! But that's no excuse for Tom.

Well, we got through dinner. Very considerate of them to let us get through dinner before they plunged us into everlasting darkness, wasn't it, Mr. O'Connor?

JIM. Ha-ha!

AMANDA. Tom, as a penalty for your carelessness you can help me with the dishes.

JIM. Let me give you a hand.

AMANDA. Indeed you will not!

JIM. I ought to be good for something.

AMANDA. Good for something? (*Her tone is rhapsodic.*) *You?* Why, Mr. O'Connor, nobody, *nobody's* given me this much entertainment in years — as you have!

JIM. Aw, now, Mrs. Wingfield!

AMANDA. I'm not exaggerating, not one bit! But Sister is all by her lonesome. You go keep her company in the parlor!

I'll give you this lovely old candelabrum that used to be on the altar at the church of the Heavenly Rest. It was melted a little out of shape when the church burnt down. Lightning struck it one spring. Gypsy Jones[1] was holding a revival at the time and he intimated that the church was destroyed because the Episcopalians gave card parties.

JIM. Ha-ha.

AMANDA. And how about you coaxing Sister to drink a little wine? I think it would be good for her! Can you carry both at once?

---

[1] *Gypsy Jones:* a thinly-veiled reference to Gypsy Smith, Southern gospel singer in great demand to perform at revivals, or weeks of intense religious exhortation and worship

JIM. Sure. I'm Superman!
AMANDA. Now, Thomas, get into this apron!

> (*The door of kitchenette swings closed on* AMANDA's *gay laughter; the flickering light approaches the portieres.*)
> (LAURA *sits up nervously as he enters. Her speech at first is low and breathless from the almost intolerable strain of being alone with a stranger.*)
> (THE LEGEND: "*I don't suppose you remember me at all!*")
> (*In her first speeches in this scene, before* JIM's *warmth overcomes her paralyzing shyness,* LAURA's *voice is thin and breathless as though she has just run up a steep flight of stairs.*)
> (JIM's *attitude is gently humorous. In playing this scene it should be stressed that while the incident is apparently unimportant, it is to* LAURA *the climax of her secret life.*)

JIM. Hello, there, Laura.
LAURA (*faintly*). Hello. (*She clears her throat.*)
JIM. How are you feeling now? Better?
LAURA. Yes. Yes, thank you.
JIM. This is for you. A little dandelion wine. (*He extends it toward her with extravagant gallantry.*)
LAURA. Thank you.
JIM. Drink it—but don't get drunk!

> (*He laughs heartily.* LAURA *takes the glass uncertainly; laughs shyly.*)

Where shall I set the candles?
LAURA. Oh—oh, anywhere . . .
JIM. How about here on the floor? Any objections?
LAURA. No.
JIM. I'll spread a newspaper under to catch the drippings. I like to sit on the floor. Mind if I do?
LAURA. Oh, no.
JIM. Give me a pillow?
LAURA. What?
JIM. A pillow!

LAURA. Oh . . . (*Hands him one quickly.*)

JIM. How about you? Don't you like to sit on the floor?

LAURA. Oh—yes.

JIM. Why don't you, then?

LAURA. I—will.

JIM. Take a pillow! (LAURA *does. Sits on the other side of the candelabrum.* JIM *crosses his legs and smiles engagingly at her.*) I can't hardly see you sitting way over there.

LAURA. I can—see you.

JIM. I know, but that's not fair, I'm in the limelight. (LAURA *moves her pillow closer.*) Good! Now I can see you! Comfortable?

LAURA. Yes.

JIM. So am I. Comfortable as a cow! Will you have some gum?

LAURA. No, thank you.

JIM. I think that I will indulge, with your permission. (*Musingly unwraps it and holds it up.*) Think of the fortune made by the guy that invented the first piece of chewing gum. Amazing, huh? The Wrigley Building is one of the sights of Chicago.—I saw it summer before last when I went up to the Century of Progress.[2] Did you take in the Century of Progress?

LAURA. No, I didn't.

JIM. Well, it was quite a wonderful exposition. What impressed me most was the Hall of Science. Gives you an idea of what the future will be in America, even more wonderful than the present time is! (*Pause. Smiling at her.*) Your brother tells me you're shy. Is that right, Laura?

LAURA. I—don't know.

JIM. I judge you to be an old-fashioned type of girl. Well, I think that's a pretty good type to be. Hope you don't think I'm being too personal—do you?

LAURA (*hastily, out of embarrassment*). I believe I *will* take a piece of gum, if you—don't mind. (*Clearing her throat.*) Mr. O'Connor, have you—kept up with your singing?

---

[2] *Century of Progress:* the Chicago World's Fair held in 1933-34

JIM.   Singing? Me?
LAURA.   Yes. I remember what a beautiful voice you had.
JIM.   When did you hear me sing?

(*Voice off stage in the pause.*)

VOICE (*off stage*).
 O blow, ye winds, heigh-ho,
 A-roving I will go!
  I'm off to my love
  With a boxing glove—
 Ten thousand miles away!
JIM.   You say you've heard me sing?
LAURA.   Oh, yes! Yes, very often . . . I—don't suppose—you remember me—at all?
JIM (*smiling doubtfully*).   You know I have an idea I've seen you before. I had that idea soon as you opened the door. It seemed almost like I was about to remember your name. But the name that I started to call you—wasn't a name! And so I stopped myself before I said it.
LAURA.   Wasn't it—Blue Roses?
JIM (*springs up. Grinning*).   Blue Roses!—My gosh, yes—Blue Roses!
 That's what I had on my tongue when you opened the door!
 Isn't it funny what tricks your memory plays? I didn't connect you with high school somehow or other.
 But that's where it was; it was high school. I didn't even know you were Shakespeare's sister!
 Gosh, I'm sorry.
LAURA.   I didn't expect you to. You—barely knew me!
JIM.   But we did have a speaking acquaintance, huh?
LAURA.   Yes, we—spoke to each other.
JIM.   When did you recognize me?
LAURA.   Oh, right away!
JIM.   Soon as I came in the door?
LAURA.   When I heard your name I thought it was probably you. I knew that Tom used to know you a little in high school. So when you came in the door—
 Well, then I was—sure.

JIM. Why didn't you *say* something, then?
LAURA (*breathlessly*). I didn't know what to say, I was—too surprised!
JIM. For goodness' sakes! You know, this sure is funny!
LAURA. Yes! Yes, isn't it, though . . .
JIM. Didn't we have a class in something together?
LAURA. Yes, we did.
JIM. What class was that?
LAURA. It was—singing—Chorus!
JIM. Aw!
LAURA. I sat across the aisle from you in the Aud.
JIM. Aw.
LAURA. Mondays, Wednesdays and Fridays.
JIM. Now I remember—you always came in late.
LAURA. Yes, it was so hard for me, getting upstairs. I had that brace on my leg—it clumped so loud!
JIM. I never heard any clumping.
LAURA (*wincing at the recollection*). To me it sounded like—thunder!
JIM. Well, well, well, I never even noticed.
LAURA. And everybody was seated before I came in. I had to walk in front of all those people. My seat was in the back row. I had to go clumping all the way up the aisle with everyone watching!
JIM. You shouldn't have been self-conscious.
LAURA. I know, but I was. It was always such a relief when the singing started.
JIM. Aw, yes, I've placed *you* now! I used to call you Blue Roses. How was it that I got started calling you that?
LAURA. I was out of school a little while with pleurosis. When I came back you asked me what was the matter. I said I had pleurosis—you thought I said Blue Roses. That's what you always called me after that!
JIM. I hope you didn't mind.
LAURA. Oh, no—I liked it. You see, I wasn't acquainted with many—people. . . .
JIM. As I remember you sort of stuck by yourself.
LAURA. I—I—never have had much luck at—making friends.
JIM. I don't see why you wouldn't.
LAURA. Well, I—started out badly.

JIM. You mean being —
LAURA. Yes, it sort of — stood between me —
JIM. You shouldn't have let it!
LAURA. I know, but it did, and —
JIM. You were shy with people!
LAURA. I tried not to be but never could —
JIM. Overcome it?
LAURA. No, I — I never could!
JIM. I guess being shy is something you have to work out of kind of gradually.
LAURA (*sorrowfully*). Yes — I guess it —
JIM. Takes time!
LAURA. Yes —
JIM. People are not so dreadful when you know them. That's what you have to remember! And everybody has problems, not just you, but practically everybody has got some problems.

You think of yourself as having the only problems, as being the only one who is disappointed. But just look around you and you will see lots of people as disappointed as you are. For instance, I hoped when I was going to high school that I would be further along at this time, six years later, than I am now — You remember that wonderful write-up I had in *The Torch?*
LAURA. Yes! (*She rises and crosses to table.*)
JIM. It said I was bound to succeed in anything I went into! (LAURA *returns with the annual.*) Holy gee! *The Torch!* (*He accepts it reverently. They smile across it with mutual wonder.* LAURA *crouches beside him and they begin to turn through it.* LAURA's *shyness is dissolving in his warmth.*)
LAURA. Here you are in *The Pirates of Penzance!*
JIM (*wistfully*). I sang the baritone lead in that operetta.
LAURA (*raptly*). So — *beautifully!*
JIM (*protesting*). Aw —
LAURA. Yes, yes — beautifully — beautifully!
JIM. You heard me?
LAURA. All three times!
JIM. No!
LAURA. Yes!

JIM. All three performances?
LAURA (*looking down*). Yes.
JIM. Why?
LAURA. I—wanted to ask you to—autograph my program.
JIM. Why didn't you ask me to?
LAURA. You were always surrounded by your own friends so much that I never had a chance to.
JIM. You should have just—
LAURA. Well, I—thought you might think I was—
JIM. Thought I might think you was—what?
LAURA. Oh—
JIM (*with reflective relish*). I was beleaguered by females in those days.
LAURA. You were terribly popular!
JIM. Yeah—
LAURA. You had such a—friendly way—
JIM. I was spoiled in high school.
LAURA. Everybody—liked you!
JIM. Including you?
LAURA. I—yes, I—I did, too— (*She gently closes the book in her lap.*)
JIM. Well, well, well!—Give me that program, Laura. (*She hands it to him. He signs it with a flourish.*) There you are—better late than never!
LAURA. Oh, I—what a—surprise!
JIM. My signature isn't worth very much right now.
  But some day—maybe—it will increase in value!
  Being disappointed is one thing and being discouraged is something else. I am disappointed but I am not discouraged.
  I'm twenty-three years old.
  How old are you?
LAURA. I'll be twenty-four in June.
JIM. That's not old age!
LAURA. No, but—
JIM. You finished high school?
LAURA (*with difficulty*). I didn't go back.
JIM. You mean you dropped out?
LAURA. I made bad grades in my final examinations. (*She

*rises and replaces the book and the program. Her voice strained.*) How is—Emily Meisenbach getting along?

JIM. Oh, that kraut-head!
LAURA. Why do you call her that?
JIM. That's what she was.
JIM. You're not still—going with her?
JIM. I never see her.
LAURA. It said in the Personal Section that you were—engaged!
JIM. I know, but I wasn't impressed by that—propaganda!
LAURA. It wasn't—the truth?
JIM. Only in Emily's optimistic opinion!
LAURA. Oh—

(LEGEND: *"What have you done since High School?"*)
(JIM *lights a cigarette and leans indolently back on his elbows smiling at* LAURA *with a warmth and charm which lights her inwardly with altar candles. She remains by the table and turns in her hands a piece of glass to cover her tumult.*).

JIM (*after several reflective puffs on a cigarette*). What have you done since high school? (*She seems not to hear him.*) Huh? (LAURA *looks up.*) I said what have you done since high school, Laura?
LAURA. Nothing much.
JIM. You must have been doing something these six long years.
LAURA. Yes.
JIM. Well, then, such as what?
LAURA. I took a business course at business college—
JIM. How did that work out?
LAURA. Well, not very—well—I had to drop out, it gave me—indigestion—

(JIM *laughs gently.*)

JIM. What are you doing now?
LAURA. I don't do anything—much. Oh, please don't think I

sit around doing nothing! My glass collection takes up a good deal of time. Glass is something you have to take good care of.

JIM. What did you say—about glass?

LAURA. Collection I said—I have one— (*She clears her throat and turns away again, acutely shy.*)

JIM (*abruptly*). You know what I judge to be the trouble with you?

Inferiority complex! Know what that is? That's what they call it when someone low-rates himself!

I understand it because I had it, too. Although my case was not so aggravated as yours seems to be. I had it until I took up public speaking, developed my voice, and learned that I had an aptitude for science. Before that time I never thought of myself as being outstanding in any way whatsoever!

Now I've never made a regular study of it, but I have a friend who says I can analyze people better than doctors that make a profession of it. I don't claim that to be necessarily true, but I can sure guess a person's psychology, Laura! (*Takes out his gum.*) Excuse me, Laura. I always take it out when the flavor is gone. I'll use this scrap of paper to wrap it in. I know how it is to get it stuck on a shoe.

Yep—that's what I judge to be your principal trouble. A lack of confidence in yourself as a person. You don't have the proper amount of faith in yourself. I'm basing that fact on a number of your remarks and also on certain observations I've made. For instance that clumping you thought was so awful in high school. You say that you even dreaded to walk into class. You see what you did? You dropped out of school, you gave up an education because of a clump, which as far as I know was practically nonexistent! A little physical defect is what you have. Hardly noticeable even! Magnified thousands of times by imagination!

You know what my strong advice to you is? Think of yourself as *superior* in some way!

LAURA. In what way would I think?

JIM. Why, man alive, Laura! Just look about you a little.

What do you see? A world full of common people! All of 'em born and all of 'em going to die!
  Which of them has one-tenth of your good points! Or mine! Or anyone else's, as far as that goes — Gosh!
  Everybody excels in some one thing. Some in many!

(*Unconsciously glances at himself in the mirror.*)

All you've got to do is discover in *what!*
Take me, for instance.

(*He adjusts his tie at the mirror.*)

  My interest happens to lie in electrodynamics. I'm taking a course in radio engineering at night school, Laura, on top of a fairly responsible job at the warehouse. I'm taking that course and studying public speaking.
LAURA. Ohhhh.
JIM. Because I believe in the future of television!

(*Turning back to her.*)

  I wish to be ready to go up right along with it. Therefore I'm planning to get in on the ground floor. In fact I've already made the right connections and all that remains is for the industry itself to get under way! Full steam —

(*His eyes are starry.*)

  *Knowledge* — Zzzzzp! *Money* — Zzzzzzp! *Power!* That's the cycle democracy is built on!

(*His attitude is convincingly dynamic.* LAURA *stares at him, even her shyness eclipsed in her absolute wonder. He suddenly grins.*)

  I guess you think I think a lot of myself!
LAURA. No — o-o-o, I —
JIM. Now how about you? Isn't there something you take more interest in than anything else?

LAURA.   Well, I do — as I said — have my — glass collection —

(*A peal of girlish laughter from the kitchen.*)

JIM.   I'm not right sure I know what you're talking about. What kind of glass is it?
LAURA.   Little articles of it, they're ornaments mostly! Most of them are little animals made out of glass, the tiniest little animals in the world. Mother calls them a glass menagerie!
   Here's an example of one, if you'd like to see it!
   This one is one of the oldest. It's nearly thirteen.

(MUSIC: *"The Glass Menagerie."*)
(*He stretches out his hand.*)

   Oh, be careful — if you breathe, it breaks!
JIM.   I'd better not take it. I'm pretty clumsy with things.
LAURA.   Go on, I trust you with him!

(*Places it in his palm.*)

   There now — you're holding him gently!
   Hold him over the light, he loves the light! You see how the light shines through him?
JIM.   It sure does shine!
LAURA.   I shouldn't be partial, but he is my favorite one.
JIM.   What kind of a thing is this one supposed to be?
LAURA.   Haven't you noticed the single horn on his forehead?
JIM.   A unicorn, huh?
LAURA.   Mmm-hmmm!
JIM.   Unicorns, aren't they extinct in the modern world?
LAURA.   I know!
JIM.   Poor little fellow, he must feel sort of lonesome.
LAURA (*smiling*).   Well, if he does he doesn't complain about it. He stays on a shelf with some horses that don't have horns and all of them seem to get along nicely together.
JIM.   How do you know?
LAURA (*lightly*).   I haven't heard any arguments among them!

JIM (*grinning*).   No arguments, huh? Well, that's a pretty good sign!
  Where shall I set him?
LAURA.   Put him on the table. They all like a change of scenery once in a while!
JIM (*stretching*).   Well, well, well, well—
  Look how big my shadow is when I stretch!
LAURA.   Oh, oh, yes—it stretches across the ceiling!
JIM (*crossing to door*).   I think it's stopped raining. (*Opens fire escape door.*) Where does the music come from?
LAURA.   From the Paradise Dance Hall across the alley.
JIM.   How about cutting the rug a little, Miss Wingfield?
LAURA.   Oh, I—
JIM.   Or is your program filled up? Let me have a look at it. (*Grasps imaginary card.*) Why, every dance is taken! I'll just have to scratch some out. (WALTZ MUSIC: "*La Golondrina.*") Ahhh, a waltz! (*He executes some sweeping turns by himself then holds his arms toward* LAURA.)
LAURA (*breathlessly*).   I—can't dance!
JIM.   There you go, that inferiority stuff!
LAURA.   I've never danced in my life!
JIM.   Come on, try!
LAURA.   Oh, but I'd step on you!
JIM.   I'm not made out of glass.
LAURA.   How—how—how do we start?
JIM.   Just leave it to me. You hold your arms out a little.
LAURA.   Like this?
JIM.   A little bit higher. Right. Now don't tighten up, that's the main thing about it—relax.
LAURA (*laughing breathlessly*).   It's hard not to.
JIM.   Okay.
LAURA.   I'm afraid you can't budge me.
JIM.   What do you bet I can't? (*He swings her into motion.*)
LAURA.   Goodness, yes, you can!
JIM.   Let yourself go, now, Laura, just let yourself go.
LAURA.   I'm—
JIM.   Come on!
LAURA.   Trying!
JIM.   Not so stiff—Easy does it!

LAURA. I know but I'm—
JIM. Loosen th' backbone! There now, that's a lot better.
LAURA. Am I?
JIM. Lots, lots better! (*He moves her about the room in a clumsy waltz.*)
LAURA. Oh, my!
JIM. Ha-ha!
LAURA. Oh, my goodness!
JIM. Ha-ha-ha! (*They suddenly bump into the table.* JIM *stops.*) What did we hit on?
LAURA. Table.
JIM. Did something fall off it? I think—
LAURA. Yes.
JIM. I hope that it wasn't the little glass horse with the horn!
LAURA. Yes.
JIM. Aw, aw, aw. Is it broken?
LAURA. Now it is just like all the other horses.
JIM. It's lost its—
LAURA. Horn!

    It doesn't matter. Maybe it's a blessing in disguise.
JIM. You'll never forgive me. I bet that that was your favorite piece of glass.
LAURA. I don't have favorites much. It's no tragedy, Freckles. Glass breaks so easily. No matter how careful you are. The traffic jars the shelves and things fall off them.
JIM. Still I'm awfully sorry that I was the cause.
LAURA (*smiling*). I'll just imagine he had an operation. The horn was removed to make him feel less—freakish!

(*They both laugh.*)

    Now he will feel more at home with the other horses, the ones that don't have horns . . .
JIM. Ha-ha, that's very funny!

(*Suddenly serious.*)

    I'm glad to see that you have a sense of humor.
You know—you're—well—very different!
Surprisingly different from anyone else I know!

(*His voice becomes soft and hesitant with a genuine feeling.*)

Do you mind me telling you that?

(LAURA *is abashed beyond speech.*)

I mean it in a nice way . . .

(LAURA *nods shyly, looking away.*)

You make me feel sort of—I don't know how to put it! I'm usually pretty good at expressing things, but— This is something that I don't know how to say!

(LAURA *touches her throat and clears it—turns the broken unicorn in her hands.*)
(*Even softer.*)

Has anyone ever told you that you were pretty?

(*Pause: music.*)
(LAURA *looks up slowly, with wonder, and shakes her head.*)

Well, you are! In a very different way from anyone else. And all the nicer because of the difference, too.

(*His voice becomes low and husky.* LAURA *turns away, nearly faint with the novelty of her emotions.*)

I wish that you were my sister. I'd teach you to have some confidence in yourself. The different people are not like other people, but being different is nothing to be ashamed of. Because other people are not such wonderful people. They're one hundred times one thousand. You're one times one! They walk all over the earth. You just stay here. They're common as—weeds, but—you— well, you're—Blue Roses!

(IMAGE ON SCREEN: *Blue Roses.*)

(*Music changes.*)

LAURA. But blue is wrong for—roses . . .
JIM. It's right for you!—You're—pretty!
LAURA. In what respect am I pretty?
JIM. In all respects—believe me! Your eyes—your hair—are pretty! Your hands are pretty!

(*He catches hold of her hand.*)

You think I'm making this up because I'm invited to dinner and have to be nice. Oh, I could do that! I could put on an act for you, Laura, and say lots of things without being very sincere. But this time I am. I'm talking to you sincerely. I happened to notice you had this inferiority complex that keeps you from feeling comfortable with people. Somebody needs to build your confidence up and make you proud instead of shy and turning away and—blushing—
Somebody—ought to—
Ought to—*kiss* you, Laura!

(*His hand slips slowly up her arm to her shoulder.*)
(*Music swells tumultuously.*)
(*He suddenly turns her about and kisses her on the lips.*)
(*When he releases her,* LAURA *sinks on the sofa with a bright, dazed look.*)
(JIM *backs away and fishes in his pocket for a cigarette.*)
(LEGEND ON SCREEN: "*Souvenir.*")

Stumble-john!

(*He lights the cigarette, avoiding her look.*)
(*There is a peal of girlish laughter from* AMANDA *in the kitchen.*)
(LAURA *slowly raises and opens her hand. It still contains the little broken glass animal. She looks at it with a tender, bewildered expression.*)

Stumble-john!
I shouldn't have done that— That was way off the beam.
You don't smoke, do you?

(*She looks up, smiling, not hearing the question.*)
(*He sits beside her a little gingerly. She looks at him speechlessly—waiting.*)
(*He coughs decorously and moves a little farther aside as he considers the situation and senses her feelings, dimly, with perturbation.*)
(*Gently.*)

Would you—care for a—mint?

(*She doesn't seem to hear him but her look grows brighter even.*)

Peppermint—Life Saver?
My pocket's a regular drug store—wherever I go . . .
(*He pops a mint in his mouth. Then gulps and decides to make a clean breast of it. He speaks slowly and gingerly.*)

Laura, you know, if I had a sister like you, I'd do the same thing as Tom, I'd bring out fellows and—introduce her to them. The right type of boys of a type to—appreciate her.
Only—well—he made a mistake about me.
Maybe I've got no call to be saying this. That may not have been the idea in having me over. But what if it was?
There's nothing wrong about that. The only trouble is that in my case—I'm not in a situation to—do the right thing.
I can't take down your number and say I'll phone.
I can't call up next week and—ask for a date.
I thought I had better explain the situation in case you—misunderstood it and—hurt your feelings. . . .

(*Pause.*)
(*Slowly, very slowly,* LAURA'S *look changes, her eyes*

*returning slowly from his to the ornament in her palm.)*
(AMANDA *utters another gay laugh in the kitchen.*)

LAURA (*faintly*). You—won't—call again?
JIM. No, Laura, I can't.

(*He rises from the sofa.*)

As I was just explaining, I've—got strings on me.
Laura, I've—been going steady!
I go out all of the time with a girl named Betty. She's a home-girl like you, and Catholic, and Irish, and in a great many ways we—get along fine.
I met her last summer on a moonlight boat trip up the river to Alton, on the *Majestic*.
Well—right away from the start it was—love!

(LEGEND: *Love!*)
(LAURA *sways slightly forward and grips the arm of the sofa. He fails to notice, now enrapt in his own comfortable being.*)

Being in love has made a new man of me!

(*Leaning stiffly forward, clutching the arm of the sofa,* LAURA *struggles visibly with her storm. But* JIM *is oblivious, she is a long way off.*)

The power of love is really pretty tremendous!
Love is something that—changes the whole world, Laura!

(*The storm abates a little and* LAURA *leans back. He notices her again.*)

It happened that Betty's aunt took sick, she got a wire and had to go to Centralia. So Tom—when he asked me to dinner—I naturally just accepted the invitation, not knowing that you—that he—that I—

(*He stops awkwardly.*)

Huh — I'm a stumble-john!

(*He flops back on the sofa.*)
(*The holy candles in the altar of* LAURA'S *face have been snuffed out. There is a look of almost infinite desolation.*)
(JIM *glances at her uneasily.*)

I wish that you would — say something. (*She bites her lip which was trembling and then bravely smiles. She opens her hand again on the broken glass ornament. Then she gently takes his hand and raises it level with her own. She carefully places the unicorn in the palm of his hand, then pushes his fingers closed upon it.*) What are you — doing that for? You want me to have him? — Laura? (*She nods.*) What for?

LAURA. A — souvenir...

(*She rises unsteadily and crouches beside the victrola to wind it up.*)
(LEGEND ON SCREEN: "*Things have a way of turning out so badly!*")
(OR IMAGE: "*Gentleman caller waving good-bye! — gaily.*")
(*At this moment* AMANDA *rushes brightly back in the front room. She bears a pitcher of fruit punch in an old-fashioned cut-glass pitcher and a plate of macaroons. The plate has a gold border and poppies painted on it.*)

AMANDA. Well, well, well! Isn't the air delightful after the shower?
I've made you children a little liquid refreshment.

(*Turns gaily to the gentleman caller.*)

Jim, do you know that song about lemonade?

> "Lemonade, lemonade
> Made in the shade and stirred with a spade —
> Good enough for any old maid!"

JIM (*uneasily*).  Ha-ha! No — I never heard it.
AMANDA.  Why, Laura! You look so serious!
JIM.  We were having a serious conversation.
AMANDA.  Good! Now you're better acquainted!
JIM (*uncertainly*).  Ha-ha! Yes.
AMANDA.  You modern young people are much more serious-minded than my generation. I was so gay as a girl!
JIM.  You haven't changed, Mrs. Wingfield.
AMANDA.  Tonight I'm rejuvenated! The gaiety of the occasion, Mr. O'Connor!

(*She tosses her head with a peal of laughter. Spills lemonade.*)

Oooo! I'm baptizing myself!
JIM.  Here — let me —
AMANDA (*setting the pitcher down*).  There now. I discovered we had some maraschino cherries. I dumped them in, juice and all!
JIM.  You shouldn't have gone to that trouble, Mrs. Wingfield.
AMANDA.  Trouble, trouble? Why, it was loads of fun!

Didn't you hear me cutting up in the kitchen? I bet your ears were burning! I told Tom how outdone with him I was for keeping you to himself so long a time! He should have brought you over much, much sooner! Well, now that you've found your way, I want you to be a very frequent caller! Not just occasional but all the time.

Oh, we're going to have a lot of gay times together! I see them coming!

Mmm, just breathe that air! So fresh, and the moon's so pretty!

I'll skip back out — I know where my place is when young folks are having a — serious conversation!
JIM.  Oh, don't go out, Mrs. Wingfield. The fact of the matter is I've got to be going.

AMANDA.  Going, now? You're joking! Why, it's only the shank of the evening, Mr. O'Connor!
JIM.  Well, you know how it is.
AMANDA.  You mean you're a young workingman and have to keep workingmen's hours. We'll let you off early tonight. But only on the condition that next time you stay later. What's the best night for you? Isn't Saturday night the best night for you workingmen?
JIM.  I have a couple of time-clocks to punch, Mrs. Wingfield. One at morning, another one at night!
AMANDA.  My, but you *are* ambitious! You work at night, too?
JIM.  No, Ma'am, not work but—Betty! (*He crosses deliberately to pick up his hat. The band at the Paradise Dance Hall goes into a tender waltz.*)
AMANDA.  Betty? Betty? Who's—Betty!

(*There is an ominous cracking sound in the sky.*)

JIM.  Oh, just a girl. The girl I go steady with! (*He smiles charmingly. The sky falls.*)

(LEGEND: "*The Sky Falls.*")

AMANDA (*a long-drawn exhalation*).  Ohhhh . . . Is it a serious romance, Mr. O'Connor?
JIM.  We're going to be married the second Sunday in June.
AMANDA.  Ohhhh—how nice!
Tom didn't mention that you were engaged to be married.
JIM.  The cat's not out of the bag at the warehouse yet.
You know how they are. They call you Romeo and stuff like that.

(*He stops at the oval mirror to put on his hat. He carefully shapes the brim and the crown to give a discreetly dashing effect.*)

It's been a wonderful evening, Mrs. Wingfield. I guess this is what they mean by Southern hospitality.

AMANDA. It really wasn't anything at all.
JIM. I hope it don't seem like I'm rushing off. But I promised Betty I'd pick her up at the Wabash depot, an' by the time I get my jalopy down there her train'll be in. Some women are pretty upset if you keep 'em waiting.
AMANDA. Yes, I know—The tyranny of women!

(*Extends her hand.*)

Good-bye, Mr. O'Connor.
I wish you luck—and happiness—and success! All three of them, and so does Laura!—Don't you, Laura?
LAURA. Yes!
JIM (*taking her hand*). Good-bye, Laura. I'm certainly going to treasure that souvenir. And don't you forget the good advice I gave you.

(*Raises his voice to a cheery shout.*)

So long, Shakespeare!
Thanks again, ladies—Good night!

(*He grins and ducks jauntily out.*)
(*Still bravely grimacing,* AMANDA *closes the door on the gentleman caller. Then she turns back to the room with a puzzled expression. She and* LAURA *don't dare to face each other.* LAURA *crouches beside the victrola to wind it.*)

AMANDA (*faintly*). Things have a way of turning out so badly.
I don't believe that I would play the victrola.
Well, well—well—
Our gentleman caller was engaged to be married!
Tom!
TOM (*from back*). Yes, Mother?
AMANDA. Come in here a minute. I want to tell you something awfully funny.
TOM (*enters with macaroon and a glass of the lemonade*). Has the gentleman caller gotten away already?

AMANDA. The gentleman caller has made an early departure. What a wonderful joke you played on us!
TOM. How do you mean?
AMANDA. You didn't mention that he was engaged to be married.
TOM. Jim? Engaged?
AMANDA. That's what he just informed us.
TOM. I'll be jiggered! I didn't know about that.
AMANDA. That seems very peculiar.
TOM. What's peculiar about it?
AMANDA. Didn't you call him your best friend down at the warehouse?
TOM. He is, but how did I know?
AMANDA. It seems extremely peculiar that you wouldn't know your best friend was going to be married!
TOM. The warehouse is where I work, not where I know things about people!
AMANDA. You don't know things anywhere! You live in a dream; you manufacture illusions!

(*He crosses to door.*)

 Where are you going?
TOM. I'm going to the movies.
AMANDA. That's right, now that you've had us make such fools of ourselves. The effort, the preparations, all the expense! The new floor lamp, the rug, the clothes for Laura! All for what? To entertain some other girl's fiancé!
 Go to the movies, go! Don't think about us, a mother deserted, an unmarried sister who's crippled and has no job! Don't let anything interfere with your selfish pleasure!
 Just go, go, go—to the movies!
TOM. All right, I will! The more you shout about my selfishness to me the quicker I'll go, and I won't go to the movies!
AMANDA. Go, then! Then go to the moon—you selfish dreamer!

(TOM *smashes his glass on the floor. He plunges out on the fire escape, slamming the door.* LAURA *screams—cut by door.*)
(*Dance-hall music up.* TOM *goes to the rail and grips it desperately, lifting his face in the chill white moonlight penetrating the narrow abyss of the alley.*)
(LEGEND ON SCREEN: *"And so Good-bye...."*)
(TOM'S *closing speech is timed with the interior pantomime. The interior scene is played as though viewed through soundproof glass.* AMANDA *appears to be making a comforting speech to* LAURA *who is huddled upon the sofa. Now that we cannot hear the mother's speech, her silliness is gone and she has dignity and tragic beauty.* LAURA'S *dark hair hides her face until at the end of the speech she lifts it to smile at her mother.* AMANDA'S *gestures are slow and graceful, almost dance-like, as she comforts the daughter. At the end of her speech she glances a moment at the father's picture—then withdraws through the portieres. At close of* TOM'S *speech,* LAURA *blows out the candles, ending the play.*)

TOM. I didn't go to the moon, I went much further—for time is the longest distance between two places—

Not long after that I was fired for writing a poem on the lid of a shoe-box.

I left Saint Louis. I descended the steps of this fire escape for a last time and followed, from then on, in my father's footsteps, attempting to find in motion what was lost in space—

I traveled around a great deal. The cities swept about me like dead leaves, leaves that were brightly colored but torn away from the branches.

I would have stopped, but I was pursued by something.

It always came upon me unawares, taking me altogether by surprise. Perhaps it was a familiar bit of music. Perhaps it was only a piece of transparent glass—

Perhaps I am walking along a street at night, in some strange city, before I have found companions. I pass the lighted window of a shop where perfume is sold. The window is filled with pieces of colored glass, tiny transparent bottles in delicate colors, like bits of a shattered rainbow.

Then all at once my sister touches my shoulder. I turn around and look into her eyes . . .

Oh, Laura, Laura, I tried to leave you behind me, but I am more faithful than I intended to be!

I reach for a cigarette, I cross the street, I run into the movies or a bar, I buy a drink, I speak to the nearest stranger—anything that can blow your candles out!

(LAURA *bends over the candles.*)

—for nowadays the world is lit by lightning! Blow out your candles, Laura—and so good-bye. . . .

(*She blows the candles out.*)

The Scene Dissolves

**FOR DISCUSSION**

**SCENE 1**

1. When the curtain rises on *The Glass Menagerie*, the audience first sees the Wingfield apartment through a scrim, or transparent curtain. What effect or mood is conveyed through this device?
2. Do you detect any difference between Tom-as-narrator and Tom-as-character? Do you feel the two should be alike? Why or why not?
3. Williams states that the narrator is "an undisguised convention of this play." Why is a narrator unusual in drama? How does he affect the exposition at the beginning of the play? What advantages are gained when a narrator is omitted?
4. Her first speech reveals that Amanda is fussy and nagging, but also that she is much more complex than that. What can you deduce about her background, her education, and her view of herself? What in subsequent speeches confirms these impressions?
5. When Tom teases his mother about her former lovers being

dead, what does he imply about Amanda? How does Amanda manage to avoid his implications and still preserve her fantasy?
6. Why is it so important to Amanda to pretend Laura will have a caller? Laura's final statement suggests that being an old maid is in Amanda's view the worst of all possible fates. Why would Amanda feel this way?

## SCENE 2

1. Laura is the person on whom this scene focuses. What do you find out from your initial glimpse of her? How is this impression reinforced by Laura's confrontation with Amanda and by the details revealed in this scene?
2. Williams says that the glass menagerie is Laura's image. In what ways do the glass animals symbolize, or represent, Laura?
3. Discuss the dramatic qualities and implications of Laura's gesture when she crosses the stage to wind up her Victrola (page 284). What does this gesture confirm?
4. What poetic associations does Williams assume you will make when he suggests that a winter scene be flashed on a screen which the audience can see?
5. What do you learn about Laura through the information about Jim O'Connor?

## SCENE 3

1. Why does Tom compare the Gentleman Caller to an "archetype of the universal unconscious"?
2. How does Amanda's preoccupation with gentlemen callers begin to affect Laura? What does Amanda's course of action prove about her? What impression is made by such a line as "You're a Christian martyr" (page 288)?
3. In this scene you learn about Amanda's taste in literature. What kind of stories does she like? What does her taste reveal about Amanda?
4. At the climax of the family argument, Tom performs a symbolic action when he accidentally breaks some of Laura's glass animals. What is symbolized by this event? How does Williams show that he means the moment to have symbolic overtones? What particularly effective stage business underscores the importance of the moment?

## SCENE 4

1. Those who have encountered Tennessee Williams' plays only through reading them are always surprised at the amount of humor in a staged production. Scene 4 of *The Glass Menagerie* is full of humor when produced. On what does the humor depend? What reliably funny devices does Williams include?
2. To what does Tom compare his life in his first long speech? Is his comparison accurate? Is it fair? What conclusion about his relationship to his family does Tom's speech suggest?
3. When Amanda begins to nag Tom again, saying "Most young men find adventure in their careers" (page 299), Williams originally planned for a pirate ship to flash in view of the audience. If used, the ship would foreshadow the end of the play. What else in this scene furnishes that same foreshadowing?
4. This scene explains why Williams considers, or wants his audience to consider, Amanda a lovable character. What lovable qualities does she display here?

## SCENE 5

1. Several minutes of this scene are devoted to describing the Paradise Dance Hall. Why do you think Williams brought this establishment into his play? By mentioning the dance hall, what points does he make about Tom, about young people Tom's age, and about American society?
2. Amanda says, "The future becomes the present, the present the past, and the past turns into everlasting regret if you don't plan for it!" (page 307). Does the play as a whole suggest that Amanda is right or wrong? Explain.
3. In this scene, Amanda jumps to many hasty conclusions about Mr. O'Connor. Many of her guesses turn out to be quite shrewd. Point out those conclusions of hers about the Gentleman Caller which are accurate.

## SCENE 6

1. At this point in the play, Amanda says to Laura lightly, "You're as pretty as you'll ever be." In retrospect, this statement is significant and moving. Why?
2. Point out the different ways in which the playwright shows his audience (who can't read his stage directions and commentary) that the evening is to be the most important one of Laura's life?

3. The jonquils Amanda carries in this scene become as accurate a symbol for her as are Laura's glass figures. Discuss the symbolic meaning of the jonquils.
4. Did Jim serve successfully as the "emissary from a world of reality" Tom said he was in Scene 1? How does the playwright establish Jim O'Connor's "normality"? How does he show *dramatically* that Jim represents a world from which the Wingfields are "somehow set apart"?
5. What did you think of Amanda's behavior in this scene? Why would Amanda appeal to Jim? Throughout the scene runs a discrepancy between the way Amanda talks and the obvious facts of her life. What effect does Williams achieve by emphasizing this discrepancy?
6. The scene closes with an excellent example of dramatic irony. What is ironic about the final moments?

## SCENE 7

1. In this scene, Laura's view of the world is contrasted with Jim's. How did each see himself or herself in relation to other people? What information is Williams striving to give us by putting these two views together?
2. The nickname "Blue Roses" defines Laura almost as accurately as her glass menagerie. Explain why.
3. When Jim chides Laura for exaggerating the importance of the brace she once wore, he sounds much like Amanda. How else are Jim and Amanda similar? How do they differ from Tom and Laura?
4. In this scene, Laura discusses her collection of animals for the first time. Do any of her statements surprise you? What do they reveal?
5. Amanda's girlish laughter is heard offstage as Laura states, "I do have my glass collection." Dramatically, this coincidence suggests several things: Amanda seems, unconsciously, to be making a judgment of Laura's statement and also to be contrasting herself to Laura. When and how, later in the scene, is Amanda's laughter once more employed symbolically?
6. Why is the glass unicorn an appropriate favorite for Laura? What symbolic meaning is conveyed when the unicorn's horn is broken? Why is the moment at which this accident occurs especially appropriate, symbolically?
7. It is, of course, ironic that just at the point when her own illusions are destroyed, Amanda accuses Tom of living "in a dream"

and of manufacturing illusions. Is she being unfair to Tom, or do her words apply to him as much as to her? Prove your answer.
8. Until this point in the play, either Laura or Amanda has seemed to be the main character. Perhaps at this moment, however, the play becomes Tom's story. Why? What sign in Amanda's next speech (page 347) reveals that she has finally stopped fighting for her illusions?
9. What does Tom mean when he says that he attempted "to find in motion what was lost in space"? What does he mean when he says he has been more faithful to Laura than he meant to be? Why does he want to "blow out her candles" (page 349)?
10. The candles are the last symbol introduced into the play. Like the glass animals and the blue roses, they express an aspect of Laura. What does Williams suggest about Laura through the candles? What do you think he meant when he had Laura blow the candles out at the end of the play? Remember the history of the candelabrum as you give your answer.

## FOR COMPOSITION

1. Decide which Wingfield is the major character of this play. Write a theme explaining why your answer is the best one.
2. Write three paragraphs on "Amanda, the mother" or "Tom, the brother." Limit your comments to the one relationship or role you choose to explore.
3. Williams states that such apartments as the Wingfields' "burn with the implacable fires of desperation." Take one of the Wingfield family and write several paragraphs explaining why he or she is desperate, and why his desperation is implacable.
4. Write a theme comparing Amanda with Birdie in *The Little Foxes* as aging daughters of old Southern families.
5. Williams states that the "Wingfield apartment is in the rear of ... one of those vast hive-like conglomerations of cellular living-units that flower as warty growths in overcrowded urban centers ... and are symptomatic of the impulse of this ... fundamentally enslaved section of American society to avoid fluidity and differentiation and to exist ... as one interfused mass of automatism." Prepare a short theme on one part of this sentence, proving why it is true or untrue. Use specific evidence in your theme.
6. Pretend you are a professional set designer. Describe the set that perfectly conveys the "dim and poetic" interior of *The Glass Menagerie*. Especially explain why the props you plan for the set are poetic.

# ABOUT THE PLAYWRIGHTS

**Frank D. Gilroy** (1925-    ) was born in New York City. Like Timmy Cleary, he went into the army as a very young man and served in World War II. When he returned home, he went to Dartmouth College, from which he was graduated in 1950. By this time, he had firmly decided that he wanted to write for the theater and took a year's postgraduate study at the Yale School of Drama.

Within a short time, Gilroy established himself as a writer for radio and TV. His credits included most of the major dramatic shows of the 1950's. He also wrote the scripts for such movies as *The Fastest Gun Alive* with Glenn Ford and *The Gallant Hours* with James Cagney.

At the same time, Gilroy was attempting to write for the legitimate theater. His first play, *Who'll Save the Plowboy?*, was completed in 1957, but it was not produced until 1962. (This time element will help to explain why he continued to write for movies and TV.) The play was a critical, if not a popular, success and won the Obie Award, given for the best American play of the year.

Gilroy then turned to *The Subject Was Roses*, which he worked on for several years while employed as a screen writer in Hollywood. For fully two years, producers wrestled with the difficulties and uncertainties of converting this obviously brilliant script into a finished production. (Gilroy himself has told the story in a delightful and revealing book-length essay entitled *About Those Roses or How Not to Do a Play and Succeed*.)

The play finally had its New York premiere in May, 1964 and experienced a rather mild reception. In fact, it was not until its 136th performance that it had a sold-out house. But it has since been widely recognized as one of the finest dramas of the contemporary American theater.

*About the Playwrights* ☙ 355

**Lillian Hellman** (1905-    ) was born in New Orleans, but educated in New York City, at New York University and Columbia University. Her first play, *The Children's Hour* (1934), established her as an important new talent in the American theater. One of her greatest successes was *The Little Foxes* (1939), which was revived on Broadway with an all-star cast in the 1967-1968 theatrical season. It was also made into an opera called *Regina* in 1949. Among her other plays of note are *Watch on the Rhine* (1941), *Another Part of the Forest* (1946), and *Toys in the Attic* (1959). She has also written for the movies.


**Thornton Wilder** (1897-    ), winner of three Pulitzer Prizes, was born in Madison, Wisconsin, and attended college at Oberlin, Yale, and Princeton. His literary fame began in 1927 with the publication of his novel, *The Bridge of San Luis Rey*, which brought him a Pulitzer Prize and an international reputation. At the time, he was a teacher and housemaster at a boys' preparatory school, and for several years thereafter he combined academic and literary pursuits.

*Our Town* (1938), his first full-length play, was a resounding success and won for its author a second Pulitzer Prize. His next play, *The Merchant of Yonkers*, failed on Broadway, but when he rewrote it as *The Matchmaker* in 1956, it won praise from critics and theatergoers. It was made into a successful motion picture and into a musical comedy, the Broadway hit *Hello, Dolly!* Wilder won a third Pulitzer Prize in 1942 for his experimental play, *The Skin of Our Teeth*, a comic history of the human race.

Wilder's other literary works include three novels; two collections of one-act plays, *The Angel That Troubled the Waters* and *The Long Christmas Dinner*; and two cycles of one-act plays, *The Seven Ages of Man* and *The Seven Deadly Sins*, on which Wilder is still at work. Three of these cycle plays have already been performed in New York, where they received a warm reception.


**Tennessee Williams** (1914-    ) was born Thomas Lanier Williams in Columbus, Mississippi, but took *Tennessee* as his pen name. In his early life, he lived in various parts of the South—the region which was later to furnish the setting for many of his plays. He then studied at the University of Missouri, Washington University in St. Louis, and the University of Iowa, before making a definite decision to become a professional playwright.

His first successful play, *The Glass Menagerie*, was produced in 1944 and won the New York Drama Critics' Circle Award. An even greater success, *A Streetcar Named Desire* (1947), won the Drama Critics' Circle Award and a Pulitzer Prize and made a star of Marlon Brando. Outstanding among his other plays are *The Rose Tattoo, Cat on a Hot Tin Roof* (awarded a Pulitzer Prize in 1955), *Sweet Bird of Youth*, and *Night of the Iguana*.

Williams has been one of the most influential of American playwrights. His works have reached audiences not only through the professional theater, but also through the movies. The list of Williams' dramas is a list of distinguished films which have become vehicles for many well-known actresses, including Vivien Leigh, Katherine Hepburn, Elizabeth Taylor, and Geraldine Page.

# ROLLING STONES

I FUCKED IT UP